In Realms Beyond:

Study Guide

Questions and Answers for
The Peter Chronicles

By AL MINER and LAMA SING

CoCreations Publishing

Cover and book design by Susan Miner

Library of Congress control Number: 2010942984

ISBN: 978-0-982878620

1. Spirit writings 2. Psychics 3. Trance Channels

I. Miner, Al   II. Lama Sing   III. Title

Printed in the United States of America

For books and products, or to write Al Miner,
visit the Lama Sing website: **www.lamasing.net**

Contents

A Message from Al Miner
Note from the Editor

A Message from Al Miner

In my early tenure as a channel, I began working with a growing number of individuals who were following the information given in the Lama Sing readings, calling ourselves "Voyagers." We had a list of topics we were interested in exploring, and would take these one by one until we or Lama Sing felt we had concluded that topic and were ready to embark on the next. Some of these projects lasted for four or five readings, while others went on for twenty or more. The project members were given the opportunity to submit questions throughout the project based on what was being given that were then put to the Lama Sing group in follow-up readings. So the projects included open readings by Lama Sing, as well as question and answer readings. Those members participating in the project were then privy not only to the "open readings" but also to all the questions submitted and to Lama Sing's answers to those questions.

We were finishing up on one of these projects and I had asked in a reading what topic would be helpful for us to explore next. The suggestion was: "The Nature and Influence of Colors." Imagine our surprise when the reading actually began exploring the experiences of a man who was in a hospital, dying. This began a 10-year series of readings on the journeys of the man called "Peter" with people just like you, who were enthralled by the question "What lies beyond?" To our knowledge, no such work had ever been endeavored.

The book, IN REALMS BEYOND, is the collection of the first twelve readings chronicling Peter's journey beyond life on Earth. What is included in this accompanying study book are the seventeen readings of questions submitted by the project members, and Lama Sing's answers to those questions.

Lama Sing's answers were and are intended to not only answer the questions themselves but to help those participating and those who would follow to set themselves free – free from the illusions of the limitations of finiteness and from the fear of death and beyond.

I invite you to use this study guide alongside IN REALMS BEYOND. You might find it interesting to write your own questions for the chapters and compare your questions with those asked. Look for answers to your questions in this and later study guides.

It is my prayer that these readings serve you well.

Warm Blessings,
Al

Editor's Note:

Lama Sing's use of words such as *ye, thee, we, they, he* is often contrary to convention, but the meaning will be clear. With two opposite views as to how to present Lama Sing – those who feel the grammar should be corrected, and those who find it endearing – it has been decided to keep the text verbatim, except for the frequent incorrect use of *whom*, which is too often a distraction because of how often it occurs.

Even though the name *Lama Sing* has been assigned to these readings, there is always a group involved. Depending upon the topic, sometimes the number is massive, and sometimes it is a handful; sometimes they are speaking to a group, and sometimes to an individual they know will one day get the message – in essence, speaking to one and all, as well as to only one and only all... curious, but true. Throughout the reading, they defer to one another just as we do when in a group discussion. This information may be of value as you read, so you don't stumble when they sometimes change, even in a single paragraph, from an archaic form of speech to a more modern one, or from the singular to the plural.

The name *Channel* is used by Lama Sing in place of *Al* because to use the name *Al* would essentially serve to call him from that consciousness to which he is taken that prevents his personal involvement and influence in what is given in the reading. There is only one known occasion in which Lama Sing used Al's given name; the reason given was that the depth of his channeled state was being tested.

When referring to life on Earth, Lama Sing uses the term *in Earth*. This is because Lama Sing is referring to living within the consciousness of Earth, finite experience, rather than *on* the consciousness of Earth and that expression. It is similar to using the term *in Heaven*.

There are places where Lama Sing emphasizes a thought by speaking the words *quote/end-quote*. To let the reader know that those emphases are Lama Sing's, as opposed to the transcriber's, the words *quote/end-quote* have been left in the transcript along with the quotation marks themselves.

The word *dis-ease* is used by Lama Sing to mean, not only illness and such, but *"first and foremost, a lack of ease in spirit, mind, and/or emotion, which are then precipitated into the physical body."*

Finally, the single space between various paragraphs denotes where Lama Sing has paused in the narrative, usually indicating moving from one question and answer to the next.

Q&A READING #1

Questions After Chapters 1 and 2:
BEYOND THE BLACKNESS (V-630)
IN THE GARDEN (V-631)

Given April 11, 1990

AL MINER/CHANNEL: This reading is code number V-632. It is the next in the Voyager sequence, Voyager Project #6, dealing with the general topic of Colors and Their Influences.

In this reading I will submit a number of questions generally based upon the same theme or topic, and that is "colors." These are all questions received from the Voyagers. In some cases I have consolidated questions that were very similar from a number of different Voyagers, and so you will find that if you have submitted a number of questions and that they are similar to others, you'll probably hear your name mentioned, even though you may not actually recognize the phrasing of your question. Hopefully, I have maintained the integrity of your intent.

QUESTIONS SUBMITTED

#1 - In the movement through the layers of light, like the layers of atmosphere around the Earth, Peter encounters different colors that are probably related to his thoughts during this lifetime. Please tell us about this. What causes the yellow color, the green, the red? Why did Peter get a jolt with the red color? What does the red color represent? Is the indigo color like a higher consciousness?

#2 - If different times in Peter's life are represented by different colors, do those colors correspond to his effective experience of those times? Example given: All sad times represented by one color, happy by another, et cetera. If so, are those colors the same for all persons experiencing the same effect? If so, what is the correspondence between colors and the emotional experience?

#3 - Does everyone experience the same colors as Peter saw, or different ones, when they depart the Earth plane? Do the colors represent different realms of habitation? In other words, different realms where souls exist, collectively? Or are they only associated with emotions? Is the movement through the colors related to one's mental, physical, emotional and/or spiritual state at the time of passing over?

#4 - When leaving the body, does every entity go through the indigo-colored veil of darkness? Even the two-day turn-around? Do the colors we have in our auras (in other words, while we are here in the Earth in physical body) have any significance on or association with the colors we will experience?

#5 - Can one envision a color in meditation and move to that state of awareness immediately? If one uses certain colors for meditation (example given: lavender) would this enhance one's ability to channel an entity from that plane (lavender) which is, again, corresponding to that specific color? This is assuming that different planes correspond to specific colors, as seemingly implied from the reading.

#6 - Do thoughts affect the various colors of the chakras or seven endocrine glands (or centers) and lotus petals? (I'm presuming here that the reference to lotus petals is similar to the crown chakra of Eastern extraction.) How, and which color corresponds to which chakra? Is there a resultant effect on the health and consciousness of the total entity? Is there a different set of colors related to each of the different bodies? (In example: etheric, astral, et cetera.)

#7 - What were the colors of the endocrine gland system of Jesus before and after crucifixion? What was the effect on his aura?

#8 - As Peter, in the earlier readings, saw the various colors, did he also hear various sounds?

#9 - Please explain what light is and where does it come from? What causes it to be of various colors? (Let me add here that, although I felt that that was probably a rather Earthly scientific question, I've included it here with the hope that the answer will be in accordance with what is intended in the question, in case that isn't meant in the way I took it.)

#10 - Are there, as fashion color analysts suggest, some colors more than others that suit each individual? Or some colors more than others that suit certain environments? If so, why? How does one determine the best colors for themselves and their environment?

#11 - Apparently, all the different realms or the "primary realms" are related to certain colors. Now, as we leave our homey realm in order to reincarnate into the Earth or elsewhere, do we all come in on a particular color that is associated with our individual spiritual consciousness or soul vibration? Would we share that predominant color or vibration with all the other members of our soul grouping residing in the same realm? Would this likely be the color or colors we'd be particularly fond of while in the Earth? Why do we prefer some colors and dislike others?

(I guess that every one of us has had this experience:)
#12 - We close our eyes for a second and, spontaneously, a specific color pops up and floods our inner vision. Why is that, and what does it mean?

Those are the extent of the questions that I received on tape number V-630 that had to do more predominantly with the general topic of "color." While the questions that will follow may cross over and deal with color here and there, all of these, I felt, were fairly closely correlated and, as you look them over, I'm sure that you'll realize that some of them ac-

tually overlap and approach redundancy, but I felt that, again, it was inappropriate for me to attempt to interpret some specific subtle differences that I noted in the questions, and therefore, rather than miss some objective that the requestor was seeking, I ran the risk of being redundant. I think these are a marvelous collection of questions, and I think they typify the deep reflection and contemplation that is being given to the topics that we are receiving during this project.

And so now, Father, we prayerfully submit these questions to You, asking as we do that You would guide us to that which is of the best and most purposeful in accordance with Your will and purpose and those of each individual who has submitted questions above. Thank You, Father, and a special thanks and blessings to all those souls in other realms who will be providing this information, and an echo of this from nearly every one of the individuals who submitted questions. They extended their love, their gratitude, and their thankfulness for the beautiful material that we've received to date in this project. Once again, we thank You, Father. Amen.

THE READING

LAMA SING: Yes, we have the Channel then and, as well, those references which apply to the topic, those individuals involved with same, their inquiring minds, and that of the intent and purpose of same, now before us.

As we begin with this work, Father, we call upon Thee, as ever, to be our guide, the mentor of that information as shall be humbly offered to those seeking. And thereof do we pray, Father, further, that it shall be the blessing of Thy joy and light that shall surround each soul in all realms presently in some need and about who there are none reflecting thy joyous light. It is to our joy and humbleness that we accept this offering of service in Thy name. Thank You, Father. Amen.

We reciprocate the gratitude for this opportunity to share with those of you in the Earth who shall perceive this information, this opportunity for mutual growth, understanding and service, in the purpose and intent of our Father's Spirit.

Understand that all functions that occur in terms of events of consciousness are not necessarily sequential nor mandated to conform to that which is called *absolute order*, in the sense of the scientific interpretation of the Earth. Paradoxically, all things are in order, and harmoniously so. It then remains the task of the seeker, the perceiver, to determine how that harmony exists; and by finding such, using each harmonic as an equally spaced or equidistant step towards the ascension unto the reclamation of their spiritual consciousness, fully and irrevocably.

The movements of Peter, in the earlier commentary, through those spheres of illumination (as could be described, "colors" or "color representations") are, in essence, ordered. They form, as such, rather a standard, perhaps in the manner that they reflect the accepted level of consciousness of the realm adjacent to which they exist. In many respects, they typify that which is the emotional counterpart in the Earth, and thereof they are representative of certain levels of emotion in accordance with that level of glandular activity ... chakridic activity, as might be also correlated or associated with same.

The specific colors do not necessarily conform in the absolute sense to certain types of emotion for each individual. This perhaps obviously having to do with a number of other factors, inclusively certain group thought-forms and certain race thought-forms, as well as individual societies, sub-groupings of same, and varying dialectical or, as could be called, certain provisions or provinces mandated within certain social strata (or *stratae*, if the latter is more correct).

Thereof, then, do we find that, as Peter progressed through these colors, his assessment, reaction, and individual interaction with each of these, was somewhat aligned with his just-previous experience ... that is, his just-previous lifetime in the Earth. More subtly, but yet ever-present, these were further conditioned by the collective assembly of all earlier experiences and by, as well, the potential of all future experiences. (We are cognizant that the latter might give you a bit of difficulty intellectually, so don't concern about it just now, just here. See?)

Each color, then, had to do with activity that was primarily influential upon the emotional body first, in the Earth plane. Next, in association with the emotional and by the responsive stimuli obtained through the physical body, in terms of the standardized (as accepted in the Earth) five senses. Then, next, all of this information was intellectualized or actualized through the experience of that lifetime, augmented catalytically by the sum and substance of his consciousness (which would be called his id or personality of that experience). These, then, basally stimulated by collective experiences existing in the subconscious, yet not superficially influential, nonetheless, underlying streams of influencing energy.

Above all of this, then, in the supra-consciousness, we find in existence (as given just above) the collective assemblage of the intent, the purpose of this incarnation, the general soul pattern or past experiences, and the plan pattern or ideal, which is generally the imprint of individuality of this soul.

The earlier colors as experienced would be associated with the lower chakras or glandular centers. Then, as these progress, correspondingly, they had to do with the ever-heightening step-wise progression up these centers or glandular positions, until correspondingly the entity reached the pinnacle, which, in the description as we defined it to you of his journey (in this instance), resulted in his sleep of spirit.

A differentiation needs to be made here for the purposes of reference in the Earth: Categorically, in the Earth, you recognize two types of color. One is called reflective or has to do with pigmentation and deals with certain absorption levels of some materials or particles in suspension called color or pigment, which actually enhance the reflection of some rays (rays being vibrational frequency wave-lengths) and deter or angularly dispel or absorb others. The properties as just given in this example, then, collectively denote the different categories of pigment so that, for example, an artist might select certain carrier media as oil or water or the like, which is occluded or saturated with certain types of pigment known to produce a type of reflected light. So, *reflective light*, with that definition as we find it given here, about the Earth, is the first.

Next, we would move away from the Earth towards what is called *source light* (or *living light*, colloquially given). This light, then, has to do moreso with, not the reflection off an object, as such, but rather projection of light rays through varying media, which are, in and of themselves, acting somewhat as filters or diffusers. In the case of the former, the filter does, in essence, the same or similar as the reflected light (dealing with the pigment), and the diffuser tends to split these and yet not absorb them, but define them into a pattern. Oft times [it is] perceived and described as a rainbow, such as might be perceived by moisture or dust particles in the atmosphere, or by the bending or reflecting through a prism or a crystal.

Therefore, we find that all of these colors, then, as they are referenced in the Earth, tend to become symbols in terms of the ethnic and in terms of the specific mores, oddly conditioned often by, in your current time, advertisement or by culture, by varying traditions, dogmas, even religious philosophy. So that red can depict, in the religious sense, one thing and, in the sense of aggression, another, both representing blood: one representing the blood of Christ, the other simply representing blood on a battlefield. The connotation being quite diverse, and yet the actualization of the data being identical in the sense of the source and description. (These are matters which need to be dealt with in the Earth and not here. We are merely giving them for reference. See?)

And so, then, to turn to the more specifics of the questions ...

Peter had the reaction based upon his own influence as a Christian, and based upon his own society. In his earlier incarnation, at early age, he had reactions which were very traumatic and dealt with blood. Thus, the heavy, blood-like color which was alive and pulsating had an initial fragmentary recall reaction upon him. As this was tempered, it moderated.

But, in essence, the colors represented memories, influences, emotions, as were fragmentally a part of Peter's yet somewhat physical recall. See? This is not to imply that he'll lose that totally, but he will temper (and has) the emotional reaction to that. That's a part of the spiritual progression.

The indigo color is, in a sense, like a higher consciousness. In this instance it is the level of inter-between, or the level of the highest attainment of consciousness within the sphere which is defined as Earth. In other words, each level or realm of consciousness has an outer perimeter and an inner core or heart perimeter (which, if one were to move within same, they would find another outer perimeter and an array of inner concentric spheres and another core or heart or inner perimeter of the level which is on the other side of the Earth). Have you thought about that? (Given with a note of loving humor, see).

The colors do correspond to his effective experience and, as such, generalize themselves into categories. However, take a given experience, for example, his fifth birthday. He'll remember some influences of that day from the sounds. The soul records the sound as well as the color and, as such the sound will give off an emanation which is the equivalent in color, and vice-versa. The colors remembered will give off an emanation at the other end of the vibrational frequency which the soul perceives in its sensory perceptive mechanisms as sound. See? (We're not just three-dimensional in this perspective now, mind thee, so that limitation doesn't apply. What is colored isn't simply color; what is sound isn't simply sound.) The inter-relationship between these two expressions of vibration are visible, detectable, audible, perceptible … tactically, emotionally, spiritually, and intellectually. See?

In the general sense, they are similar for all persons detecting same. In that sense, the correlation between color and emotional experience has to do with direct parallels to the conditioning factors of society, theological belief, interracial doctrines as might have to do with race karma, collective soul group intent … purposes, karma, and such as these.

But, more generally, yes, they relate to the influences of emotion and can be patterned most generally after one of your gradient charts of vibrational frequency. Moving from infrared to ultra-violent to X-ray and et cetera, the spectrum generally aligns itself quite comfortably with the denser, more heavy, slower vibrational frequencies of mottled browns or mottled blacks, and then upwards correspondingly through the chakras. A divergence occurs here when we reach the crown chakra. Some societies will interpret this as the golden; others as the white or silver; and yet others, if they have specific sight, will perceive this as having touched the hem of God's robe, which, in their interpretation, must be, logically, black, for black is the presence of all vibration (from source light, not reflected light, see.) We hope that helps. We understand your intent.

Association with colors as Peter saw them: The colors represent different realms and, to an extent, these are realms of habitation. But they are not in the true interpretation of the term *habitation* but, rather, the title *gravitational levels* (in other words, implying that this is the level to which they have gravitated, by choice, by habit, by desire) then that is where they exist. You can traverse these realms. In a sense, for your perspective, this would be lateral. However, the range, in terms of height and breadth, of such a realm would be interpreted as infinite from the finite perspective. From the spiritual, it would seem as a simple band of color, vibration, sound, et cetera. A paradox, see? Within that realm, entities will interact, largely because of choice. And those who associate with this color will generally have similar attitudes, emotions, needs, doubts, fears, guilts, desires, et cetera. Don't presume that those from the Bowery are the only ones there. There's quite a number of preachers there, too.

In other words, it's not the nature of the desire that generally confines an entity to a certain realm, but the desire itself and the way the desire is manifest. If it's obsessive, you'll find it generally in the thicker yellows. If it's possessive and has to do with carnal desires, you'll find it in the mottled browns near the basal chakric centers. If it has to do with certain attitudes of abuse, of domination, you'll find it in some of the severe colors, as are reds, even those who have strong spiritual connotations and yet they lie about such because of carnal desire or because of a need for self-gratification, you'll find the presence of blue in the yellow band. And so, it could be interpreted that those certain colors would seem to be, generally, expected to be more purely that base color. Other colors can be present, as well.

As you broach the area of intersect between two colors, a curious event occurs. You generally approach or broach an intersect of many colors, as you will recall from Peter's experience. This occurs when entities come to the point of realizing the need for balance or moderation. Then, as these colors come together, if they temper or balance and become subtle, soft and yielding, and can be penetrable by the sense or by the will, and entities of equal or higher vibration are able to move through these, they provide a portal ... a sort of shortcut to the inter-between or the next veil of darkness. See?

In other words, an entity can move from the yellow realm directly to the Veil of Darkness in the event that entity only had several things which held him or her in that realm. And by gravitating to the understanding that the tempering or moderating of such was their own choice or will, they released themselves from this spectrum of consciousness completely. See?

Yes, movement through the colors is related to one's mental, physical, emotional, and spiritual state. Not necessarily or just at the time of passing from the Earth but, rather, the sum or summarial sense.

However, influences which are dramatically present at the moment of departure from the Earth do have a preponderant effect upon the soul in these realms. Such instances are tended to by experienced workers from this realm, where such workers move immediately to assist that entity, in conjunction with that entity's guide or guides.

When leaving the body, physical, every entity goes through the indigo-colored Veil of Darkness. All entities. There are no exceptions. Some will pass through on the light of their own spiritual consciousness or *silver cord*, as it's called. In such instances, when the cord is unbroken, those entities can return. Those are NDE, or near-death experiences. And oft times OBE, or out-of-body experiences, also fall in those categories.

Auric colors do not necessarily have to do with the association with the colors you will experience. However, conversely, a predominance of a certain color indicates, by way of its measure in the aura, certain emotions and attitudes. True? Then those are like building, in essence, the next step, which is departure from the Earth. If the preponderance is such as we've given above, then those will be the colors that are dealt with first, if they are binding or limiting to the soul's movement. Paradox.

Conversely, certain colors are predominant in entities' auras from the instant they are in acceptance of that physical vehicle to the end time that that vehicle is useful to that entity in the Earth. There are many different factors involved with this, and an entire realm of discussion is possible on this singular topic.

Generally, you have those souls who can enter the Earth and have no karmic purpose but, rather, a mission. In other words, this isn't individual karma; this is group work or as an emissary of those of light or of God.

The Master enters the Earth on such a ray, such a light, maintains it and departs upon it. See?

Certain guides, certain soul-group workers, will choose

to enter with a certain power. That will be evidenced in their aura. Understand why this is a broad and expansive topic?

Envisioning a color in meditation enables an entity to move to that state of awareness immediately, providing the entity has that capability. In other words, just envisioning a color isn't a magical wand that enables you to break free of all constraints you have builded (given with a note of loving humor).

Conversely, if you select a vibration of personal power to you (in other words, generally, let's call it your favorite color) that color has personal power for you. If you focus upon it, it will provide you with a state of ease. That state of ease makes the way more passable and you accelerate your movement. Immediate? This depends upon the individual, see. Accelerated? Yes.

Continual concentration upon certain vibrations enhances one's movement. Therefore, if consistency of use of certain colors is the watchword, then that certain color becomes a catalyst or a triggering mechanism to accelerate movement. Try that one. You'll find it productive.

Movement to a certain color, in terms of focusing upon that as a catalyst to make contact with an entity at that level or realm, should be used advisedly. Be certain that the color that you want to choose is the type of expression or entity that you want to channel.

The highest and best is that of the pure light. The pure light as it is expressed in your realm is pure white. The level of consciousness, which is demarcative between your realm and the next realm, does not appear to you in the Earth as pure white, because you are still in the Earth. Therefore, it is called the Veil of Darkness for your perception, for your understanding.

It's not that complex. We'll try again. It's our error, and we'll make a greater effort here. But simply understand this:

Many things of consciousness are relative to the perspective and the acceptance level of the individual who is the perceiver. If that entity is in physical form, generally they are limited to physical sensory tools. If they have educated themselves in terms of becoming free, they may have gained the adequate use of other tools ... perspective and tools. We'll attempt to exemplify this with some brief analogies extracted from your realm:

As a child, you perceived construction to be the building with paste and paper. You may also consider it to be the filling of a container with sand and the inversion of same in a sandbox. Building with various types of container gives you various types of structures. As you gain in Earth-year duration (or age), you begin to perceive construction differently. You look to that which is more complex, more integrated, and that which is produced by those who are skilled in terms of artisanry of the varying trades. As the cycle continues, you perceive mechanical devices, electronic devices (aeroplanes, and such as these), and you may desire to become a part of the activities associated with same. Those are the devices of construction, of development, of perception.

As you were a child, simplicity existed. If you did not like that which you builded, you simply ran your hands over it and started over again. As you gathered age, you gathered knowledge, experience, influence, patterns. You were subjected to certain expectations ... the evaluations of emotions on the part of those around you. In other words, if your peers perceived certain things to be desirable, you were influenced by that. As you became subjected to advertisement, whether through printed form, broadcast or televised or thought patterns (and yes, these are used), the matter is the same. You began to subtly expect for yourself that which was pronounced to you or presented to you.

The collage of all of this influence, then, brings you to the point where your attitude of expectation is tempered by the collection of expectations imposed upon you by existence in the Earth. (We hope we've made ourselves clear to this point.) Then the sensory perception that you have, as you see, is tempered by all of that. Associated with this during the process of influence and growth are colors. Certain colors are denoted to be good; other colors are denoted to be bad. Evil is thought of as black; and good or righteousness is thought of as white. That which is golden is to be revered; and that which is brown or black or mottled is considered to be rubble. That which is pink and fragrant is desirous; that which is brilliant red and repugnant is not.

Emotion is a subject which is dealt with by brilliance. Expectation is heightened by the presence of brilliant colors. Which color is most prevalent in advertisement to attempt to get your attention? (Yes, you've said red.) What do you color red in the Earth? The heart, the lips upon a female entity (given with a note of loving humor ... Those Egyptians really started something with that, didn't they?) And then from here we find that green is lovely... it's a meadow, it's a field; it's also, in the North American, money. Yellow is very beautiful as the rays of this color dance upon the surface of a body of water; or there is the vile yellow of bigotry, of hatred, of dispassionate attitudes of violence, one against another.

And so it is, do you see, what senses you have, have been influenced. The perception of your consciousness as is introduced to new experience must thereby also be influenced. And if your thoughts and your attitudes and your emotions are all that you have when you leave the Earth, in the sense of being finite or infinite, isn't it logical that you should attempt to balance those colors, those vibrations, and to restore to good health your sensory perception? Isn't it further logical that a worker would wish to regain the full and complete individualization of their tools?

Thoughts are color. Thoughts are music. You are moving into a realm where thought is very important. It is what the Master as the man called Jesus expressed, "So as a man thinketh in his heart, so is he in this realm of my Father." In other words, what you are within is what you are here in the total, in the sum and substance. What you hold in your heart denotes what's upon your spiritual cloak. Becoming clearer? That would be our prayer.

And so as you would turn again back to the questions as given above, "Is there a different set of colors related to each of the different bodies?" well, actually, yes, there is. The astral body won't respond to the colors in the same way as the physical body because the astral body isn't carrying all the baggage the physical body is.

Similarly, the etheric body is even less bound by habit, mores, expectation, ideological doctrine and such. But the true body, the spirit body, is to become unencumbered. The objective upon departing from the Earth is to return to the spiritual body. In order to do this, one must pass through back along the conduit or passageway ... the river of light[1] (do you recall that?) ... the channel of blessings, the silver cord. If this can be completely removed from within the sphere and concentric realms of influence around that sphere, the entity is freed to progress. Think about it. If you can move through each of those realms symbolized by varying colors and interactions between the colors, you will be free.

What exactly does it mean to be free? (Well, with a note of loving humor, when we return to Peter, you'll find out. Until then, let's proceed with your questions.)

As Peter moved before the massive array of influences, of potentials, each color was as an offering. In essence, saying to him or any vestiges of his human, emotional, physical

---

[1] River of Light - Lama Sing first spoke of the *River of Light* in 1977, reading: "Changing the Body with Thought." Subsequently, it has been referred to frequently in various projects and workshops. Ex: "...you are without limitation within ... a river of God's Grace, a veritable *River of Light*." –Lama Sing

tendencies, "See me? Here I am ... a realm of existence. Wonderful. I'll provide your every wish. Look about you. There are entities here. They think as you do. Join them. Come with us."

That's the kind of influence that's present in the Sea of Faces.[2] It's that sort of thing that is dealt with. See?

Each of the colors do represent not only different bodies, in a sense, but an entire spectrum of color is representative of that body, dependent upon the individual's relationship to the attitudes and emotions as are aligned with those colors, physically, mentally, and emotionally (all-important), ... and, to a degree, spiritually.

The colors of the glandular centers, the colors of the chakridic centers of the man who was called Jesus were consistent from the moment of entry until the moment of departure. To the perceiver who had eyes to see (which is an important point, isn't it) His aura was consistent until the instant he stated, "It is done," at which point the shift was from the physical to the spiritual body.

Because of the prophecy and His intended purpose, the physical, astral, etheric, and spiritual bodies did not comple-

---

[2] The Sea of Faces - In the early 1990's the Al Miner/Lama Sing readings coined the term "Sea of Faces." Al asked in a reading about faces he would see while moving out of the Earth realm in a meditation or reading. Lama Sing explained that these are entities dwelling in various realms formed by entities with like desires or habits who seek to perpetuate their realm by luring others to it. It is often encountered when one departs life, when from off to the side someone may call to them – for example, an old friend with whom perhaps they used to share drinks at happy hour, a former neighbor who apparently is sitting on a porch on their beloved neighborhood street, a nemesis with whom an old grudge was never finished, the memory of an event that has caused anguishing guilt, or sorrow, or hatred, or a desire for revenge or to conquer a fear, or even an event where love was not completed. The "departee" might think about pausing the journey, just for a bit, to participate in the call. And as easily and smoothly as that, can be tempted, lured, to a realm, built around that habit, desire, fear, regret, love, etc.

ly disconnect in the manner that you understand the process of death or dying or departure in the Earth. Therefore, after this conclusive point, the aura remained consistent. But, again, to those who could perceive, there was a difference because the life force was not empowering the body in the physical sense. The spiritual force was totally in control. Therefore, the color was not, as such, vibrant in the sense of depth and breadth, but translucent, glowing.

To try to become specific for you, one of the observers states that: He was preceding the moment of His final comments aglow in a silvery orb. At the moment after His last word, the entirety of existence seemed to take on a tremendous orb of velvety darkness, as though the sky no longer was separate from the Earth, and the body and those of the faithful took upon themselves glows, which illuminated that which was about. And that was perceptibly the only light. Moments thereafter, the shift in coloration became golden 'round and about Jesus and remained such until the last perceptible moment of this observer. See?

In the Earth there are those who would tell you this or that color suits you, and they will be correct to an extent that their evaluatory methods can tell which colors seem to blend with what they'll call an elusive harmonic or an elusive reflective coordinance. While we are told here that they have definable criteria from which this occurs and reflectometer-type activities which prove it, only understand this: If one's aura possesses a rather heavy, scarlet color, certainly some colors in the spectrum will balance with that and blend well. But supposing that that heavy, scarlet color is a part of the karma you're carrying in the Earth. If you complement it, aren't you supporting it? (Given with a note of loving humor.) Let thy colors be chosen from within self and in meditation. And here's the procedure. It's very simple:

Meditate, seated erect in an Eastern style before a mirror large enough so that you can see the entirety of your body seated in the form as you would see Buddha seated: the crossed legs and the opened-upwards palms resting in the lap. The room should be dimly, if at all, lit. Let it be lit by candle-light, either between you and the mirror or off to the sides one or two on each side. Pray, meditate. And with your eyes closed, seat yourself erect in front of the mirror until you feel the urge to look. Then do so. You'll perceive beautiful colors. One or more will be predominant. Those, you see, are your colors. That simple. See?

Now, looking at the other side, using the Earthly senses and other intuitive guidances, you are intuitively attracted to those colors which are best for you in terms of arriving at a state of balance and ease in the Earth. While these may not be your best colors in terms of an authentic, genuine evaluation of what's right for you on the part of someone else (given with a note of loving humor and compassionate understanding), they are still the colors you should choose. If you like them, they're good for you, aren't they? If someone tells you, "That color looks awful on you," agree. And tell them that you simply like it anyway. See?

The color which is good for you is a color which you choose. That color may differ day to day, week to week, month to month. Last year's favorite color may be the one on the bottom of the list this year. You've grown. Your needs have changed. Your spirit has awakened here or there, and now you are looking to the next level of expression. See?

Next paradox: Entities who have difficulty in the emotional sense tend to rigidly conform to the color spectrum in the Earth. Line this up with the chakras and with emotions that correspond to those chakras, and you have a ready-made treatment method. Certain criminal mentalities also respond to this without fail. Give a brutalizer who's in the dungeons of solitary confinement a pastel, feminine pink surrounding, and you'll change him in a fortnight. (Those who don't believe need to try, see.)

Color is powerful. You can use it to heal. You can use it to influence. You can use it to guide or to remind. Color is a tool. Color creates resonance within you, the perceiver.

Music is a tool. It influences you. It guides you. It directs you. It can remind you. It can stimulate you. It creates color within you. Music creates color, and color creates music. Combine the two, and you have a dynamic healing environment.

What's the next sense? Well, perhaps the tactile sense. Give an entity several objects to touch. Plug their ears, cover their eyes, block their nose, and such, and let them feel different fabrics. You can wire them up to your electronic devices and you'll detect a difference. That difference will correspond to the dielectric rhythm of the electromagnetic nature of the body. Galvanically, they are capable of being measured in terms of all of your monitoring devices, whether you wish to measure brain waves or respiratory changes or the cellular salt reaction (if you've developed that good enough as yet). All of these things will manifest themselves and be capable of being defined.

Put a bit of salt on that same entity's tongue and watch the meters measure. Irrigate the tongue and the oral cavity, allow two-three minutes to pass to allow the neuron endings to neutralize themselves, and sprinkle a few grains of sugar on the tongue or, better yet, a bit of honey. Watch the meters. Experiment similarly with other spectrum extremes ... pepper, onion, you know, such as these ... the more exotic pleasures of the Earth (given with loving understanding).

So you know about sight, about hearing, about touch, and about taste. The remaining sense has to do with the olfactory. And, paradoxically, this perhaps is one of the more dynamic senses for you in the Earth, and yet has not, as yet, been recognized as such. If you stimulate the sense of smell, it automatically activates all of the other sensations. If you stimulate the sensory perception tactically, it doesn't do this, at least not for a delayed period of time. The delay/reactive factor is prolonged. The same is true with hearing. The same is true with sight, and somewhat similarly, but less so, with taste. Taste and smell are closely correlated. Of course, many of you know this, being medically oriented and scientifically oriented. But what you may not have (possibly) realized is that the connective link, then, here tends to activate the next level of sensory perception. In other words, we are dealing with the pineal and pituitary glands here, and a very small center (gangliae or nerve collection) which tends to act as a fulcrum or springboard for the next level of sense.

It is in this interactive state of your physiological structure that stems the basis for what is called the third eye ... which isn't an eye at all but, rather, the third level of expression of man: body, mind, spirit. See?

In the spiritual, then, at the level of the third eye, the entire spectrum of color takes on new dimension. It no longer exists in the sense of the finite expression. Nor can it be corralled, in the sense of the Earth nomenclature, for a singular purpose. It begins to take on the characteristics of its true nature, which is as to say it becomes a living expression of those who perpetuate it.

For some of you, little doors are opening into a new realm of understanding with these last few words of commentary. And we applaud you lovingly and warmly, and welcome you here with your knowledge. It is our prayer that it becomes for you the gift of wisdom.

As you pass through the portal which is symbolically (and in a sense, literally) symbolized by the third eye and the conscious perception of what this is, you begin to play, as it were, the game of consciousness with an entirely new set of tools. Do you remember the analogy of the child in the sandbox? Their reality was simplistic by design and in terms of their potential control over it. And so *Ye must be likened unto these little children before ye might enter into the Kingdom of my Father.* See the meaning? The truth is before you. And now it awakens.

Through the portal of consciousness, then, comes the understanding that all of existence, as you are about to move into it, is the end result of someone's thinking.

The first colors are not actually colors, after all, but thought-forms. If the thought-forms correspondingly relate to activities, attitudes, and/or emotions from the Earth which have to do with lower glandular associated activities (lust, excessive sexual desires, and all manner as ye can imagine perhaps better than we) then these living thought-forms combine in this strata to become the realm of the murky, rather collage-like assemblage of those heavier, thicker, denser, lower chakridic-origin thoughts.

The desire for expression of love in a union of matrimony and the wish to bear children is not a brown thought-form. It is one of love, of light, has a silver hue, dances and sparkles with golden and pastel pink colors ... oh, yes, could be a blue one here or there (that's the symbol for the boy, isn't it).

And yet, all of these have to do with the same center. How can it be then that in these realms of thought a sexual activity can be such a beautiful collage of music, color and experience on the one hand, and on the other be almost thick and syrupy like mud upon your boots in the Earth? (Speaking from the spiritual perspective, colloquially not literally see. There's considerable humor here over that comment.)

Color. Thought. Desire. What's important to you in the Earth will continue to be important to you here. If a color is associated with that in the Earth, it tends to symbolically be the depictation of that desire here. Universally? No, not necessarily. But, generally. See?

The best colors for you and for your environment are the ones that make you joyful. And if what's joyful also seems to be burdensome, then find out why. And look for the influence of other thoughts. Look for attitudes of excess. Remember, as above, where the colors come together and join in their pastels, oft times many, if not all, colors will be found there in a brief or narrow strata. This is a type of accelerated growth.

Moderation is a state of balance. The balanced aura is the aura which has, literally, the indicator of an entity who has made significant spiritual progress. A balanced aura is capable of projecting the primary thought-form as is the best and highest for the situation in which that entity exists. And, thus, that entity (as might be appropriately and lovingly called an adept) would project what's needed by an entity at hand to their physical body because that is how they perceive them and that is their extension of love. They are beginning to use the tools of their spiritual consciousness, of which one is love.

Have you ever, in the Earth, thought of love as a tool? Well, if you haven't (with a note of loving humor), advertising agencies have. We're not speaking of that, of course. We are speaking here of the viability and power which is present in you, if you voluntarily choose to deal with an individual or a situation in an attitude of unreserved, unrestricted love. Not the abandonment of your ideal, your purpose, your goal. Not subjecting yourself to the needs or expectations or even the desires of another. But to express to them through the mechanism of your unlimited potential for love. Not sexually, not even physically. Actually, though, a bit of a gentle touch here and there doesn't hurt. See? No, nor does a well-intended hug. But let's not split straws ... hairs. (That's the term?)

The question is an attitude of spiritual intent. If your intention is from the level of your spiritual form, then what's your tool? Well, one of your tools is the power of love. The child in the sandbox can create with a container. You can create with love. See?

If you leave your homey realm here and decide to incarnate in the Earth, you will no doubt choose a primary color upon which to enter.

The common vernacular for this is called "the ray" (R-A-

Y), upon which the soul has entered. Those who can see or who have gained (through their dedicated efforts) access to the Akasha (or the Universal Records) can define that or interpret it for you. But be mindful that, just as in all given above, the primary ray or color upon which you have entered does not necessarily mean that you won't choose or be perceived as having predominant other colors. The primary ray is associated with the overview or theme or ultimate goal of this or a series of incarnations that you, as the soul, have chosen to embark upon. Generally, though, the ray does have to do primarily with that lifetime in the more specific sense, because no souls are dealing in the singular consciousness with one lifetime at a time. See?

There aren't that many who can juggle more than one lifetime at a point of consciousness. Not that many dealing with simultaneous existences, contrary to what might be the impression you have. Multiple awareness levels, yes, but that's different; you having two, three, four bodies walking around at the same time ... we don't see many of those here. A soul has the power to choose and to create in accordance with its will. If that is your will, you are capable of it, providing you don't violate universal law and the prime law or thought-form for that realm. Then it's within your possibility.

But, as you choose a ray, it generally defines your intent and purpose, your alignment with specific works for that lifetime in that primary incarnation. Soul groupings do not always all choose the same ray or color, as should seem obvious to you at this point.

Soul groupings will choose, intentionally, a multiplicity of rays, and the higher the consciousness, the less likely is the ray to be definable in Earthly terms. It will be seen as a shaft of light or silvery or indigo or violet, something in that nature. This would likely be your color of preference, or a color which makes you feel good or right. See? But not necessarily a color in the sense of, let's say, that's what you need to work upon. In other words, this is not necessarily a color which depicts a karmic need, though it can. It may be a spiritual blessing. (We regret if this sounds complex. It's not. It's just that there is considerable latitude and individuality available to you all.)

Now, then, when you close your eyes and a certain color pops before your eyes, if it's not the afterglow of an incandescent light, then it has to do with a guidance for you and possibly for that which you are encouraged to seek out. Follow that color and become a part of it. It's a good experience.

Prayer, as you might assume from what we've given above, is a part of the thought-form of the person praying. Wouldn't they project in color?

We are grateful to those who have come forward here to provide this information. We know that their intent has been pure, and we pray that the material is found in your hearts and minds to be joyful and of small illumination to your footsteps in your paths in the Earth.

May the light of our Father's wisdom be that which ever guides you in all realms. Fare thee well, then, for the present, dear friends.

Q&A READING #2

Continuation of Questions After Chapters 1 and 2:
BEYOND THE BLACKNESS (V-630)
IN THE GARDEN (V-631)

Given April 12, 1990

AL MINER/CHANNEL: *This reading is code number V-633. It is the next in a series of readings in Voyager Project #6. This reading stems from the topic titled "Colors and Their Influences," and it is comprised of a series of questions submitted by the Voyagers having to do with the experiences of Peter in the tape number V-630, as told to us by Lama Sing.*

QUESTIONS SUBMITTED

#1 - Were all the entities Peter met on this journey (with the exception of Abe) still in physical bodies? Or were they aspects of himself from this world and/or from alternate existences, or were they entities at the same level of spirituality as Peter? Was Abe at the same time both a guide and a personality on Earth?

#2 - After Peter passed from his physical body and then through the veil of darkness, at what point on this journey does he stop seeing the planet Earth and anything from the physical realm? When Peter started to inquire about where he was, did he ask at any point if he was in heaven? And how did Paul respond?

#3 - At the point where Peter fell asleep because he was at his level of highest acceptance of his consciousness, does this mean he cannot go any further without reincarnating again? Or else, how can he go on to full awareness? In other words, if he doesn't have to reincarnate, what happens next?

#4 - Are Peter, Paul and Abe associated presently in other incarnations? And are they a part of the Lama Sing group?

#5 - Some people say they cannot meditate, as they only fall asleep. Is this because they relax and the body really sleeps? Or have they quickly reached the point Peter did where he "moved within himself for a period of balance"? Trying to relate the experiences of Peter to Monroe, Monroe's Levels, *(that's Robert Monroe)* I suspect that he has moved through the ten state to the twelve state and may be moving to the fifteen state when he has fallen asleep. Can such a correlation be made? What are your comments? In movement out of body, are there places that one is drawn to and places that one likes to rest? Would you please talk to us about rest points in eternity?

(As an aside for those of you who aren't familiar with Robert Monroe's work, the numbers that have been stated in the question are sort of indicators of levels of out-of-body accomplishment levels of altered states of awareness, and the increase in the number value indicates a, generally speaking, more distant or higher accomplishment. And that's certainly a greatly paraphrased commentary. It's some fascinating work that Mr. Monroe has done.)

(And the following questions generally have to do with the transitional experience.)

#7 - Lama Sing, you mentioned that Peter has completed a lifetime without any karmic baggage to accompany him. Would the transition process been different had there been a lot of karmic baggage? *(I can envision people carrying his bags here, can't you? Some days I feel like I'm going to need a lot of porters when I leave.)* Can you please elaborate on this so that we can move towards living our lives without accumulating more karmic baggage?

(Again, let me point out that these questions have been combined, to a great degree, to form composite questions, summarized from an array of questions generally kind of circulating around the same theme. So, if you are one of the Voyagers who have submitted questions, you should find the essence of your question in these composite questions I'm reading. Now to number eight ...)

#8 - I work with people who are dying *(I believe she's a member of a hospice program or something like that.)* And it seems quite apparent that people can choose their moment of death, whether they are alert or comatose. Can we choose our moment of death? In our work we suggest that families say goodbye and tell the patients that they love them and that it's okay to die. Some people can do this, and some cannot. Should we continue to suggest this?

#9 - Peter felt a tug on his upward progression when Abe was grieving for him. Sometimes family and friends cannot get over their grief or sense of loss, and they continue to tell the patient, "Don't give up. Keep fighting. I can't live without you," et cetera. How does this affect the person who has passed over and the material process of death? Some people mourn for years and years, especially if they've lost a child. Is there a mechanism to release the deceased person from that? What about the effect of mass grief on famous people? Example given: Elvis Presley. People just can't seem to leave him in peace.

#10 - We in our [Hospice] work often encourage people to take their pain medication regularly and sufficiently so that their pain is relieved. We feel that once they are pain-free they may be able to let go and make the transition peacefully. Is that okay, or is it against any natural laws in some way? What more could or should we be doing? Are there any methods or techniques that could be learned to help a person make the transition from the physical body to the spiritual without fear or pain? How different would Peter's journey have been if he were in pain or had no friends or family members present (or not present)? Would the route be the same? And with an accompanying guide?

(We might point out that these questions on this topic came from all over the United States and Germany.)

#11 - Recent studies of near-death experiences [NDE] indicate a bright white light to be followed, and a summary of life experiences to be reviewed. As this was not mentioned in the reading, does it occur on transition or only for those returning to consciousness after the "near-death" experience?

#12 - Coincidentally, I guess, a person who had played a very big part in my life made the transition on the very day this reading was done. *(She's referring to 630.)* Therefore, I am feeling a close affinity to the material. About three or four nights after he had left the Earth, I had a very strange night. I seemed to never "go under" but stayed just barely below the edge of sleep, feeling that I was aware all night long. And strangest of all, I felt this wonderful sense of anticipation, as though something wonderful were going to happen. I have likened it to the night before Christmas when we were children. You can barely sleep for anticipating the wonders ahead.

Question: Does this experience relate in some way to the passing of this man from the Earth? Does it perhaps relate to Peter's situation when he is at a place where colors are blended, though separate, pastel ... and he sees the entities on the mound? One of them raises his hand and waves, then nods, turns, and goes in a different direction. Paul tells him that this is his guide. I believe it's stated that Abe was a guide, but I think to those people that were with him. I could stand to be corrected on that. You tell us that this was the spirit of his friend Abe. Could this relate to my experience? Were our souls communicating during this time? Was the message being given to me that all was well with this man, or was something else entirely happening during that night? Though I felt I hadn't slept all night, I wasn't tired or sleepy the next day, but continued to feel the anticipation, the happiness, that had been with me all that night. *(Quite an experience, hmm?)*

(The following questions have to do with the cloak.)

#13 - What kind of emotions or state of mind creates what kind of colors or vibrations in the cloak that we are wearing? What are the more desirable colors, or must one work on all colors (i.e., rainbow) alike? Or is that each person's choice? But to become perfect, perhaps one works on developing a perfect blue, and so on. Does each individual perceive the same color in the same way? In other words, I see Peter's cloak as green, but someone else sees or perceives it as blue, depending on when or from what point I perceive.

#14 - Does one earn certain colors through various activities and experiences for our cloaks? For example, an adept in meditation might earn the color purple in their cloak. *(Sort of like Scout merit badges, isn't it? Forgive me.)*

#15 - When Paul provided the envelopment for Peter, what does this protect him from? The Sea of Faces? Is the experience of "envelopment" as done by Paul to Peter something we all experience?

#16 - If an individual forms a cloak of spiritual consciousness around him or herself, then does any grouping (example given: family, nationality, race, creed, and the planet) also create a cloak around themselves? Can the cloak limit us in any way?

#17 - Can we learn to consciously work with our cloak of light while still in the Earth, to make changes in our psyches and move towards mental and emotional healing? While in the Earth it would seem more effective to work directly with the emotion than the light.

Those are the extent of the questions I have for this point -- for this reading.

So now, we prayerfully and thankfully present them to You, Father, praying that You would guide us to that which You would know to be the very best. A special blessing on those souls who are serving with us in other realms. Thank You, Father. Amen.

THE READING

LAMA SING: Yes, we have the Channel then and, as well, those references which apply to the topic, questions, and inquiring minds as have submitted same.

Father, we thank Thee for guiding us in this work, that we might herein accomplish Thy will and purpose. We pray and call upon Thy light to embrace all those souls in all realms that are presently in the darkness of some need and for whom there are none illuminating the way. Humbly, joyfully, we thank Thee, Father, for this wondrous opportunity of oneness with Thee and our brethren in the Earth. Amen.

It should be noted here that some of the inquiries now before us have, to the greater or lesser degree, been addressed in the earlier information as has been given and has not, as of this point in your time, been heard by this, our Channel.

The relationship between the entity Peter and those entities met or observed during the proceeding from the Earth to the realm of his spiritual sleep were not aspects of himself. Neither were they, as such, alternative existences. They were, and are, entities who are at that, or those, levels of consciousness for the purpose of resolving some issues or works which yet remain therein for them. The exception here being, of course, Abe, who is and was a worker in those realms.

Abe can be both a guide and an expressed entity in the Earth, because of his spiritual stature. Abe has no karma to fulfill of an individual soul need or purpose in the Earth. Therefore, at some level of his spirituality he is conscious of his multiple expressions. See? (We told you there were exceptions. Abe is one of them.)

In essence, Peter stopped seeing and being aware of the Earth and its more broad influences almost immediately upon departure from the Earth. Though his sensory perception was still functioning and his attitude of expectation was still Earth-oriented, and even is at this moment as we speak, he was, as given, nearly immediately uninfluenced by sensory perceptions from the Earth ... the exception being those emotions which remained somewhat unresolved or needed additional balance.

We can't find any indication here of him inquiring of Paul whether he was in heaven or the *opposite place*. Actually, you see, those connotations are moreso Earthly-oriented. There is only, as one passes from the Earth, the awareness of a sense of being alive. In other words, there is so much of a concentration and focus upon the fact that existence continues most entities don't have the wherewithal (we believe would be your term) to think about asking that question. Isn't that odd? Especially since it's such an important one while they're in the Earth.

Here again, there are some exceptions and, ironically (it might seem to you) these are more often than not those heavily steeped in dogma or religious rote or such, and very often those who fill roles of leadership in such capacities. They are much more conscious of, what they call, error or sin. See?

The mental-emotional-spiritual attitude of the entity upon departure from the Earth has much to do with an entity's immediate reactions here. And so this, you see, is a tempering influence to the experiences that are perpetuated and the actions and reactions that occur on the part of entities who are (quote) "new arrivals" (end-quote). (Just a colloquial term from here.)

The level of spiritual sleep and the term *level of highest spiritual acceptance* does generally have to do with that point in consciousness. It doesn't mean that there is a rigid ceiling upon where they can go and can't go. It's moreso of certain constraints holding them back ... an inability to function at these other levels, rather like an entity rising to high altitudes, geographically in the Earth, and finding difficulty in breathing for the first several days of residency there. After that, they make adjustments and change habits and/or schedules as were previously in place from the lower altitude levels. See?

How he can go on to full awareness? Well, that's ahead. You'll hear about that when we return to Peter.

Peter, Paul, and Abe are not associated presently in other incarnations. They are not in multiple levels of existence, carnally, physically. They are expressed on multiple levels of consciousness, but not physically and not in the specific individualized sense, as the question infers. Abe, of course, as we've given it, you know about. Paul has a broader range of awareness than Peter at the moment. Peter is changing, though, as you'll see.

Yes, they are a part of our grouping, as you suspected.

The differentiation between meditation and falling asleep can at times be a very fine line. For as one enters into the sleep period, they are as free or fluid to move about from their physical body as they are in meditation. Very often, the sleep-time movement is even freer and less limited. However, at the same time, it is influenced by other factors. And what you call lucid dreaming doesn't seem to be as commonplace in the Earth, as yet, as it might be.

In a sense, the falling asleep during meditation is reaching a stage or resting point, and that resting point does have an impact upon the body-mind connection to the spirit, and so the memory is placed into a rest state and, therefore, the true experience as it is encountered is still there, but the recall of it hasn't registered in the Earth consciously. It's in the registry of the subconscious, however. See?

So, in a sense, relatively speaking or comparatively speaking, yes, they have moved within themselves for a period of balance, just as Peter did. And that period of balance can be as productive to them as a meditative experience which is recalled. Such should not be minimized, even though often such entities are disappointed that they merely fell asleep.

The relationship between the entity Monroe's work and demarcation points in the comparative analyses of Peter's movement are difficult for us to make here. Monroe doesn't visit our group, and we haven't a personal contact with him in the manner which you would expect us to have to answer that question. Why? Universal records are subjected to Universal Law. Were we to delve into those records as applied to the entity Monroe without his approval, we would be in violation of Universal Law. On the outer extent, based upon your willingness to answer and your knowledge, a correlation can be made based upon what you have extrapolated from the experience. The indicators are comparatively close to what you have assessed them to be. However, don't be limited by those demarcations. Peter can just as well move to 29 in the twinkling of an eye. Or beyond. See?

There are places to where one is drawn for purposes of spiritual rejuvenation or balance. There is an aspect to the spirit which is likened unto a physical sense in the Earth. And curiously, it is inversive. In other words, it is the inverse of an aspect. If an entity is without fear, they have the possession of a spiritual sense. That is, in essence, inversely, faith. Faith is a power which creates additional illumination or luminosity to their spiritual cloak. This is adjuncted with yet another tool, spiritually speaking, which we will simply call love.

Both of these have connotations in the Earth which are somewhat different here. In other words, love here is an expression of the soul's potential, just like your senses or ...

A moment please ...

Very well. What's expressed here is that if an entity has sensory perception in the form of tactile movement, they might be particularly skilled at playing the piano or the cello, as one of the Voyagers does, and so, therefore, this entity (in an analogy here) in the realm of spirit might find that the sense of faith enables the entity to move about many different realms freely, fluidly, without interfering with them or being encumbered by them. See?

Such levels of (as one could call) rest are precisely where you find Peter at this point. The garden-like area is that which is used by a number of souls who are very active members of our grouping, and other groupings, as well. This, we'll call it, *existence* is supported directly by souls in other realms beyond the one we are speaking to you from at present. And this support comes in the form of another spiritual sense, which is called (or has been titled, for your understanding) quite simply, grace. See? And so the Law of Grace permits the existence of this realm. It is an oasis, a rest area, on a spiritual freeway (given with a note of loving humor, though there are many more comforts here than on your rest areas).

Completing a lifetime without karmic baggage is a matter which is dealt with on the individual level of each soul. The potential for releasing karmic baggage is ever-present in front of each of you. Find those things that frustrate you, that anger you, that sadden you and, ironically, that make you joyful. Explore, understand, and balance these so that you have a state of ease across the breadth and depth of your life, and you will have released your karmic baggage. Things that are exceptions in your life tend to relate most probably to karma. As with all things, there are always those aspects to be looked upon as blessings ... the light of your soul, the gifts that you bring in, and those things which are available to all under Universal Law. Thus, these things as stand out about you or in your life do not necessarily apply under that description.

People can and do choose their moment of death, even in the case of an accident where it would appear otherwise. Thus, you have those who miraculously escape an event which should have consumed their life.

Suggesting that entities release other entities is something that should be done all through their life, not just at the moment of departure. To love an entity is not to hold them, to bind them, to cling to them. It's to cherish and nurture them, openly, in the palm of your outstretched hand. If you admired a lovely songbird in a flowering bush just in front of you, would you think of reaching out and grasping it and clutching it in your hand because you loved its presence and its song so much that you didn't want to let it go? That's the whole issue there. If you hold it a bit too long, you'll harm it, you'll damage it. You'll prevent it from being the thing of beauty that you loved in the first place. See?

Yes, continue to suggest this, and even more emphatically. Be a bit bolder. The time is in the Earth where that's needed. But it's not your responsibility. This should become a way of life, that entities realize that life is eternal. As those who are to be the preparers of the way are awakened, you'll see this more and more.

The tug from Abe was, indeed, as you have defined it. Tell an entity not to give up, keep fighting, and also that life will be less brilliant without them. But don't tell them not to give up and keep fighting to stay in the Earth, but to not give up and keep fighting to be joyful, and to be as God wishes and is right for them. And if that includes moving from this realm to the next, then be assured that so as there is purpose and joy for you both, you will be together again ... that simple, that straightforward.

There is no offering here that can temper the loss of a loved one in the Earth. For as surely as one gathers the light of joy and happiness from friendship or family or child about them, and that light moves from their presence, would there not be a sense of loss? But the recognition needs to be focused and emphasized upon the fact that that light does not go out nor diminish, but becomes more brilliant as it passes through that veil of separateness between your realm and these. The love which is a part of being together in the Earth does not cease. It expands and multiplies. And those moments which are together, ye and those who are loved ... Let them be meaningful, and let each moment be as precious as the bird which might fly from the branch in the next moment.

Those who are well-noted or famous are protected and preserved in certain ways, and the Veil of Separateness is a part of that mechanism which protects. When there exists a bond between that entity and one or more entities back in the Earth, that is the exception. In the case of an entity who is notorious, that bond usually doesn't exist on a personal enough level to have impact upon them. So, Elvis is, in that sense, in peace with the exception that he is having to deal with his own choices and his own experiences in the Earth.

Encourage entities to do that which is in accordance with their belief. If you counter that belief, then you are attempting to lead them. Offer your suggestions, and if pain medication makes their life in a state of greater ease and tolerance, then that's a suggestion offered from that level. But if you add to this that the pain medication is an aid to transition, that's getting just a bit to the point of leading. *You* know it; that's sufficient. Entities need to be encouraged to find their own way, but not to be led or forced. Those are the signets, the indicators, or a good guide.

If Peter had been in pain, he would have remained in the Earth. When Peter left the Earth, he left the pain behind. In other words, pain and transition are not bedfellows, necessarily. Peter experienced pain only when he was briefly in the body. Most of the time in those latter stages, he wasn't. That's true of most. Exceptions? Of course.

Everyone has a family member in the spiritual sense. The power of the presence of those in both realms who love and care for an entity should not be minimized. This greatly enhanced the movement of Peter, and is a work which should be sought after, desired, on the part of all of you. True friendships are one of the best, the greatest, accomplishments of any lifetime. If you have a true friend or are a true friend, you have that much more light to make the passing brilliant. This can't be over-emphasized here. One of the greatest expressions of true love is being or having a true friend.

If each entity entering into a matrimonial relationship sought first as vigorously to develop an attitude of true friendship between their potential mate and self, all would stay together. Or they wouldn't have the relationship in the first place. They'd be such good friends, they'd recognize their differences were too great.

All entities have guides. Some can refuse them. Some choose to ignore them, just in the manner as some choose to ignore the existence of God. But they still have both.

Near-death experiences involve the activity of following a path of bright light because that path of bright light is the soul connection. In other words, that light between the soul and the existence of that soul in physical body in the Earth is the bright light that they perceive. In effect, that's as though they move immediately from the Earth to the point of spiritual rest or sleep, as Peter did after his side journey, so to say.

Peter had the advantage of knowing that he was moving from the Earth and knowing that he was met by a guide and, thus, his spiritual awareness was greatly enhanced by those activities. Now, all of you who are a part of this grouping [Voyagers] also know that. So, when it comes time for you to come here (to return home, in a manner of speaking), you'll have those advantages, too. Try to keep them conscious, foremost in your mind.

The white light is that which is perceived in the state of spiritual sleep. Even though Paul perceived Peter as becoming, in a manner of speaking, inactive, the experiences had by Peter would more closely match those of the near-death experience. See? Generally speaking, the opposite is the consistency of occurrence: Near-death experiences rarely, if ever, have the type of experiences that Peter had. While Peter had the same experiences as they did, but in a different way and accomplished through different procedures, Peter's was and is the more desirable for the attainment of greatest spiritual growth.

The sleep of spirit can occur at any level, even within the Sea of Faces. It does not necessarily have to occur at the highest level of that realm. But Peter's did. He ascended through that realm and then went into his spiritual sleep. NDE's don't always do that. See?

In the inquiry as was expressed with the (quote) "coincidentally, I guess" (end quote) commentary, we have the following to offer: As we gave just above, the period of sleep or rest is not always as it would seem to those generally in the Earth. The sleep state can be as productive and/or as active to the experienced sleeper (or worker, in the more appropriate sense) as can those well-practiced in the activity of OBE's. And as such, your knowledge, your experience, and the information you have absorbed, brought you to a point in that time of what we'll call spiritual and emotional change, where those forces which are adjacent to you were able to create an environment which was productive to your soul, your mind, your emotion, and your body.

Another way of stating that to you (perhaps more understandable) is, because of your efforts to better understand your true nature and your expressions of, in essence, reaching beyond self to higher levels of awareness, this formed sufficient bridging between the semi-conscious state and the spiritual state to enable the experience to take place. It was and is as the experience you described that Peter had. And so, a duality of accomplishments was made. Those which you have defined for and from yourself, and those which the entity who had part in your life also experienced. The entity, perhaps curiously to you, wasn't as bound to the Earth in some ways as might be expected. And actually, in the last several Earth months accomplished much in terms of realizing his more eternal nature (though he wouldn't have nor didn't express it in quite that way).

Expectation is a form of joy in the spiritual sense. And as one has expectation, no matter how it is expressed, this awakens the potential of the soul, the spirit. And so, as such, you became a vehicle which enabled not only those who are a part of his grouping or who are guides to him, but also the awareness and subsequent presence of your own spiritual light to be a lamp to guide his footsteps. Your spiritual cloak and awareness were used to aid him. It was very much like the love and true friendship of Abe to Peter, and the obvious love and true friendship of Paul to Peter. And so, between the two realms and the two individual workers, the transition was made passable with considerable ease, and some joy, as well. See? You should find more frequently now your sleep periods different, in ways which will be, we should think, of curiosity and joy for you.

It's not necessarily desirable to have a certain color in your aura predominantly, as we gave earlier, but rather, to be capable of directing thought-forms which have as their resulting effect the production of color. In other words, remember, in the next realms thoughts will become reality very swiftly, and the realization of that will impact your soul all too quickly when you enter those realms. The reaction of those thought-forms (as we told you, the heavily embodied red impacted Peter with a jolt, a thud, recall?) ... well, that emotion, you see, is symbolized by that color. It's not just the color. It's the thought-form behind same. Those thought-forms exist primarily in that realm because they are associated with the Earth-plane to that color, and therefore, that realm or strata. (We hope this isn't too confusing. It's quite simple. It only gets complex in the explaining.)

Here is a suggestion ... If it seems too complex, experiment with it: Go out and look for one of these colors and ask for guidance, for the presence of God's spirit, and one of those who are with you will protect and envelop you, along with your own envelopment. See? Always remember that when you travel, and you are in physical body in the Earth, that your life force is one of the strongest and most pure and powerful cloaks that you could ever wish for. Affirming its presence amplifies it. See?

If you seek to develop a certain perfect blue, there is a good aspect to this. Not just because you can turn to others and say, "Did you know I've developed a perfect control over blue in my cloak?" They may look for another table to sit at if you say it too often, we fear. However, what's important in this is, as we gave or inferred earlier, as you exercise or as you develop or use those gifts and blessings that are yours, you become adept at them. And that's desired. So, if you can project a color and work upon a perfect blue, also remember what you are attempting to convey with that. What's the thought-form that you are building or projecting with that perfect blue? Just developing the ability to project a perfect blue is likened unto an artist in the Earth just putting several blobs of color on a canvas and walking away. Develop a thought-form with it. Make a portrait or a picture out of what you are doing. See? Whether it's a monograph or what-not, be in control. Direct the power of your potential. Then it's a good idea.

Well, if you see Peter's cloak as green, then that means you can see Peter. In which case, if you can see Peter, you're not in physical body, and Peter's cloak *is* green. And that's that. However, if you are in the Earth plane, and you perceive the aura on someone else, and it appears green, it may not be. You may have yellow in your aura cast upon ... (what's that color ... blue?) and you'll perceive green, while another may not, and they'll perceive blue. And that's that. See? (Given with a note of loving humor.)

Perception is all-important, but it's not so much a position in terms of where do you sit or stand physically as much as where does your thinking and acceptance stand or sit? If your acceptance level is high, then you are in control of your spiritual senses. That means that even though you are in physical body and conscious thereof, your ability to control your spiritual senses gives you the ability to see. And therefore, you would be looking through what, in essence, would be a clear cloak, and you would perceive what is. That's what makes seers seers and prophets. They can get themselves and their emotions out of the way sufficiently soas to perceive what is. That's the ticket. See?

The question of earning colors for one's cloak (that humored the Channel) is not that far from accurate. In other words, look at it this way: If you gain the ability to control thought-forms that have to do with, let's say, charity and hope and long-suffering and/or forgiveness, these tend to relate to very high levels of energy, and ofttimes have to do with the upper chakridic centers. And, therefore, may gain you that certain corresponding color, which, in this case, approaches the indigo in the spiritual sight, or the white or silver or golden in the Earthly ... the function, then, of that being, essentially, again, the accomplishment of having control. And as you have control, that's evident in your cloak or in your aura. The aura is the physical counterpoint of the spiritual cloak, and vice-versa. And so, therefore, you can find that correlation useful.

If an entity has a preponderant beautiful control over purple in their aura, you can be reasonably certain that they have gained some significant spiritual control. An alternative to this, possibly, is the presence of a highly evolved guide or mentor or some such who is channeling same to the entity. But the end result or conclusion amounts to the same; generally, you wouldn't find the one without the other, see.

The envelopment for Peter in his movement was to prevent an over-reaction on the part of Peter from allowing him to be caught in that corresponding color. The concern here is that the guide has a certain degree of participation with those whom they guide ... their chelas, as is called in the Eastern philosophy. And therefore, those who are their flock are one with them.

The bonding, you will note, took place early on between Peter and Paul, and as the movement progressed, the spiritual bond between these two entities was quickly reawakened. And so that bond, then, provides Paul with some latitude and some participation with Peter. Therefore to protect Peter is no different than Paul protecting himself. He has that right and, in a manner of speaking, that duty. Peter was being guided by Paul, and is being guided by him. Therefore, Paul has certain rights under Universal Law that do not hinder him from stepping before Peter in some instances.

Peter has work to do ahead. Paul is the guide to help Peter reach that point and realize it, and make that decision. And therefore, the presence of his cloak is a blessing, and protects him from being vulnerable while he is in an accelerated state of growth. Entities of such a state of accelerated growth are subject to ... or more vulnerable than normal. Entities who are moving at a lesser pace (so to say) are not subjected to these influences because they are moving only to the extent that they are completely capable of balancing with all around them. Peter's movement was and is much more rapid. See?

What's being protected is the integrity and the right of free will of Peter. He's being protected from the thought-forms and those who are perpetuating same in that area of consciousness wherein you heard the action take place. Paul's cloak remains around Peter even as we speak, even though, as you recall from our report from them, that Peter was off with Zack. Paul's cloak is very elastic. It reaches wherever Peter goes.

The experience of envelopment is, indeed, something you all experience, and you do so often. It is also something that you do for others. You do this when you pray. You do this when you care, when you love, when you feel a sense of compassion ... not an attitude of interference or whatnot, but of understanding and of love and of support, compassion.

The forming of an individual cloak of consciousness, spiritually speaking, around one's self as an individual, a group, a society, a planet ... is ... How can we convey this to you? A moment, please. It's not an option. It's not something you choose to do or don't choose to do. It's there. Once you affirm it's there, it becomes a tool, an extension of your senses, your awareness, by which you can do works.

The following has been given in response to the second aspect of that question: Yes, a cloak can limit. Anything which protects and preserves the integrity of that which is within it, in the containerized sense, also limits, does it not? If you limit something from getting into the container you must therefore also, to a degree, limit that which is within from getting out. Being conscious of the presence of this *buffer* (as it were) enables you to selectively choose which energies you wish in and which you wish to reflect or transform, i.e. filter (in the manner described, as with light, above). Therefore, choose that which is benevolent and useful to you.

You also, as you have command of your cloak, have the

ability to transform that which comes at you. If a force comes towards you in the form of a vibration or frequency, and you recognize this to be deleterious to you and in essence in discordant existence with Universal Law, since it's directed at you intentionally or by the free will act (voluntarily or involuntarily) you have the right to purify it and reflect it back in that pure state. The recipient, then, will become conscious of this and has the right to choose to accept or reject. They also have the right to reflect it back to you, in which case it's amplified back to you. And since it's good and joyful and in accordance with Universal Law, you can't lose, can you? Prayer is like that, see?

As you deal with the forces of emotion and those things which limit you in the Earth, you are working with your cloak. As you recognize that you are so doing, you enable yourself the availability of certain tools. It's as simple as having a set of tools in front of you to do works and choosing to ignore them, or to use them.

You are correct. Better to deal with, and work with, the emotion being cognizant of the presence of the cloak (how it functions and you can use it as an adjunct) than to simply focus upon this or that color, or whatnot. The value, as we indicated it to reflect and to filter, however, is productive in your evolution. You can use this to rid yourself of excess karmic baggage. That's one of the good tools, see.

Very well, we're going to pause a moment here. We'll return briefly.

...

Very well, we are returned and we continue. We invoke our earlier affirmation and prayer and continue in Thy Name, Father. And we thank Thee. Amen.

Let us turn to some of the other questions unexpressed by the Channel here to the present point.

When a soul has consciousness of their intended purpose or spiritual work for an incarnation before coming into the Earth, and then presumably after being incarnated, awakens somewhat spiritually and asks themselves one morning, "Now what was it I came here for?" the answer to the question is generally very visible before you. The tendency is to ignore it and to look for something that isn't what's before you. Most of the time, those things which are the elements of your labor are those things which are important to your soul in terms of the individual consciousness.

Guidance to attain understanding of the soul's purpose, or the greater collective work, can be attained best by attuning to that source within and allowing self to be guided by same, perhaps using some of the information given earlier on this topic of colors. And that yet to come on the remaining topics might also be helpful.

The potentials that you follow in life are not by happenstance, even those which you make which seem to be just free will choices (and perhaps not the best ones). Your opportunities follow you, no matter what path you take. You can't take a sharp turn here at this road at age twenty-one and lose your karmic baggage. It will follow you no matter how twists and turns you make in the road of freewill on the pathway of life.

Karma doesn't need a roadmap. It's a part of you. Karma is your purpose, your work. Group karma and soul karma are different things. They have much more latitude. But free will choices and voluntary efforts ... Those abound at every turn.

Raise yourself to higher spiritual consciousness and ask this simple question: What things would our Lord have me do, were He at my side at this port upon the road of life? One of the first that would be an encouragement to you, dear sister or brother: *Art thou joyful? How may I serve you to bring you joy? For I love you.* Your good works usually begin within self and spread from there.

There are life forces on many different spheres in many different levels of consciousness, and that includes the focal point in time and space called Venus... not in the physical form as you know it. The potential of you becoming aware of this is increasing and does not necessarily mean that you have to make a transition from the Earth physically before becoming aware of it. That's all we can give on that point. It's not our work to be that much involved with that subject matter (as it might collectively be called). Those souls who are part of that sphere of consciousness are often present here. But not in that form as is their expression there, but in their spiritual form ... just like Peter's here.

It's not so much so that God wishes you back (to answer a question which is unspoken) for you've never left. Your question presumes that you've departed from God. God doesn't want you back, because you haven't left. God wants you to have the highest and best, the most joyful, the most wonderful of consciousness. You and others have chosen paths which have progressively limited that joy. In essence, His wish is for you to become aware of what is being given to you. It's like someone sleeping through their own birthday party. Unheard of. See?

Your use to God, when you do reawaken, is that one entity, joyful, alone is a wonder to perceive. But if there is only one, who does the perceiving? Two entities are not just twice as joyful but perhaps four times as joyful. Four entities are so much more joyful that it is immeasurable ... not an exponential value, but far more than this because you'd need to move in multiple dimensions and directions. And so with the adjunct or addition of each new awakened soul it's like adding another perfectly tuned instrument to a symphonic orchestra. The depth and breadth becomes even moreso inspiring.

If you feel that you should be doing more in your life, then stop doing what you're doing (given with a note of loving humor). The question was, "I often feel I should be accomplishing more or doing more in life." What you are doing in life, more often than not, will remain in that life. What you are doing in spirit while you are in physical body will go with you no matter where you are. This is not to become idle or ... (is it larconic or lactonic) [lethargic] ... well, colloquially, it's lazy, but, rather, that you would become a balanced entity in the Earth, joyfully functioning, knowing that you are not of it. And the greater work that you do at this point of your life is to be the example. If you look for great ways to measure your life you will find it takes a great effort. But if you look for the little ways to measure great opportunities and actions, you will find it easy.

You never know the form or the manner in which the Master might confront you ... a weary passerby yearning for a smile, a greeting, a confirmation that someone cares. Could that have been the Master yesterday at the counter at your elbow? Could it have been He behind the wheel of the automobile parked at the same stoplight next to you? And so forth. The one in need is the great opportunity. Those who aren't in need are blessings. See?

You have, as the potential, a direct communication or link to God. If you choose to allow yourself to realize this, then there are no expressions between you and God. The more you are unable to accept this, the more likely you are to have additional levels or points of demarcation between yourself and God. For that, the question was, "If we are expressions of God or of our soul, are they direct or are there expressions in between?" There often are expressions in between, but not as individuals. They are sort of like protective envelopments of limitation. Follow that?

When two or more members of a soul grouping are expressed finitely and physically in the same place, the potential for the accomplishments of either or both is dramatically enhanced. This has to do with spiritual Laws. The elaboration on this is simply the power of reflection. Even though this may be conscious or unconscious, all such forces travel. And as they travel, they impact the thought-form in which that existence is being sustained. Therefore, the greater is the light within darkness, the less dark is the darkness.

There are those guides in the Earth who function like Paul to Peter. Paul has been with Peter (and vise versa) for much consciousness ... a great deal of time. Each entity has, for the specific incarnation, another entity who is a counterpart of Paul, though this may change as entities grow or realize that you might need some different assistance. But generally, the guide that is with you (or if that's plural, as it is in most cases) at the time of your entry remains with you until you return. That continuity and connective link between you is important. And, again, this approaches a complex subject matter, but we believe that sufficiently answers your question. Does it not?

Those who are of a higher level of spiritual acceptance or consciousness are generally not detectable or visible to those in levels beneath them. This is a graduated thing, you see, and the lower the level or the more finite or dense the vibrations are for that higher-consciousness entity, the less visible they are. Visibility, then, becomes a matter of application of Universal Law, the request on the part of the less conscious entity to one of a higher consciousness, or to God, in which case, the changing or altering of the energy patterns, i.e., controlling the energy patterns of their spiritual cloak (color, see) ... understand that? Controlling the color then enables the entity in that realm to perceive them. If that entity is in a realm (for example) which is predominantly red, then lowering or changing the vibration of the spiritual cloak makes the higher consciousness-entity visible if that color is red. See? Entities perceive what they are willing to perceive in those realms.

Abe is an entity who is, indeed, very beautiful. Abe is

capable of knowing that he exists in a multiplicity of expression, though consciously in the Earth does not. This preserves the integrity of Abe in that individual expression. Abe can have that consciousness if it's needed or useful or called upon by him. It may come to him in varying form, but it's there.

Universal Law prevents a *bad guy* (as this Voyager has questioned) from being a guide. In other words, you can't be a guide and be of lesser vibration than the entity you are guiding. You must be at least the equal or higher, and in most instances you need to be one complete level above that entity you are guiding, or at least on the highest possible spiritual level equal to that entity. This means that the entity may have chosen a lesser level of incarnation spiritually, and the guide is at the highest potential for that entity. See?

Universal Law is like a cloak in and of itself. Universal Law is God's spiritual cloak. See? It's around us all.

If Peter remained completely unaware of Paul's presence, little difference would be affected, with this exception: Peter would have progressed much more slowly. He would not have had the movement rapidly through the colors, the Sea of Faces, and into his present realm without Paul's assistance. This would have been a slow, measured, and probably involved lateral movement, as a pace. Inability to recognize the assistance of a guide is not different than the inability of being able to recognize someone who is striving to help or guide you in the Earth. The same, see?

A guide is a very handy person (with a note of loving humor) to have if one is wandering about in the Sea of Faces. That's not a good area to ... What's your term? Hang about, to loiter in.

There are no precise schools of guides (with a note of loving humor), though all of existence is a school for guides.

Guides are not, in that sense, an orderly flock. But on the other hand, they are indeed so. The moreso the subject is spiritually aware, the moreso must the guide, then, be capable of helping them at least to the next major level of consciousness, which means, in your vernacular, where Peter is now, Paul should be able to take him completely through, and to the same parallel level beyond the next spectrum of colors and through the next realm of existence, which Paul is capable of doing.

Each entity has the opportunity to guide frequently. Being a guide is equally valuable to the soul's consciousness as is incarnating.

And so, then, we would ask that each of you would think of yourselves as guides, as teachers, to those who are in need, in your prayer and in your daily actions.

And for the present, we shall now conclude. May the grace and blessings of our Father's wisdom illuminate your path and your works. Until next we meet, may the Christ Spirit be a lamp in your heart in these times.

Fare thee well, then, for the present, dear friends.

Q&A READING #3

Questions After Chapter 3:
ABOUT GOD (V-640)

Given June 2, 1990

AL MINER/CHANNEL: *This reading is code number V-641. It is the next in the series of readings for Voyager Project #6, and it is the first follow-up reading on the topic of "About God," which was code number V-640.*

I had to chuckle just a bit to myself as I realized after working with the questions that the first category that I have here of the Voyagers' questions is generally titled "The Flowers." And I guess if you were coming in from the outside, you might wonder how in the world we'd have such a topic or sub-topic under the title of "About God."

Nonetheless, once again, we have some superb questions, and let me go right into them. The next series of questions are a composite and a collection of questions received from a number of the Voyagers, including David and Leiko in Florida, Rudy in North Carolina, Patty in Florida, Ken in North Carolina, and several others of you who might recognize your questions sort of merged in with these.

QUESTIONS SUBMITTED

#1 - Please explain Zack's disinterested behavior regarding the manifestation of the flowers. Did Zack cause the flowers to become temporarily invisible?

#2 - Referencing the comment that the flowers came into existence through a "mutuality of love, of appreciation, and of wonder," wonder may simply imply surprise or astonishment. What was the intended meaning here, and does it apply to God?

#3 - Can we co-create a field of flowers here and now, if we want?

#4 - Lama Sing, the tape, "About God," reminded me of one of the most beautiful dreams I ever had. It consisted of looking at the center of a yellow cruciate (meaning four-petaled) flower and being overwhelmed by its beauty. Could you talk to us about the meaning of flowers when seen in other realms?

Next: I've had two other dreams that feel like the dreams of the beautiful flower given above. These were seeing a woman who was so beautiful as to be breathtaking. I remember looking into her face and being overwhelmed by her beauty. Peter is dealing with women and men in the realm that he is in, but it doesn't sound as if any have affected him this way. Who is, or what is, the meaning of an overwhelmingly beautiful woman? *(Admittedly, now, that question sort of skirted the fringe of being included in this topic, but I felt there were enough aspects pertinent that I did include it.)*

(Next, I have a category which is generally relating to the "book" itself ... from Reading V-640. These questions come from Dave in Maryland, Patty in Florida, David and Leiko in Florida, Marie in Washington state, Ken in North Carolina, Aida in Florida, and Patty in Florida.)

#5 - What exactly is this book? Is it just a representation of something else... something that is hard to describe in material terms? What, exactly? Do each of us have a book of our own? Does the book represent the presence of the Holy Spirit or the Christ Consciousness?

(And here, one Voyager wrote about as concise a question as you could ever hope to get:)
I would like to know more about the Book of Wisdom. *(I think we all echo that question.)*

Please tell us more about the Book of Wisdom. Does it simply open Peter's acceptance of higher knowledge and wisdom? Or is its literal presence important? Is it helpful to have the icon of a book near us while moving in other realms, to help attune us to higher knowledge?

Is there a correlation between or with the Book of Wisdom and the book which appears in the life seals, for example, of several of the Voyagers and, coincidentally, including mine? *(And that's from a Voyager in Florida.)*

(Here's another great question that several people have expressed to me verbally and only one put into writing:)

#6 - Who is the female entity in the garden with the book? And why haven't we had her name yet? *(Well, Patty, maybe you'll inspire the Lama Sing group to give us her name.)*

(The next group of questions deals generally with soul groups. And these questions are primarily from Dorothy in California, Lois in Florida, and Jud in North Carolina.)

#7 - Is Peter a member of the Lama Sing grouping? Is his aim now to reach higher and higher levels within the grouping? How does the Lama Sing grouping differ from others? And where does the grouping stand in relationship to others?

#8 - How many soul groupings are there, altogether?

#9 - Are most of the Voyager Project members part of the Lama Sing grouping?

#10 - It was mentioned in an earlier Voyager reading that one does not necessarily belong to any one soul grouping on a permanent basis. How would this affect Peter? Is a "tribe," as mentioned in a personal reading, the same as a soul group, and can one also join and leave, as in a soul group?

#11 - The names and souls, Peter, Paul, Abe, Zack, and unnamed souls ... What relationship do they have with the historical Peter, Paul, and et cetera? Why were they chosen, or why did they volunteer to be the examples for us here in the Earth?

Well, I will conclude with the submission of questions at this point, and we'll see what we get on these.

As always, Father, we pray that you would guide us to the very highest and best possible information. And we, again, thank you most gratefully for the wonderful information received, and we pray on behalf of all those dedicated and loving souls who have contributed to our receipt of that information. And let me also include a prayer for every one of the Voyagers who, no doubt, have inspired this caliber and quality of questions ... being mindful of earlier readings here and from Edgar Cayce that the posture of the people inquiring or participating has a great deal to do with the material that's received in readings. So, thank you, Father. Amen.

THE READING

LAMA SING: Yes, we have the Channel then and, as well, those references which apply to the questions, the grouping, and the entities now before us. As we commence with this work, we shall first pray in this manner.

Lord God, we thank thee ever for thy presence in all things. As we affirm your presence, we know that your spirit shall be that force and light which shall guide us herein. As we do so, we also pray, Father, on behalf of all those souls in all realms who are presently in some need and for whom there are none in joyous prayer. We thank thee, Father, for this opportunity of joyful service in thy name. Amen.

The entity Zachary was not, as such, actually disinterested in the manifestation of the flowers but, rather, was fulfilling a role which was part and parcel of an activity engaged in by all of the entities involved, and others.

His participation or actions of disinterest did not, as such, cause the disappearance of the flowers or to make them invisible but, as such, created a focal point in the mind of those involved, particularly Peter, which thereby produced a more rapid result. He was serving, then, in essence, as a catalyst of sorts. See?

Wonder used as the term, in essence, [is] associated with the word in your plane *miracle* or that which could be called admiration. Not, as such, in the sense of surprise or astonishment, for the result was perfectly anticipated and predictable. The intent and meaning here is that as God sees a work and finds it good, then there is joy and resonance, and the perfection of that goodness endures. This is the completing aspect of creation as is associated with that force which emanates, ever, from God. See? It is sort of a resonance which occurs between the co-creator and God, or, in those cases where such might be plural, co-creators.

You could create a field of flowers there in the Earth, if you wanted to bad enough. (In that sense, we do not mean bad in terms of good and bad, but strong enough ... given with a note of loving humor). The relationship between wanting something and creating it is not all-powerful. (There must first be the realization within self of all those factors which are evident throughout these and earlier works on such topics, of course, some of which you are completely aware of.)

The environment in which creation takes place has much to do with the degree of its manifestation or materialization in that realm. Here, in this realm (the Garden), all factors are in harmony and accept and agree on the possibility of such creation manifesting itself. Therefore, there are no limiting forces. All present are in agreement. In the Earth plane, not all agree. Therefore, that needs to be dealt with and may be, as such, a limiting facet.

We should think here, in terms of the cruciate or the brilliant flower ... The resonance of God's promise and the hope which is ever-inspired by the presence of His Spirit, again, is thought of here by those gathered as being emblemized or being made manifest in the form of flowers. We think of flowers, then, symbolically and literally, as the presence of God ... His hope, His promise there, ever, to inspire us. Wouldn't hurt for those of thee in the Earth to think of that each time you see them. It would strengthen. See?

The meaning of flowers in dreams, in visions, and travels beyond the physical, is profound. The stimulus from the flower, as is known in the Earth, has much to do with the sensory perception. Therefore, they are a particularly powerful tool, as it were, for creating and inspiring and for motivating the learning process. Thus, these are often chosen by the guides or by self or others who are the helpmeets to that purpose for invoking same. Growth. See? Whenever these are seen in the vision, in the dream and such, pay particular note. There are those forces striving very diligently to assist you when such are present. There are certain souls and soul groupings who use certain flowers as the hallmark or as the signet ... or perhaps the term (quote) "calling card" would be most stimulative of the appropriate thought-form in your Earth realm.

The presence of an overwhelmingly beautiful woman (or, conversely, a particularly handsome man, if you happen to be in a female body in the Earth) has to do with several factors, one of which depends upon the individual perspective. But, basically, it sums to this: Whatever facet of stimulation or whichever indicator is the most likely to gain your attention, to garner your focus, that then is, more oft than not, used as a mechanism of choice by those forces who are seeking to answer in God's Name your search, your quest, or your need. Therefore, again, it is the particular inspiration of a certain pivotal indicator that should be made note of in any dream, vision, or meditation. In your case, this particular emphasis has several-fold meanings beyond that, one of which has to do with your own individual soul grouping and a unique polarity that exists between you and the entity. More than that would require your individual records to be present. We have your group records here and the presence of the entity whom you speak of, and the entity conveys: This is sufficient for the present.

The book is not a symbol, in the sense that a symbol is thought of as being innate or inactive and typifying something which is elsewhere or has, as such, only a superficial implication of what is typified or emblemized but not present. The book is a literal expression, particularly in this instance, which is formulated in the expression of a book for the greater understanding of those involved. You'll understand that more later, in the future, as other works are to unfold. For the present, then, suffice it to state that no, it is not just a representation of something else, something that is hard to describe in material terms. It is specifically, precisely, a book. You could touch it, you could feel it, you could lift it. It has mass, it has weight.

Beyond that, then, the similarity to a book in the Earth departs. For this is a book not made of simple vegetative pulp or such, or fibers; nor is it just a book printed with a mechanism or by quill or such and ink. It is a book which contains the essence of knowledge or wisdom, and particularly as applies to the entity whom it is for. Therefore, each of you do have a book of your own. It is often thought of in some reference circles as your Akashic record. This would not be precisely how we would identify it here in this case. We would opt moreso for what's called the soul record, which is indicative of a complete essence of your being, while the Akasha tends to relate moreso to karmic influences and patterns which are moreso the result or recording of patterns and influences found in sojourns. The soul record has the resonance of your soul potential. The Akasha may, but doesn't always. (This is a topic which can become very broad and very deep, but we believe, or are hopeful, that this answer suffices.)

Your book, your individual book (as it might be called) would never be delivered to you by anyone other than the keeper of the records. Thus, the entity who bears the book is the keeper of your record. That entity, then, has a particularly important role and/or association with you, and you with they. More oft than not, this entity is of a perfectly balanced polarity with you, and you with they. And so we find is the case here, as you will learn in the future … once again, as we are permitted to join with our colleagues and the experiences of Peter as they unfold further.

The book represents the presence of the Holy Spirit and

the Christ Consciousness as these are found within every soul. The book is the direct lineage or link, in a manner of speaking, between that soul point of creation and the current and projected potential and choices of the soul. In other words, the book represents (both literally and symbolically, dependent upon the realm in which that information is given or brought) the complete knowledge, experience, and wisdom that your soul possesses inherently as its potential, and through the experience as it has unfolded. See that, then? Certainly, these comments will raise many other questions. Of this we have little doubt.

The Book of Wisdom does not simply open Peter's acceptance of higher knowledge and wisdom. Its literal presence is important, but the book does not, as such, in and of itself, do this. The mechanism is a bit more complex than this, in terms of explaining it to you, but, in actuality, it is remarkably straightforward. The presence of the book is the presence of Peter's completeness. Therefore, when the book is present, the completeness of Peter is at least potentially present. More often than not, you will find that entities, when they are preparing to (as you would call it) advance in terms of their consciousness, will most likely have the book present or brought to them. The mechanism which is involved there, in brief, in short, goes something like this:

Each time the soul transcends a level of consciousness, there is a completion of sorts which takes place within and about the entity. That completion, then, requires, in essence, contact with the summation or the polarization of that soul with its Source. Dependent upon the level of consciousness which is being sought after, this will determine or influence the method of presentation. In this instance, with Paul and Zack and the others, there is a significant growth opportunity for Peter. Thus, Peter is, in essence, honored by the presence of this female entity whose sole purpose in this particular point of consciousness is as the keeper of this holy record, or book.

The question arises as you hear this: Do you have a holy keeper of your book? Indeed so. Every soul does. See?

Is it helpful to have such as an icon or symbol near you while you are moving in other realms, to help you? The consensus here is, yes and no. And here's why: If you are intending such activity as we have just attempted to humbly describe to you, then it would be particularly beneficial, if not important, for the book to be there. However, if your sojourns were for the exploration and exercising of your spiritual development and consciousness, the presence of the book would be (potentially, at least) a disrupting force (albeit, the keeper or those present around such an event would likely prevent that from occurring ... [pause] We stand or sit corrected here: Not likely ... Would. See?) So, if you seek to have the icon present simply because you wish to have that knowledge, we do not believe that that would function for you. You could have the Akasha present, which is likened unto an abbreviated form of the Book of Wisdom but not the same. See?

The Akasha is that which is observed and used for providing information to the Earth by many such entities who serve as channels to others and themselves. The Akasha is that which is, generally speaking, available to most, within the constraints, as it might be called (or loving embrace, as it's more accurately defined), of Universal Law.

The Book of Wisdom is of particular import. It is not idle. It is not a symbol. It is not an icon. It is a source of wondrous, beautiful potential. See?

The correlation between the Book of Wisdom and certain life seals does exist. In other instances there are references to books of knowledge which have to do with the awakening of the soul consciousness within that lifetime. The life seal is the pattern which has to do with the nature of the soul's potential, opportunities, and soul purpose for the current incarnation. And as such occurs, frequently there will be a depiction of a book or books in the life seal. This, then, may be thought of in several-fold perspectives. Firstly, that there is something important that is to be learned and/or gained in that incarnation. Secondly, the potential for service, in terms of being an example or a teacher or a mentor, or a channel of blessings to others in the Earth, is also a potential. Thirdly, that certain wisdoms are being offered to the Earth in terms of a method of conveyance which has to do with the consciousness of minds. And as souls awaken and focus upon what could be called their own life pattern or seal, this forms a bridge of sorts that makes available that knowledge or wisdom to other souls in a like manner who are attaining (or have attained) that same consciousness. It forms, then, somewhat of a communicative link. We do hope this is not too abstract. We are attempting to convey this as concisely and clearly as possible.

The female entity in the garden with the book is the keeper of the book, the keeper of the record or records. This entity has not identified herself intentionally. We have not identified the entity at the entity's request. In due time, as is appropriate, the entity may permit our identification of her in a manner which you would comprehend. For the present, such identification would be considered premature and might disrupt the processes (in other words, the proceedings here) until Peter has awakened a bit more. We would humbly ask your indulgence in that regard. See?

Yes, Peter is, indeed, a member of our grouping. He is, in fact, a member of our soul grouping. He is in the process of reaching what you'd call higher levels. That is a part of his purpose and, as given above, one of the reasons why the Book of Wisdom is present. See?

Our grouping differs with others in essentially very few ways. And yet, as you might from the Earth look upon our grouping and other groupings, you might see the differences as being profound. That is, perhaps, because of the mannerism in which each soul grouping might choose to manifest their works, and also the particular ray or tenet or vibrational frequency which is chosen as the primary force for that grouping. In such cases, soul groupings choose certain forces, certain primary tenets, to be that which is the mainstay or communicative link or supporting flow of consciousness for the works which they are about. In some instances, this could be interpreted (by those who can *see)* as a color; by others as a sound; and by yet others as a substance. Depends upon the perspective and the potentials ... that is, the forces which are exercised by the viewer.

We are a part of that force which is supportive to Peter. And, as such, and as will be seen in future, Peter's activities are important to this grouping, just as your activities as a grouping in the Earth are equally important.

In terms of the definition of the word *important*, we have it here as follows: We consider service and work with Peter a privilege, an honor, a joy. And, thus, it brings resonance to our consciousness to be a part of any growth or experiencing which is to take place in that regard. We also experience (if you would like to use that term) the same in our service with you, your grouping in the Earth.

Differences between soul groupings actually are minimal, in the sense that once the soul grouping reaches that point where they have a consciousness of their heritage, this forms an instantaneous bond of awareness (at least potentially) between the groupings. Now, be mindful that we are referring to the term (quote) "soul grouping" in the context in which you have thought of it, not just in the words you used ... what you thought of it in terms of soul groupings in realms beyond the Earth. For those who don't know your thoughts, let us also state here that there are soul groupings which are not in these realms or not in those levels of consciousness which are outside of finite or, perhaps more appropriately defined, as three-dimensional expression. Such soul groupings, then, could be thought of as being much less than this, in the sense of being aware of other soul groupings. Such soul groupings could be in a state of consciousness and expression which is, in essence, of choice and/or limitation because they desire it. There is a difference. See?

We are searching for the answer to the next question above … [pause] We regret that we do not know how many soul groupings there are. The first response which comes from our assembly is that there is but one soul grouping, but many derivations or divisions thereof. Just like one central nervous system with many branchings and many sub-branchings. The further one moves into finiteness or finite expression, the greater are the number of tributaries and/or branchings, and so you have this … Would you call it a splintering effect in the Earth?

Wherein soul groupings divide and subdivide and specialize and subdivide, and so forth, until ofttimes it's difficult to recognize them as such, as functioning soul groups, rather than as independent thought form expressions collectively assembled around a grouping of souls. There's a difference there which we hope is evident in that which we've given here. See? Perhaps we could get that information from the keeper of the records. We'll see in future. As associated with the Earth plane, there are a certain number of what we see as (you could call them) primary groups. Of these, there are, generally speaking, seven.

We are searching out the records here in answer to the next question. As we do so, let us respond, as well, that soul groupings do not necessarily need to be thought of as defined and compartmentalized, segmented, but rather as entities who would gravitate around a central focal point. In other words, you could be passing by our soul grouping and (as an analogy that might be explicit from the earth) were that to be gathered around a campfire, you could join our campfire. And so it is here, see, in essence, that souls can come and go. They're not bound. They don't take an oath and that's it, see?

We think of all of you as members of our soul grouping. What does that mean to you? We don't know. It would have to depend upon the individual. If you wish to be a part of our soul grouping, as we would wish you to be, then you are. That's all that's required. There's no initiation nor any fee (given with a note of loving humor). Let us turn for a moment to a bit of recapitulation, we believe is your term, of what we've stated above. First of all, the relationship between an entity in the Earth and their soul is not as distant or as striated or as demarcated as you might gain the impression by what we have given. Conversely, the mechanisms which we have defined here are as much opportunities for those who are involved with them on these and other realms, as they are for you. In other words, as you ask or as you seek, it is a privilege, an honor, to be here and to be associated with such efforts on the part of self (that being your grouping) or any other entity who is in askance.

The book, as it were, is not hidden or secret or anything of that sort. Conversely, it is preserved. It is regarded with reverence and love and particularly attuned compassion to the entity who is represented through and of same.

The term (quote) "tribe" (end-quote) is somewhat of a colloquial term that has to do as much with a heritage or a lineage, defined somewhat by terms which could be ensconced by the following: racial karma, primary purpose karma, and variations of that basic theme. In other words, it has to do with an alignment with purposes which may have taken place earlier, historically speaking, as relates to the Earth or any other realm which is similar or comparable to same. Therefore, when the term *tribe* is used somewhat interchangeably with the term *soul grouping*, it has very much the same type of criterion (structure, order, and opportunity) as does the term *soul grouping*.

However ... (given with a note of loving humor; it seems there is always one of those, doesn't it?) The *however* in this case is simply this: The souls who are a part of such, generally speaking, tend to be a determined lot, and to the degree that they have that as their ideal and purpose, it is well-defined and they tend consistently to follow patterns which emulate that. See the difference? As opposed to soul groupings, in the freer interpretation of that descriptive term, are, in essence, not quite so confined in terms of their area of focus and/or work. Not a hard and fast dictum, but a generalization.

Well, then, the names, as the question above indicated, are purposeful and are significant, and in some instances do have a correlation to what you call your biblical references. Though there is no intent here to make much ado of this but, rather, these names seem to be those which most resonate with these souls and are, in fact, names which these souls have had in past and particularly names which were used when these souls made significant progress, gained much in their consciousness.

Here's another guideline for you: Generally, when souls are identified by a particular name, whether through here or other such references, that name is indicative of some particular accomplishment aligned with that soul and also, possibly, some particular potential as with your need. Therefore, you see, there is a duality of function involved.

The old adage, as we find it replicated here and also in your realm, *What's in a name?* ... a lot, sometimes. See? Names are vibrations. Vibrations typify certain forces and have to do, more oft than not, with an essence of that soul. Most souls would have an influence upon those who would assign the name and thereof, in a manner of speaking, could be said as having chosen the name influentially, second-hand.

The portion of your question, entity Jud, which has to do with why they were chosen or volunteered, is very difficult for us to answer. We can't find a comprehensive way of expressing an answer to you. It's not as one would in the Earth volunteer for a certain service out of duty or out of inspiration or out of a particular motive or goal. Souls are in certain positions, and in those certain positions they are in harmony with the conditions around them, and that harmony, then, is a part, usually, of a pathway through which certain works are flowing or being done. Then, as these pathways appear to those souls, it is likened unto a certain light or vibration, sound, color. The soul, then, as it chooses to join in or become a part of that, or to experience it, then in that way could be thought of as having volunteered (as we understand your term in the Earth). But it's not at all like volunteering, as such, that we can see. That's as close as we can find it. And we pray that that is of some assistance to your consciousness.

These are not idle choices, nor is that which we have described to you merely a series of constructed parables. What we are describing and what you are sharing in is actually occurring. There is actually a Peter. There is a real Abe, and also a beloved Zachary, with his mirth and joyful nature. God loves him dearly, perhaps because of that unique quality (given with a note of loving humor).

Let's turn to more of the questions, even though they haven't been stated by the Channel:

All souls are of equal consciousness. In other words, as we find it indicated here, all souls are of equality in and of God. Whether or not your term *created* or *creation* fits this is difficult to state. But the Consciousness of God is not limited to what you would call *serial time*. But, rather, would more appropriately be thought of, perhaps, in Earthly terms, as being parallel consciousness, wherein all creation occurred, in essence, simultaneously, as one grand thought or expression of God. The awakening of all of these aspects and expressions of creation may have and may be occurring serially, giving the impression of just being or yet to be created. The entire thought-form of all creation and all eternity already exists. The realization, actualization, manifestation, and expiration of eternity is still unfolding. So therefore, yes, you are correct ... It could have some dependency upon your concept of time.

With regard to a question on whether or not creations subsequently subdivided, in a sense we could find that this statement has accuracy. And if you consider your own potential it would certainly have to be appropriate, for you are capable of co-creating with God, and therefore, as your free will imposes its own choices and dictums, creation will be neverending. And, therefore, there will be divisions and subdivisions. Whether or not this would be considered the creation of individual souls by other souls, we know not this. It is a possibility, we would gather from the information before us, but we find no indication of it here as having occurred. Nor is there indication of any other soul grouping of those involved with these realms who have knowledge of such occurrence. Therefore, we would conclude from this assessment that this is not so, at least in this collage of expressions of consciousness as are directly aligned with what you would call your realm. There is moreso the alignment with what we have given just before this. See?

Turning now to the topic, generally, of co-creation ... We recognize that each of you is striving to understand and to overcome any limitations or obstacles as might have to do with co-creating with God. Much of the information which we have provided to this point in this work (this *project*, as it's called there) has been for the primary purpose of preparing you for such activity. Albeit you might conclude from the interpretation of the titles given for the subtopics of this project and assess them comparatively to the information given and see the variant as being distinct. Nonetheless, the intent here is for a certain work to be accomplished, and as it is moreso towards the completion, you will understand it. (Some of you already have, and one of you has asked a question which specifically defines that understanding has been gained.) That question will come forth in the next meeting, we believe, if the Channel functions as we presume he shall (given with a note of loving humor).

Being aware of your potential, your connection with God and your potential of functioning as a co-creator is not as foreign or distant as you think. You simply are looking for the results in a manner which is associated with something which seems to be beyond your potential. And yet, each Earth day that passes you are co-creating with God. There are those instances, many of them, which we have observed on the part of all of you, wherein you have employed your potential as co-creators with God. But because these acts of co-creation seem to be moreso the norm or moreso the commonplace, the wonder of them, the potential, has not had an impact or a registration upon your consciousness. Therefore, you overlook these. It is important to see, in the daily activity, the works and the contributing factors which are a part of God's creation and of which you are co-creating, when you choose, that you are doing and have done.

For example, when you encounter an entity who is distressed, perhaps saddened, perhaps frustrated, and you take action to supportively encourage, to comfort them, to nurture them ... in that moment you are co-creating with God. For it is God's intent that all souls shall find joy. And as you respond to that entity's presence and that call, whether spoken or nay, you are a co-creator with God ... You have become at one with the flow of God's spirit to that entity. A loving thought, a smile, a cheerful countenance, is being a co-creator with God. See?

If you look to co-create with God and to challenge the laws of your universe, your laws of physics, and the accepted thought-form of your realm, this you will approach with considerable difficulty because of these simple factors: Universal

Law preserves the right of Free Will. If the greater number of souls in your realm believe in a certain thought-form, they have the right to preserve that thought-form. If you take action which is destructive to that thought-form, then you are enacting the Law of Karma, and you will bear forth a responsibility for your actions. This doesn't mean that that will be a punishment, for you may have initiated something beneficial ... a gift, a blessing. Karma is neither good nor bad. It is simply the Law involved with action and reaction. See?

Co-creating in the sense of creating a field of purple flowers in your realm ... There are some of you who could accomplish this. Need a bit more work, but could accomplish it. The best of all environs for soul creating would be the collective assembly of a like-minded group. You will note that in the grouping around Peter they are of like-mind and in simpatico with one another. There are none in that presence who are unwilling to accept Peter's ability to create, or co-create with God. See the difference? This realm supports such creation.

Ultimately, every petal of a flower will look to its center. It will look to its point of contact with the total flower for its nourishment, for its support, and so forth. Even in the Earth, when it might seem to be the darkest hour, there is always that support from the Center of all existence. And the darkness will always give way to light in its season and in accordance with the will and purposes of those souls involved. Fear and doubt are perhaps moreso expressions of a finite consciousness. Fear and doubt are the preserving mechanisms chosen by the singular expression of consciousness which has to do with the personality of that expression or focal point of the soul and/or souls involved.

And it is this, then, which needs to be focused upon, perhaps moreso than any other singular point: that there truly is no separateness, that all are a part of the sum total of all existence. And that's a good work. That's a good contribution, and a good way of thinking. That sort of work can do more to support the potential for your ability to co-create with God a field of purple flowers, a rainbow, a green meadow, or such as you would. See?

The question about suggestions for reconnecting consciously with God and ways of eliminating doubts and fears ... Much has been given on the latter in earlier works here, and could be obtained if you so wish them. Some of you have participated in some of them; others have knowledge of those works. Nonetheless, doubts and fears can be tools. For, what is a doubt? A doubt is a position of polarity. It is a position of questioning. Fear ... This could be looked upon also in the same light but, more importantly, it is an expression, an exercising of a powerful force of mind called emotion. And as one begins to recognize it as such and, instead of denial, looks at these with acceptance knowing that they are present, this has a disarming effect, a neutralizing effect. While they yet will be present for some time, they are malleable, they can be worked with, they can be redirected. But if one suppresses or chooses to overlook certain fears or doubts, this is like placing seeds into the earth and covering them. Sooner or later, the conditions will be right for them to sprout once again. When they do, they'll bear more seeds of their own kind. See that?

"If Peter had been in the Earth when he created a thought-form of purple flowers, would they have appeared as quickly?" That was a question. Yes, they would have appeared as quickly, but they would not have been detectable by those who did not believe or could not see or acknowledge the presence of Peter. See the difference?

In the Earth, indeed, you do have elemental forces. But don't strive, in essence, to control them. Strive to know them, to become familiar with them, and to become a part of them. It is far easier to direct the flow of a stream of water than it is to block it and create your own stream, isn't it? If you bind up the waters which are flowing in the Earth, and creating and providing the supporting mechanisms to the Earth, in an effort to do your own supporting and your own creating, you are demarcating a sizeable task for yourself. Conversely, if you learn to know these forces, to become aware of them and in harmony with them, then they will work with you, not against you. They will complement and augment your intent. For example, the earth is a primal force in the expression which is called the Earth. If you had a handful of seeds, you wouldn't go plant them in the midst of a free passway, your freeway or street, would you? There's nowhere for them to take root. There is no yielding, no potential embrace. You would, rather, care for some good earth and place the seeds therein in the earth and cover and nurture them. You would provide that which you know to be their need. The difference, then, being seeing the primal forces in the earth or those which are the elemental forces as being a part of you, as well, all of them. If you are a child of God, which you most surely are, then all of God's creation is a part of you, and you a part of they. See?

The prevention of doubt creeping back in to taint or dilute a thought-form, a creative thought-form, is a matter of some individual focus. It is not a matter which is beyond the potential of any individual. It is a question of one's ideal and purpose. So doing, in essence, as we perceive it, requires in the Earth that that, quite simply, becomes important to you. If it's important to you, it will become a part of an ever-present urge or desire. The Law of Expectation will begin to act and react, and all manner of mechanisms will then begin to function in harmony with you.

The expression which is called doubt and/or fear is, indeed, as such, a thought-form which is contributed to and supported by habit. The habit can be inspired through the certain ingratiation of entities who perceive habits and similar activities to be pleasurable or of pleasure or of a desirous intent. Then such souls, as they desire this as a replication of their way of life, are contributing their life energy, their creative power, to the perpetuation of what could be called doubt and/or fear for the construct of a demarcated realm of existence ... which we have heretofore defined as (quote) "an illusion" (end quote). It is illusionary because it is defined as being all there is, when, in fact, it is not all there is; it is part of all. See? It is an expression of the sum, the total. The entity Zachary will, we believe, offer some insights to that point in times ahead with Peter.

If you think of faith as being a thought-form having a positive polarity or nature, and doubt or fear as having a negative polarity, then what you would have would be a situation of a polarized potential. If one accomplishes a state of equilibrium between these seemingly opposing forces, doesn't that, in the terminology and defined parameters of Earthly laws, equal balance? In other words, if you have a plus-5 force and a minus-5 force focused upon a median, you should be at a state of equalized energy; and as such, then, this equalized energy is capable of sustaining itself and harmonically preserving that environment. In other words, the equal push-pull force would not have a deleterious effect. There would not be a degradation of equally defined forces. See? Or, at the minimum, the degradation would be equivalent, for example, plus-5/minus-5, plus 4.5/minus 4.5 and an equal action-reaction. See?

Curiously, when such is defined in the Earth as balanced, and you have a neutral reactor, you have an idealic situation. Do you not? The correlation, then, between those forces which are considered eternal and those which are considered temporal or carnal is quite straightforward, as we should see it here. Each force, in its own media or expression, has a primal right of existence. For, so long as that right of existence is supported by the powers of creative nature, then it sustains itself, and when such sustenance is altered by the change of direction or focus of the creative force, there is a transmutation of that as a result. In many respects, what you observed or shared in with Peter's creation of the field of purple flowers was just this.

When Zachary called Peter's attention to himself through his activities and his mannerisms, it was sufficient, then, to allow for the dispersion or the dissemination of changes in Peter. These were, of course, identified as Peter's doubts or questions. Had there been the continuing focus of Peter on the field of purple flowers, this would have taken considerably longer. Thus, Zachary performed a marvelous and benevolent act, allowing this to be expeditiously demonstrated, evidenced, for all involved. Not the least of which are those of you in the Voyager grouping.

The question is: What is God's work and what is not God's work? It is not the labor of thy hand, nor that which is to thy body a certain work, or even unto thy mind; but it is the intent that determines whether or not it is God's work or not. You may have, perhaps, a potentially infinite array of variables in terms of circumstances, events, some of them perhaps never outwardly seeming as having the potential of ever being an opportunity to do God's work. But in all of expressions … in the Earth, in other realms, and such … there are always those opportunities to be a part of the pure Creative Force of God. Once you have joined in that force in a state of oneness, all that you do is God's work. See?

If (as in the case of yourself [the one asking this question]) one were an architect, then by believing and knowing that you and God are one, being an architect or doing architectural work is God's work. Because you are inspired in all that you do, then the creative power of God is before you and some blessing, some service, will be performed, whether you know of it or nay.

If you are, conversely, a cellist, and you think of your talent, your ability, in terms of having had to work to develop it, and then you come to play one melody which brings joy to a single individual, then all of the work which you performed to develop that talent, that gift, that attunement, has been God's work.

If you are a farmer and you plant a single seed which gives harvest to many ears of corn, and those ears are distributed and the seeds of same also planted, and they in turn give rise to many more ears of corn, and these ultimately come to feed an entire nation which is now in a state of starvation, have you as the initiator, having sown the single seed, not done God's work?

How can you know when the Call shall come? Ever stand the watch, and be at His side. Then, when the knock comes, thou might answer.

Each step of the pathway is taken in the presence of loving companions. Which step, then, might it be that the Master has walked with thee? Whose hand which is supported and grasped in friendship and understanding might it be that is the Master's? He will not test thee nor deceive thee, but only offer to you that which is His blessing. Be ready. Be open. Be receptive. And strive to be at one with that Force which is eternal.

There have been a number of you who have requested of the Channel and who have not expressed it but have thought it: that we might continue with further commentary about the discussion between Paul and Peter. We shall attempt to include at least a portion of that in our next meeting with you.

For the present, then, it is our prayer that this information might bring some light and joy to your hearts and minds. May the grace and blessings of our Father's wisdom ever be, as such, a lamp to guide your footsteps.

Fare thee well, then, for the present, dear friends.

Q&A READING #4

Continuation of Questions After Chapter 3:
ABOUT GOD (V-640)

Given June 3, 1990

AL MINER/CHANNEL: *This reading is code number V-642. It is the next in the series of readings being conducted for Voyager Project #6, and this reading will be Questions and Answers tape #2 relating to Reading 640 entitled, "About God." And here are the questions that I have received from the Voyagers.*

QUESTIONS SUBMITTED

#1 - Did Peter know these lessons while in the earth, or is he just now learning them? If so, then are we not at an advantage, learning these lessons now? And will we, when we pass over or go home, go to a different level? *(That's from Patty in Florida.)*

#2 - Is it possible for each one of us in the material or physical realm to ask God a question and know that an immediate answer is received? Or, do we have to wait for an answer or be uncertain? What is the answer? This seems so abstract and hard to understand. Why is this so? *(That's from Dave in Maryland.)*

#3 - I was wondering when someone was going to ask Lama Sing about "walk- ins." While we are still on the current topic, should we ask? Why don't we? *(And that's from Marie in Florida.)* Why does Peter not remember any of the previous "rites of passage" associated with transition? Since he has obviously had previous transitions in past lives, why doesn't he seem to remember that? Is this significant in terms of his final-ly being willing to accept God as God truly is? Whereas previous to this transition he has been lost in belief shaped by dogma or by a lack of self-enlightenment? Could you please describe his transition prior to his latest incarnation in terms of the differences in his acceptance of God?

#4 - Beyond balanced karma, what are the characteristics of one who is making transition and is able to find oneness with God sufficient to require no further incarnations in the earth? For example, the Edgar Cayce readings list approximately eighteen such people, and studies showed a commonality in that they all demonstrated a willingness to freely and totally give of themselves. But beyond that, they seemed to have lived diverse life-styles. In meditation, we seek to connect with our higher self or our higher Christ self. Where is Peter now in relationship to that con-nection, as he explores his oneness with God? *(And these questions are from Chip in Virginia.)*

(The next several questions really are the same, and they have to do with a general request for a continued bit of in-formation on ... Well, let me read the questions ... several of them.)

#5 - The discussion of Paul and Peter on the mind and spirit is of great interest to me. *(From Rae in Washington.)* Please continue with the discussion of the nature of mind and of spirit in the sense of infin-ity. Please define mind. *(From David and Leiko in Florida. And I've had others who have emphatically hoped or pleaded, perhaps is more appropriate, that we might get to hear more about that particular discussion.)*

So, now, with these outstanding questions, we pray of You, Father, that you would guide us to the highest and best possible information that can be given. Our thanks to You for our many blessings and special prayers to all those souls on the other side who apparently are working very diligently to help us here, and others like us. Amen.

THE READING

LAMA SING: Yes, we have the Channel then, and, as well, those references which apply to this grouping now before us, the inquiring minds of same, their questions, and the ideal, purpose and goal of this work.

As we commence herein, we pray of Thee, Father, that Thou would ever guide us by the presence of Thy spirit, wisdom and light, and we ask on Thy behalf that Your grace might transcend as a prayer of healing light unto all those souls in all realms who are presently in some need and for whom there are none in joyous prayer. We humbly thank Thee, Father, for this opportunity of joyous service in Thy name. Amen.

Peter did not know the answers to these lessons while yet in Earth, nor did he have the awareness of his potential while there. And yet, all the while he had become so at peace or at one with himself that this enabled him to break free of the final vestiges of what could be called those bonds which continually have an impact of luring, attracting, or creating a need for fulfillment by way of the vehicle and expression called Earth.

Therefore, indeed, you do have an advantage as individuals and as a grouping, in terms of the potential which is now offered to you and shall yet be offered further in those earth days ahead, by having an awareness of these as the potentials and what you might call the parameters and potentials of existence beyond the Earth. This is an important as well as an outstanding question and discovery. And, thus, we would comment a bit further here, as it has such merit and is a revelation of sorts as has been realized by this entity.

The question of existence is so tempered by the presence

of those forces which define or demarcate the realm of existence in which the consciousness of the soul is partaking of at any given point in time as measured. So much so that this presents for those souls who are involved in such wondrous opportunities for application of their collective knowledge, that it might become wisdom, which will produce, in turn, a state of balanced harmony. That state of balanced harmony is most desirous to attain. It is (as it might be called here, colloquially) the entire point of participation in the Earth. It is not defined as reticence or withdrawal and becoming involved in a hermitage, or failing to meet and exemplify what's known and felt within. It is, rather, that as one does meet and accept challenges, the spirit with which this is done and the attitude of the heart are all-important.

And so it has been the intent of the entire project, as it has unfolded for you now in this work to offer you these insights in a manner preparatory for what yet will come. And as you do discover within yourselves that this information can inspire a realization of what's behind the purposes and goals of all such information as has been and shall be given through these and other sources, as called, in the Earth (of which, of course, there is only One), then regardless of where or how that information might be conveyed or channeled to the Earth, the information as we have humbly but lovingly presented to you here might give a broader and more definitive reference point, offering you some of the *whys*, some of the answers to *Why is this so? Why must this be of such importance?* and what not. All the while understanding that no single thing, action, word, deed, tradition, dogma, creed, religion, theosophy, or what not is, as such, *The* Way ... until the entities involved with such have met the challenges of their own heart and desire, and have emerged on the other side of same in a state of balanced harmony, yet sustaining those qualities which are identified in so many writings and works as could be called *Godliness*.

And yet, this term seems to symbolize or connote something unattainable. It is just this point that we are attempting to share with you through the actual experiences of a soul not unlike yourselves, who has completed what could be called the requirements (loosely given, with a note of humor) of involvement with the Earth.

This soul, Peter, as he is called, is in the process of awakening. It is an activity which is appropriately called the *rediscovery of his own nature and potential.* And so it is well ... indeed, correct that by knowing, by learning, and by bringing even some small facet of that knowledge into a realization that it can be applied while yet in the Earth, will produce for you a wondrous bountiful result upon your transition from same. (A simply wonderful realization. Excellent question.)

Yes, it is possible for you to ask a question of God, and to know that an immediate answer is received. The question is all-important in terms of the purposes behind same. In other words, presenting a question such as "Shall it rain a week from Friday?" ... While it might be important to some, if asked in a state of idle inquiry, the answer might come in a like manner. But if you are asking because your crops are parched, your cattle thirst, and so forth, this has an entirely different impetus behind it, and the intent and purpose are for the well-being of these things. Conversely, if you ask for guidance in terms of discovering a solution to a problem, a difficulty, the answer is, generally speaking, immediately presented to you. The question is not so much so whether or not the answer is received; it's learning how to see and hear, learning how to recognize the form or manner in which the answer is presented.

It is important to preface any comments about this with this statement of truth: Remember, you have free will. That is one of God's most wonderful gifts to you. What would be the purpose in giving you free will, if God were to continually intervene, and particularly so when you are meeting opportunities which you see as challenges or problems or limitations? Those are the very times when your growth is most potentially productive.

For God to speak in a loud, clear voice to you while you are in the closet of your bedroom, meditating, "Son, the answer to your question is ..." and then the answer to be given places you in an entirely different position or relationship with God. And, as we would humbly state here, all the resources before us indicate this is not at all God's intent. Nonetheless, you have a connective link eternally to God. And as you ask, the information is presented, but in a form which is unobtrusive, intentionally so. The greater is your state of balance and harmony, and the more appropriate is the motivation for asking, the more probable the answer will come to you in a manner which is clear and concise ... but usually in the form of alternative choices, attenuated by the ramifications to taking or selecting these varying choices.

The test, as it were, of any source of guidance, in terms of its oneness with God, might well align itself with that just given. If a source of guidance tells you, "Go forth and do thus and such, and do it now," that might be somewhat in question. If that is the higher self, then that is well and good. But if this is guidance obtained outside of self (that is, through another as a channel or what not) let this raise some question in your mind. For guidance from God is presented as open-handedly as choices, as selections, with the ramifications stated to varying degree. But never in the form of "Do this or that and all will be well." The higher self or the direct guidance from within could do this, but more oft than not, you'll find it not to be the case.

We empathize with your statement that this seems so abstract and hard to understand. And yet, from here it seems so logical, so reasonable, and so appropriate. And beyond those, it seems to typify the incredible breadth and depth of God's love for you.

If you don't try, if you don't go forth and do, knowing

that at times your choices won't be the better ones, but that you will, through the process of trial and error, experiencing and going forth, learn to perceive with greater and greater clarity, wisdom, and sharpness of mind, so that, ultimately, in some point of time and consciousness, it will no longer be a question. That's what's being sought after. These are a part of the tools or mechanisms we are attempting to provide to you as an offering. And then, thereafter, it is your choice, the choice of all of you, whether or not you would try them and learn, from them, more about self.

Walk-ins do occur. They are, generally speaking, those souls who have gained the (quote) "right" (end quote) to so do. There are those souls who can enter the Earth who do not have to do so through the cycle of birth and death, the Wheel of Karma. These souls must be without karma when they so do. If they have karma, they will then be caught in the activities of the Earth by so entering. Walk-ins are also present during times of great change, cycles of intensity, such as your present time.

There are more walk-ins in the Earth at present than perhaps for the last five to twelve hundred Earth years or more. Some references here state that only in that time preceding the entry of the man called Jesus were there more walk-ins in the Earth. Choose the answer that best suits you. The topic is a broad one. You will learn more about this in a unique way if the choice is, in future, to continue following Peter as a collective work.

Peter does remember his *rites of passage* to the extent that these have produced a certain end product. That end product, collectively, makes for the foundational structure upon which his current consciousness rests. When an entity reaches that point wherein they can make major movement in terms of levels of potential, levels of acceptance, levels of existence, then that entity, generally speaking, will have a rather unique set of circumstances upon transition, just as you are participating in as Voyagers.

The circumstances around the awakening of Peter as they have been described to you, or you have observed through our commentary of them, are those which might be considered to be such works ... foundational, the collective assembly of his rites of passage. See?

He has, indeed, gained a position wherein he is capable of accepting God and is, for the most part, willing to accept God, but not just with abandon. He's questioning, he's asking. And that's appropriate, for when he does, he will move forward as he accepts what he discovers in his own consciousness. It wouldn't do for us or others like us to simply do something profound (by your references) and cause him to be fully awakened to his spiritual potential. It needs to be builded. It needs to be a complete awakening or it simply will not endure. At some point in the future, or in his sojourns, because of the lack of completeness that would result from so doing, he would, in essence, break down. And, thus, he'd have to return or move (by your references) backwards to regain or fill in that gap in his sense of completeness. Also, Universal Law dictates certain ways of existence ... not rigidly, but lovingly. And so one cannot exist in another realm of expression harmoniously or completely if they haven't completed, in the literal sense of that term, such fulfillment. See?

The transition previous to this incarnation took place in a place in your continent called Indiana. And as such, there the entity was what you'd call a tiller of the earth, a farmer's son, and then a farmer himself. The entity led in that lifetime a reasonably peaceful lifetime. The transition, however, had some emotional entanglements that were not completely capable of being released. As the result of that, upon transition the entity, Peter, who departed at about 63 Earth years mostly because of an injury he had received which later became complicated and developed into a build-up of drosses in the upper respiratory known as, then, consumption. Here, the entity made the transition, was met by several of the same entities who are present with him at this point, and one other who now has incarnated in the Earth (otherwise, would be present here at this point, as well).

Upon departure, the movement of Peter in that lifetime (when he was, by the way, called Nathan) was first to have to deal with fear because he was quite strongly steeped in theological tradition and felt he had not led a very good life. That fear needed to be dealt with. Thus, he was to spend a considerable amount of time in the more intense and denser colors. You will recall he still had a bit of reaction to some of the stronger ones for a time in this transition.

Remember his reaction to them where Paul tempered them a bit so that he could balance? Recent incarnations often do have some semblance of influence on a soul in subsequent incarnations, and so when he met the strong color red, he had a flashback of a sort that emotionally caused him some duress or discomfort. Paul was swift and accurate in his preservation of Peter at that point.

But in his transition as Nate, here we find that he dwelt heavily in the colors brown, deep dark greens, some of the heavy oranges, strong yellows, a powerful red, at which point in that experience of transition he was laterally moved (you might call it) into the sleep of spirit, for him to be able to balance and not to be drawn into that as a color and as a realm of existence, so that he could re-discover himself and, in essence, basically, forgive himself. See? (Zachary stated to us just then, "He had to unlearn some things.")

And so, then, after that he was brought to a point of some consciousness, but not in the fullness as you have heard and observed in the earlier meetings with Peter. In that state of consciousness he wasn't aware at the individual level as you see him now. He was aware, rather, at a level which is of a spiritual consciousness and looking from the position of the over-soul over the entire array, and so this was moreso like what many souls experience upon transition, wherein they are likely to return to the Earth or some other realm like same, providing they are not so intensely involved so as to be off in one of the realms of emotion where they must dwell until they are ready to release that emotion and/or have balanced it, or the same ... (both, see).

The activities were presided over quite similar to what you are observing here, but minus the fullness of consciousness and the reasoning and logic as you are witnessing Peter demonstrate here, now. Also, the communication between all of the entities involved ... those being Paul and Zack and such ... were not in this form at all. They could only, to the extent that Peter was willing (as Nate, then) to receive, offer these as he would realize them just in the framework of having had a thought or an inspiration or such. So, they were presented more as thought-forms, and only as he reached out to understand or discover did these become realized and, thus, become a part of his consciousness. Quite a difference, don't you see?

Again, returning to the question first above here, this does present you with a resplendent opportunity in the current life ... being aware of such. The question will come about, no doubt, as to why this opportunity and this information is being presented. Each time, preparatory to such a current cycle as is preponderant in the Earth and growing with each passing Earth moment, such is possible. And as more and more souls gather to know of their nature and to awaken, and as this light of the Way becomes more brilliant, it opens up the pathway. When such is opened, many more things are possible under Universal Law than in other times. That is simply explained, and we should hope understandable, because the consciousness of the souls in the Earth have reached such a point wherein enough souls are asking, enough souls are seeking and striving, so as to make for openings in the thought-form prevalent in your realm. And that's a greatly paraphrased answer to that question. See?

Beyond balanced karma, the characteristics of one who is making a transition and is sufficiently, as such, in balance or harmony so as to break free of the Wheel of Karma, or require no further incarnations in the Earth, is quite like the personality and attitude of Peter ... in other words, not greatly illuminated. In other words, Peter certainly must not appear to you as being a highly illuminated soul, we should think. And yet, the potential of Peter's luminosity is far beyond what you now anticipate. And you may be able to see what we mean in time.

The characteristics other than those which are evident in Peter, as you observed and heard, are as follows: Certainly, he is in a state of some considerable balance or polarization with what you call karma. He doesn't need karma any longer, to the extent that it represents a bond to the Earth. You'll note he hasn't had any strong thoughts or reflections about those souls who are left behind in the Earth. You've not heard him or observed his commentary about them. Had you not wondered about this? He hasn't asked how his family is, or "What's Abe doing today?" or "What's the level of the stock market?" or who's driving his BMW at this point (given with a note of loving humor ... he did have one of those).

Not at all. These things no longer have any power over him. It is not that he does not love those who are yet in the Earth. It is, rather, that this love is unconditional. In the works which were done with some of you on "Universal Law," you will recall we spoke about true love being that which held the object, entity, or whatnot which is loved, open-handedly, that ever it was allowed to have its own freedom. Peter has attained that sense of balanced love. Intuitively he knows that all is well. Intuitively he knows that what he could do, he has done. And that which he felt he could not do, he did not labor over. He did not become burdened by those things which he couldn't change, but, rather, he found a way to exist joyfully in spite of them if they were burdens.

He endured several serious bouts with dis-ease and over-came these with inspiration and hope for those who tended him. Always. In other words, he was a very good chap in the Earth ... not perfect, but good.

A goodness of heart, perhaps, is what you are looking for as the real answer to your question. Not an entity who can't be angered about something unjust or who doesn't have a bit of remorse when something loved or worked for diligently is whisked away. It's not an entity without feelings or emotion but, rather, an entity whose state of balance does not cling to or need retribution, balance, or what we could call clinging to things. See?

Another unique characteristic which perhaps typifies en-tities who are in that state (which are balanced, capable of movement) is the willingness to give and take ... in other words, the willingness to receive good or bad and, to the best of their ability, to deal with that and to look upon themselves and life as being abundant. That's an attitude of mind but it's an aspect of heart. There was never an outstretched hand to Peter that didn't have something placed in it. See what we mean? Whether that was figuratively or literally out-stretched to him, he took the time to love, whether the entity would obviously respond in kind at some point down the pathway of life or whether the entity might never be seen again. Intuitively, as the result of his progressions and his growth through earlier incarnations and whatnot, he knew that each act of kindness made him feel good. And, therefore, he adjudged that if it felt good, it must be good. (And we're not speaking of a temporal physiological feeling good ... good of heart. See?)

Don't look to complicate the matter too much, for it isn't complicated. It's the reverse of that. It's uncomplicated. And that's why it might be difficult. It's all the same with attempt-ing to hear God's answer to your question, as was also asked above. The more you complicate the matter, the more complicated will become the mechanism through which you'll have to sort to find the answer. Uncomplicate things wherever you can. Look for truth. Truth is pure and usually expresses itself in utter simplicity, the discovery of which is likened unto a revelation of light, like the sunrise penetrating darkness.

Where is Peter now in relationship to his connection, as he might be paralleled to have had one, in your example in the question as a connection with the higher self and/or the higher Christ self? Well, as we would believe you might have ascertained from what we've just stated, he was fairly well manifesting his higher self or Christ Consciousness while he was in the Earth. It's true, he didn't really know that, in the sense of intellectualizing it. He just intuitively felt this was right, and he had the strength to live by what he believed. He made manifest that which was in his heart, rather than vocalizing it or being a proponent of it, and doing quite the opposite, in life. He did not live a dual standard. He lived what he believed.

Where is he now in relationship to the scale you have presented? Well, Peter wasn't much on meditation. In fact, he hadn't really become what you'd call an adept in meditation. He did, however, have a practice which was precisely that which you would define as meditation, though he didn't see it as such: He would often seat himself in a leathered, upholstered, reclining contrivance in his study (which had a lovely view, we note) and had his own particular choice of music, and would simply look out over the greenery and down the slope and see a body of water in the distance. And he'd simply let himself be free. He'd do this as often as he could, but tried to do it daily. He felt it was simply getting out of the habit or thoughts of his business life and such, and recharging himself. That's what he called it. And it did just that. But it provided a clearer and clearer link between his composite being and his infinite being.

So, where is he at present on that scale? Well ... (There

certainly have been some challenging questions in this array, given with a note of loving humor and, as well, admiration. Our prayer is that the answers are equal in kind.) We'd state to you that he is at a point not midway between what you would call the higher self, but close to that. The higher self for Peter is defined differently than it would be were we to take someone who is still involved with the Earth. The higher consciousness for Peter would be well beyond where the higher consciousness would be for one who is intending to continue involvement in the Earth.

Peter's potential is quite profound at this point. That's the best we can do in answer to your question. Your association and your reason for asking the question might now be different than this. If you continue as you are in your development and in your application of your own realization, and you eliminate those several-fold doubts, as you have done well of recent times with regard to the worthiness of self (given with a note of loving humor), you could at this point, comparatively speaking to Peter, be at a state wherein you were in position with your over-soul or higher self. (That doesn't mean that you will have returned to the God-head, but the over-soul.)

In all of these comments as have been given, understand this, dear friends: Existence is not rigid. Therefore, when speaking from a realm which has definition of specific nature and boundaries or parameters, as you call them (which are in place as the result of a myriad of Earth years of support of that thought-form). the nature is to reference by what is known. And this, of course, is understandable. But when you leave a defined realm of existence and are attempting to grasp the concept of being unlimited, and then turn back to attempt to convey such unlimited nature, as you discover it, to the Earth, you would find that the methodology of describing same would be an extremely difficult task, without being able to demonstrate or show them what it is you are attempting to convey to them. See?

And so it is here with many of your questions. The best way for you to truly discover the answer to your questions is to apply what you know. You'll see more and understand better as we continue to follow Peter and the others through this process. Those who have provided the information here are from realms which are very much unlimited. And it is through the grace of their willingness to support and provide the information as you have received it to date that we have been enabled to provide it to you. We will continue to do so as they have advised they will continue to provide us the opportunity. It is up to you to attempt to look for and use. That is, look for the opportunities and use this information in your life in the Earth. See?

The other answers will come, we believe, as we proceed … including more about the mind and spirit and infinity.

For the present, then, we'll conclude. May the grace and blessings of our Father's wisdom be ever as a lamp to guide your footsteps.

We thank thee in humbleness for this opportunity and for the wonderful questions, as the Channel stated they were, and your willing hearts.

Fare thee well, then, for the present, dear friends.

Q&A READING #5

Questions After Chapters 4 and 5:
CO-CREATING (V-650)
THE CRYSTAL WORKER'S REALM (V-660)

Given July 31, 1990

AL MINER/CHANNEL: *This reading is code number V-651. It is the first reading to be conducted regarding tape number V-650 entitled "The Influence of Sound." [aka "Co-Creating"] The questions that I have received for V-650 are, once again, very stimulating, and I will now turn immediately to them, requesting that we would receive any and all information that would be beneficial to us in any way in regard to these and any unexpressed or questions that I have not received but that some of you may have thought of.*

The first questions have to do primarily with Peter and Zack. Let me turn now to them.

QUESTIONS SUBMITTED

#1 - Regarding the structure of the learning process that Peter is experiencing, will each of us go through a similar process in the "garden-like place"? *(From David and Leiko in Florida)*

#2 - I can't help but feel that Peter is somewhat of a representative of those of us Voyagers still here in the physical on Earth. And somehow, as he is experiencing these things, so are we, to some degree. Hopefully, by experiencing this with him at this time, it will facilitate our transition in embracing our unlimited spiritual awareness. *(Aida in Florida)*

#3 - What sets Zack apart? How has he become the great teacher that he is? I know that the answer to that is that he has greater acceptance. So that brings me to the real question: How come he's so smart (enlightened) and I'm so dumb (unenlightened)? What should we as a group do to accelerate our acceptance, that we may become teachers of Zack's ability? *(That's from Chip in Virginia.)*

#5 - What can Zack tell us about how to be more like he is ... light-hearted, protective, and playful, yet wise and supportive? *(That's from Lynne and her group in North Carolina.)*

#6 - Please discuss the present and past associations of Zack and Paul with the Master. Is that which they do in terms of teaching the result of direct guidance from the Master? Or the result of harmonic and intuitive oneness with the Christ? Do all souls serve in this manner at some point? *(That's from Chip in Virginia.)*

#7 - If we were to be able to control our thoughts, deeds, and words, to what degree could we eliminate our mental and physical illnesses? *(From Dorothy in California.)*

#8 - In Questions and Answers Reading #1, they commented something to the effect, "There is one of you who already understands, based on the question in the next Questions and Answers" (that would have been number 2). That struck me right between the eyes. I feel like I do understand, but do you think they really meant me? I thought they did. *(And that's from Patty in Florida. I think we're going to find that out, Patty.)*

#9 - It seems that having this knowledge opens up opportunities to apply this information. Opportunities such as old emotions one thought had been dealt with and were no longer an issue resurfacing. Old habits once controlled or thought to be under control make themselves known once again. This makes one feel as if little had been learned or, possibly, that a few steps backward have been taken. I realize that we alone are the ones putting ourselves to the test, which makes me wonder why we sometimes are such harsh taskmasters. *(That's from Aida in Florida.)*

(The next series of questions have to do primarily with sound ... which is, of course, the topic of V-650.)

#10 - Is there any instrumental or vocal music that in the Earth best represents or begins to express the beautiful symphonic colored sound as described when the group is responding to joyful singing and humor? *(From David and Leiko in Florida.)*

#11 - Several spiritual paths teach about different qualities of sound, like bees buzzing, violins, small bells, gongs, the sound of a flute, the sound of the wind. Would you teach us about the differences between these sounds? Is there a significant difference? Perhaps you could lead Peter into a situation where he would learn about them. Thank you, Al and Lama Sing, and please continue with the adventures of Peter if it is possible. *(That's from Ken in North Carolina. Well, as you all know, we will be continuing with Peter's adventures. Ken wrote that before he knew about that.)*

#12 - I had been reading various places that sound and light together are the creative building blocks of the universe, of life. At our or my present level of development in the Earth, what assistance can you give that will help us understand how to use sound (and light, if you care to get into that) to do the will of God in creating? How can we use sound and/or light to help ourselves and others to heal ... physically, mentally, emotionally and spiritually? Thank you very much. *(Christine in North Carolina, who's also a member of a group.)*

#13 - Could you explain about the sound that lifts Peter up into the air, up off the ground? In retrospect, I had a dream experience like this when I was eighteen. It was as if I had been engulfed in tingly lights that had a sound, and I felt lifted up into the air. It was a beautiful experience. How did it come about? What is its significance, and how can I re-experience this? *(Ken in North Carolina.)*

(Also from Ken:)

14 - I had an experience a year ago during meditation of hearing "The Carol of the Drum" (which goes something like "Come, they told me ... parum-pa-pum") and feeling chills of ecstatic feeling roll through me. Since that time, when trying to do healing exercises, I have tried to recapture that feeling by singing an inspiring song to myself (usually a Christmas song), feeling the tingling and having it cascade over the person for whom we are praying. Do you have any comments? *(Again, he poses the question:)* How could we use sound for healing? If it possible, could you instruct Peter in healing and, in that way, teach us about it? *(And, again, that was from Ken in North Carolina.)*

#15 - By recognizing our unlimited potential and strengthening our will and beliefs, how can we on Earth increase our awareness of color intensity and resonance of sound, thereby harmonizing mind and spirit? A French physician, Dr. Alfred Tomatis, has done much research on establishing the powers of toning and music to heal and balance body, mind and spirit. I am not asking for a "how to" manual. Rather, I see a similarity between Lama Sing's comments and Dr. Tomatis' work. *(For any of you who care to reference that, it's spelled T-O-M-A-T-I-S)* and I am wondering if I am on the right track or way off base. *(And that's from Carew up in Wisconsin, where I'm sure it's nice and cool.)*

#16 - We learned in this project that the entire point of our participation in the Earth is to attain a state of balanced harmony (Reference V642). One reason this is so important is because we take our mind and emotions with us after we leave the Earth (Reference V-660). Since we need to face challenges all of our lives, we have a never-ending source of opportunities. Would you agree, then, that one of the best things we can do when we are faced with a difficult situation which brings out our negative emotions within us ... such as anger, jealousy, worry, hurt, and so on ... is to recognize the situation as a learning possibility and then thank God for the opportunity? The next step could be to set about balancing those negative emotions with positive emotions, such as love, faith and joy. In addition, we could use the age-old techniques of prayer, meditation, and affirmations to reinforce the balancing process. What about other techniques new to our society, such as sound and color for balancing? In what way do they help? I'm thinking in particular about your "Music for Transition" reading dated 11-2-89, code number M-11. *(And that's from Dorothy in California. I might mention here that Dorothy and another researcher by the name of Maria co-sponsored that particular topical reading, and it is available for any of you who wish to have it. They are also doing research, by the way, in that topic, which I'm very excited about.)*

(The next question:)
#17 - What is the Music of the Spheres? *(And that's from Marie in Washington, who is the other researcher I spoke of.)*

That will conclude the questions for this reading.

And so, we now present them prayerfully to You, Father, asking as we do that You would guide us to the very highest and best possible information that can be given. We thank You, Father, and we ask for special prayers of blessing for all of the Voyagers and their friends and relatives who've recently written or phoned me, who are in need of prayer. If there's any way that that could be helped during the course of this reading, I would appreciate that. Special prayers of joy and blessing for the Lama Sing group and, of course, for Peter, Paul, Zack, Wilbur, and all the rest. Thank You, Father. Amen.

THE READING

LAMA SING: Yes, we have the Channel then and, as well, those references which apply to the questions, the topic, and those inquiring minds now before us. As we commence with this work, we shall first pray in this manner:

> *Lord God, we know that Thou art ever with us in all things. And thus, it is our prayer that we might herein accomplish Thy will and Thy purpose. We pray further on behalf of all those souls in all realms who are presently in some need and for whom there are none in joyous prayer. We ask, as well, special blessings for all those whom the Channel has referred to just above, and call upon those who serve with them in unseen realms, that this might form a bridge in answer to those of the inquiring or seeking hearts. In humbleness and joy for this opportunity, we thank Thee, Father. Amen.*

It could be stated in answer to the first question that, in essence, all entities will experience something similar to what Peter is experiencing, albeit that such entities in the individual sense may perceive or interact with these differing levels of expression in yet differing ways. But, in essence, all entities will experience a passage through all levels of expression which lie between, in essence, their current form of expression and their ultimate form of expression … which is as to say their soul consciousness. Do you see?

It could also be stated that Peter is representative of those of you in the Earth who are Voyagers and others who are not, in the sense that, as he is experiencing, these things could clearly be drawn as a parallel to experiences which you are also having unbeknownst to you, to a certain extent.

While some of you may feel or intuit a certain degree of participation with Peter and his experiences, others may not quite as clearly. Nonetheless, indeed, Peter is, both literally and symbolically, important to you ... all of you, your grouping and the many other entities who will hear this information, these works, in the Earth years to come.

The entity Zachary has potential which is very much ... we'll use the term *unlimited*, to the extent that he is capable of interacting with Peter in a resplendent way. Nonetheless, this does not minimize the participation of Paul, Peter himself, and the female entities and others, such as Wilbur, who will come to the forefront of these experiences in those times of the Earth which lie yet ahead.

Zachary has balanced to a great degree many of the aspects of his consciousness to such an extent that enable him to express himself, his thought, and, perhaps more importantly than all of these, his chosen work, in manners which are very much unrestricted. And so, while some of your grouping might look upon Zachary's ... we could call them antics, with a bit of a calloused eye, opting moreso for Paul's more gentle, steadfast approach, nonetheless, Zachary is indeed of a nature which is most cherished here and, as indicated by the references made from Paul, in most all realms.

In order for you to become as Zachary, you would first need to do just several very straightforward things. One of these is not to take yourself or things, events, people in the Earth, all that seriously. Note that Zachary is as quick to find humor in and of himself as he is in anything about him. And equally swift in providing insights which, delivered in Zachary's personality and methodology, tend to have crisp and clear interpretive quality. Such attributes are, indeed, indicative of considerable achievement and do also clearly imply his unlimited nature. You'll see more of this and understand, we should think, much more profoundly the breadth and depth of this again, as Peter continues on. Also, you'll see aspects of Paul and Peter, himself, emerging that perhaps at present will be considered unexpected.

Again, to our companions in North Carolina, you are on an appropriate pathway to become as Zachary. Continue to look at yourselves as you have been, holding not too firmly, holding nothing too intensely, but gently and lovingly, as though you were its creator. We believe that more will be given sufficiently to address this area of questioning quite clearly as we continue. If not, and you still have questions, submit them here. But remember, first and foremost: Treat all of existence, yourselves first, in an attitude of *passiveness* (perhaps is the term that will inspire within you the best connotation) ... not too intense, not too seriously, moderation and balance, allowing things to come and go; not to disrupt you too severely, even though some of them may be intense; always remembering to fall back upon your own basic truth and tenets, and fall back upon them frequently, with such as meditation, prayer, and a reminder to self frequently of your own eternal and unlimited nature. As you'll note as has been stated frequently, not a problem, then don't make things problems. Make them opportunities, and look for solutions which are stimulating, expanding, and which promote for the greatest good for all involved. See?

The relationship between Zachary, Paul, Peter, Wilbur, and the other, with the Master, is indeed significant. The associations with the consciousness which is called the Christ Consciousness is heavily involved in all that is taking place. For this, then, as it is titled the Christ Consciousness, is looked upon by most here as being that pathway which leads the entity back to their soul expression. It is that continual source of (quote) "Light" (end-quote) and guidance from God, expressed through the formation of your own individuality, much likened unto being an aspect of God ... which, in many respects, is precisely what you are. See this, then? All souls serve in a manner such as this much more often than they recognize. What's happening here is that the souls are recognizing it, affirming it, and, thus, they are claiming it.

Peter is in the process of unfolding himself to the point wherefrom he might be completely enabled to claim his heritage. In some respects, the Book of Wisdom represents this potential. And, thus, its presence in any of the activities is significant. It is being used, as such, as a tool to awaken Peter on higher levels, that the connective *tunnel of light*, or the filament of light which connects all expressions of a soul into oneness, is being developed, intensified, and being made more passable. See?

Mental and physical illness are issues which have to do primarily with thought-forms. Thought-forms, then, use such tools as emotion, habit, and such, as a means of their expression or manifestation in the Earth. If you are capable of controlling and directing such as your thoughts and emotions, you would certainly escape the thought-form of dis-ease and/or illness. Functioning within a greater realm, such as the Earth, containing a myriad of thought-forms and one primary, overriding thought-form which enables the existence of the Earth, makes this a difficult accomplishment. But, nonetheless, there are numerous examples in your realm, historically, and even in the more recent Earth times, of entities who have done just that. You are capable of doing so, as well. Other aspects or ramifications of that would have to do with the aging process also, and other factors which are equally stimulating in their potential. See? The greater the degree of your ability to control and to moderate your thought, primarily as has to do with the emotional reaction to same, proportionately that degree would then apply to the reduction of dis-ease or illness … physical or otherwise.

With no intention to single one of your grouping out, yes,

we were referring to you (to the entity Patty). There are others, as well, and others who are beyond this to some degrees of thinking and understanding, but the comment was made specifically to you. (With a note of loving humor, why not you? See?) Good to think about that, each of you.

Certain entities are capable of performing works which are beyond the norm in the Earth, and as they escape the norm in that sense as a calculation or a schedule, then this falls into the area of extraordinary or in the scientific, called, in some cases, mystical or miraculous. But that which is actually called a miracle is, and will be demonstrated frequently, commonplace when one escapes the illusion of limitation.

Putting yourselves to a test as being difficult taskmasters for yourselves is approached here with a note of loving humor. It is better that one choose their task and be their own taskmaster, is it not, than to allow this to be given into the hands of another? For your choices are those which are intentionally designed or selected because they will bring about the best of all result. For example, if you, dear friend Aida, would hold much more firmly to the concept of developing an idealic way of life, a joyful thought-form that you are holding out (perhaps in a sense, symbolically) at arm's length in life, that thought-form, then, becomes the goal that is sought after. And the pathway, as you are experiencing it in the day-to-day life, will be thereafter oriented towards the accomplishing of that ultimate goal.

As things change, as your ideas and concepts change, moderate, alternate the goal. Don't fix it or cast it in iron or stone. Let it be a living thing that grows as you grow, that experiences as you experience. Be alive. Not just physically, but be alive spiritually. Let your spiritual life grow and move with you. If you force yourself into a certain rote or dogmatic approach to being a spiritually aware entity, you could well end up in realms far lesser than that of Wilbur's current residency (which is actually not at all limited, but only by the perception of those involved). As you strive for the development of new habits, you'll replace the old. Much was given in this regard in that called the *Universal Laws Project*. Might be well to review that again. Make changes by dis-placement, by replacement. See? Don't force old habits out by focusing on them, as much as developing and focusing upon new ones. We should think this to be the far easier method.

There are many different forms of musical production that can approach in a fragmental sense the beautiful symphonic-colored sound that our grouping is expressing. But in terms of expressing this in the Earth, much is dependent upon the entity who is the listener, who is perceiving these sounds. While sounds which are produced in the physical sense of the Earth (for example, through the abrasive or friction between a bow and a taut string on a stringed instrument) produces many forms of sounds which are often undetected by many entities for varying reasons, but the best of all methods, we should find here, are those where many instruments are used to provide a collage of sound, rather than simply presenting a singular form, one instrument or just a few. (As ever, there are exceptions.)

In meditation and when one is attempting to accomplish a certain meditative work or to move beyond their physical body, focusing upon a single produced tone which has for the opportunity the production of overtones as resonance, these then might often be the better for such conditions. The reason, quite obviously, being that as one is focusing upon a particular objective, then the singular tonal quality augments and amplifies that focus, making it much more profound. See the difference? The broad orchestration provides a broad spectrum, whereas the singular expressed tone provides the singular focal point. See that?

When relating to the various sounds of nature (violins, small bells, gongs, the flute ... sounds of the wind) the differences here do relate somewhat to the individuality of the person perceiving same. Peter will experience more about this as we proceed. The difference has to do with the objective, the goals being sought after, then selecting those tonal qualities which best provide harmonic resonance towards that accomplishment. For example, if one is meditating to free themselves beyond that which would be in the form of nature expression, then the sounds of nature (wind, waves, bees, and such as this) might be the better to provide an environment which takes one's consciousness from the creation of man to the unlimited creative power of nature. Conversely, if one is seeking to provide some insight or gain some understanding for something which is more finite in the expression of man's needs, then these might be through the instruments, as given.

The building blocks of the universe have many forms, many expressions. Some of these are defined already in the form of light, color, sound, fragrance and such. But, in essence, the methodology for healing one's self or another (physically, mentally, emotionally and spiritually) begins as a form of preparation for the recipient. In other words, if you are seeking to heal self, then the preparation of importance is to begin within self to make the way passable for the healing to take place. Healing is about you at all times, in many forms and in many expressions. It can be found all throughout expressions of nature … in herbs and such, through the diet or through the olfactory, or through simple contact to the physical body through the vibrational frequencies. But as one has these all about self, habits and patterns of consistency tend to cause these to be repelled or not to remain consistently within the body. Begin within self or as in the subject who is seeking healing, to make the way passage.

This should be in this manner: Using the positive concepts of suggestion to open the mind, the will, the emotion, and the spirit, then use tones, colors, use fragrances, use all those which are of relationship to the five physical senses, and then go beyond. Following a tonal quality as it is first expressed and then, as it seems to taper off or the sound fades, follow the sound. Similarly, with color, strive for in meditation merging yourself into that color and, in essence, bringing it back with you as you awaken. That is one of the better approaches. See?

The experience of being lifted off the ground, as was the case with Peter, has much to do with one's own level of acceptance. In the dream state, you reach that level of acceptance wherein your conscious minds, limitations, were no longer involved. While out of body, one can find that limitations, normally thought of as imposing or the norm from the Earth, no longer apply. In many cases, the dream state seems to be surrealistic or unrealistic because of this. And yet, from the dream state, looking back, it is the Earth that seems to have this quality of being unreal or surrealistic. So, one's abilities and talents, or such as you might call them, are dependent upon the perspective of the entity who is experiencing. To repeat or replicate your experience at age 18 (actually, it was a bit later), this then would we find, beginning with the experience of unlimiting self.

You can create this at will, if you can become sufficiently unlimited. You'll see through Peter's experiences just how important each little thought, each little hesitancy or doubt, can be, exemplified already to this point in the example of the purple flowers. Remember that? A moment's doubt and the creation falls prey to the defined limitations of the realm of expression in which it exists. The difference being, that in Peter's garden-like place, all there are open to such potentials and are actually contributing to an environ which is conducive to them. If you can make the Earth, or a small area of same in which you are functioning, similarly conducive, you may find yourselves capable of doing many things, particularly within your group and such. You've already done this, as we see. Do you see?

Using sound as a form or media of expression to promote healing for self or others is encouraged very strongly here. To incorporate color, or the visualization, in with the experiencing of sound is also encouraged. For those of you who cannot truly visualize, then move into the phenomenon, as you call it, of feeling or experiencing. Color (as you will recall Peter's passage through the realms of color) has a distinct and dramatic impact upon the body, mind, and spirit ... whether it is visualized, perceived, or not.

Using such as a Christmas song brings into play or into focus other ramifications, as well, these being (not the least of which) the attitudes and mind-set of entities around that time period. Many entities whose emotions and habits are dramatically different the other eleven and one-half to eleven Earth months, approximate, are moderated dramatically during this time period in the Earth. It is that mind-set which you are (quote) "tapping into" (end-quote) when you are performing your work in the manner as you have described it. We would encourage you to continue in that manner and to experiment with other forms of song, or mental expression of sound, or sound, which has similar attributes. See?

Returning to our commentary regarding sound and healing, we would concur with your observation, entity Carew, and note the similarity (although there are some deviations and some constraints). There are excellent correlations between the works you have defined and that of the information which we find given here. Once again, we believe that you will find this amplified and becoming more specific as time progresses here and with the continuing journeys of Peter.

As relates to both of your experiences and those of the question asked by the entity Dorothy, all of expression has vibration. All of expression has a certain finiteness which differentiates one point from another. That finiteness could be measured on varying types of scales of measure. One of these could be in terms of the number of vibrations per second or

Earth minute or some such as this. Another could be the measure of the amplitude or the soundwave oscillation, and other such as fall into the more technical methodologies of defining and describing the range and breadth and depth of sound. And these, as we have indicated them, are only cursory, moderate, references. We note you have many, much more defined and specific forms of such definition. But look at the entire matter of healing.

As the entity, Dorothy, indicated in her question above, opportunity is what you are seeking in the Earth. If you did not seek opportunity, then you would have little, if any, purpose for being in the Earth. An entity who is at a point of total idleness or inactivity in the Earth will rarely endure for a long period of your time measure. They will fall prey to some state of dis-ease or imbalance, or will (more often than not) become reclusive, withdrawn, and such. It is the quest for experience that motivates the majority of souls who are in the Earth. The ideal, then, being, as we perceive it from here, to exemplify the results of certain information and works and application of same so that ye might become the examples which are sought after by those who are in turn seeking experience or opportunity.

When an opportunity inspires or invokes within self the emotions of anger, hostility, frustration, jealousy, worry, and so forth, then you know you have a good experience, albeit from the Earth plane you might not like it, it might not be pleasant to you. Well, that is a part of the spectrum of the Earth itself, one which contributes significantly to the value and importance of incarnating in the Earth. For such stimuli are those forces which motivate you to seek out, ultimately, the very best which is in within you. If you were not so motivated, it might be a different matter. You would not seek to grow, you would not seek to become what you are now becoming. And so, while there are those opportunities to lament or to become despondent or silent or whatnot over the lot which appears to have befallen you in life, also remember to be thankful for them as you perceive them as opportunities for growth.

We know, dear friends, sufficiently from here that this is not always an easy task. Nonetheless, think about it. Keep it a bit to the forefront of your mind as you go through life. And as you see others, let them be the example for you. Try to encourage them in their times of challenge or opportunity. The more supportive you can be to another in such an instance, the greater will be the support which is returned to you in a similar instance. See? Or a similar time of need.

As the entity called Ken reiterated the cascading down over his being of the impact of sound, music, the thinking of the sound, he was exemplifying precisely what Zachary and Paul are attempting to convey to Peter. As Peter realizes that he is in command or control of his own destiny, we believe that he will take that command and use it in a responsible manner. This is not to imply that he will do so immediately, in a perfect way. But that through the experiences he will encounter through what you call imperfect application, he will learn, he will grow, and he will respond to new stimuli, well-armed with the experiences of his past opportunities. Building one upon the other, one can rise to a state of great awareness and great potential, not the least of which is the ability to be a channel of blessings to others. Do you see?

New techniques for your society, in terms of sound and color for balancing, are many-fold and they are being given to the Earth or (quote) "discovered" (end-quote) in the Earth with great frequency in your current time. Begin where you are with what you have, and be unlimited. Color, as it is close to the physical body, tends to create a sympathetic reaction in the energy field around the body. Color, as it is radiated upon the body (i.e., from a light source), tends to be absorbed into the body, or to react upon the cellular photo-reactive properties of the body. Therefore, as would logically be deduced, correlating radiated color and what we might call as refractive or reflective or absorbent color, you can promote an environment which is remarkably conducive to healing.

For example, wearing a swatch or a small patch of brilliant color (for example, green) on or about the body, particularly as relates to the abdominal, the digestive, tends to promote for healing very rapidly. Radiating the body, particularly in this one-third segment of the body, approximate, also tends to react immediately upon the cellular structure, reacting to the electrochemical mechanism of the body. As the radiated green color is absorbed or excites the cellular patterns of the body, particularly as relate to the neurological and the fluidic systems, then placing the green swatch as closely paralleling the color frequency or hue as the radiated light induces and promotes for a prolonged residual effect by sympathetic radiation or vibration. See? So, then, radiated light begins the activating process. The reflected or reactive light, which is the color swatch on or about the body or the clothing, tends to keep it in action and continues to draw those wave-lengths or frequencies from the forces of nature. See? So that's a step in the healing cycle.

Sonically, or as expressed in terms of sound, color frequencies are expressed in a parallel sense, dimensionally, to sound frequencies. As the entity Kendall noted, the passage of these undulations of sound, even in mind, created a cascading effect down through the glandular centers or chakras. Then, as you find the color frequencies and tonal frequencies that are best sympathetic for the individual and the individual's need, continuing with them and modulating them as we discussed in the (as called) M-11[3] will promote for an environment which is conducive to rapid healing. Then apply the

---

[3] The M Series – This was a code designation in the Lama Sing readings for (loosely) medical topics: diet, massage, various therapies, etc. M-11 was on a topic called "Musical Massage Sound Therapy," a term coined by Dr. Maria McKinney and Dr. Dorothy Gundling, a form of music that could assist people with the process of dying. Lama Sing provided the basic structure of the composition. www.musicalmassagesoundtherapy.com

other modalities, then apply such as the electrical impedance device, the castor oil packs, the herbs, the dietary, the massage, the manipulation, and, most emphatically, the prayer and magnetic healing. And you'll have the best of all environs to provide for a healing platform or foundation upon which the recipient can then build.

Now comes the point of pivotal transition, and that applies to the recipient. Preparing the recipient to be open and to seek a change, an expression of healing, is an important key here. In your control group, it's good to note the attitudinal posture of each entity towards change, finding through such as the MMPI[4], which is quite limited as we see it, but would provide some insight to the attitudinal base of the entity. As the entity is emotionally clinging to certain patterns, then those patterns need to be addressed to release the entity to move into a posture of ease. As you seek it, more can be given on this, and we would welcome such here, as it would provide a spiritual, mental, and emotional bond for healing, making the way passable for many, not just one or two.

We'll pause a moment here and continue, requesting from the Channel additional questions.

Fare thee well, then, for the present, dear friends.

---

[4] MMPI – Al Miner assumes this is a reference by Lama Sing to the Minnesota Multiphasic Personality Inventory, one of the most frequently used personality tests in mental health according to Wikipedia, which does, though, have its critics.

Q&A READING #6

Continuation of Questions After Chapters 4 and 5:
CO-CREATING (V-650)
THE CRYSTAL WORKER'S REALM (V-660)

Given July 31, 1990

AL MINER/CHANNEL: *This will be reading V-652. Apparently I didn't submit enough questions. Next questions are:*

QUESTIONS SUBMITTED

#1 - Please try to explain again why a butterfly was created by Peter when he wasn't consciously thinking of a butterfly when he made the sound. The sound went to a golden orb of light to a creation, a butterfly. Is this the usual process? Sound to light to creation? The "word was with God" (In the beginning was the Word, and the Word was with God and the Word was God ... *Word* equaling vibration equaling sound, and sound equaling color/light equaling creation? Yes?)

#2 - When God created the realms, universes, and souls (all that we know about currently) did he have the thought first and then created it by sending forth a "sound"? A note of vibration that caused things to manifest because in his being he held the thought of them? Then within his being he thought of a creation that could also create and would co-create with him and keep the creation process going. But in order to have that happen, he had to allow the creative ones to have free will. Was that thought what we call the Christ? The first created manifestation with free will? Also known as The Word? Is the Christ energy or spirit a sound? *(That's from Joan in Pennsylvania. That's an absolutely pro-*

found and stimulating series of questions, Joan. Thanks.)

#3 - Was the butterfly created complete in the biological detail Peter was familiar with on Earth; i.e., made on the cellular level, complete with DNA and organelles? *(Whatever they are. Rudy, I don't know what they are.)* If not, how does this process differ from that which we know of on the Earth? *(And that's, as you can tell, from Rudy in North Carolina.)*

#4 - Regarding the creation of the butterfly, as I understand it, each of us has an individual light, sound and color, all of which are vibration. Do we also have an individual aroma, also? I suspect so. Remember the old ghost stories when you knew the ghost was there because of her perfume? Do these vibrations precede the manifestation of physical body? And as such, influence its form and appearance? I assume the appearance, et cetera, is also influenced by purpose, karma, et cetera. In essence, when the physical body is no longer useful, do we return simply to that vibration? Manifesting various degrees of forms of the body, in those dimensions where it is useful or necessary? *(That's from Anita in Florida. Well thought out, too.)*

#5 - Did Peter create a new awareness as he did the body, or did the butterfly's awareness come from a soul pool? Or is the butterfly somehow an extension of Peter's own awareness? Lama Sing, you have mentioned a cat being with you at least one time. Have the animals that manifest in that realm reached that point which you have indicated in the past where they are attached to a soul and that is how they get to those realms, rather than returning to a "soul group"? Does any soul there have a beloved pet companion with them as the result of that attachment? Or is that considered a bond to Earth and exists in lower realms? Is the pet manifested in its furry little body in higher realms, or is it an extra light or sparkle or energy in the attachee's cloak? I have the vision of St. Francis surrounded by a multitude of animal forms. *(And that's from Anita in Florida also, as was the previous question. Great questions.)*

#6 - The garden-like place seems familiar. I remember co-creating a very blue bluebird. Is this the same place as Peter is experiencing? Why do I and certain others remember it? *(From Jud in North Carolina.)*

#7 - Regarding Peter and Paul's discussion about the bench being in motion, alive and warm, are physicists' unified field theories on the right track? Was Albert Einstein spiritually aware? Who in the group co-created the detailed design and appearance on the first bench, and then the additional benches? *(That's from David and Leiko in Florida.)*

These are terrific questions, and I thank you all for them, and I'm going to conclude here and turn this back to Lama Sing.

We ask for the highest and best always in Your name, Father, and we thank You. Amen.

THE READING

LAMA SING: Very well, we are returned, and we continue, invoking the presence and power of our just-previous prayers and affirmations.

Turning to the last to be first, as seems appropriate here (with a note of loving humor): The entity Albert Einstein was and is most assuredly spiritually aware. For the power of the creative force as it flows through an entity is very specifically associated or connected to spirituality, for creativity must reach through and into the infinite nature of self, which is the spirit.

The relationship between the Universal Forces and all of existence does, to a degree (at least as viewed from the Earth), parallel from a certain point to a certain point the (quote) "unified field theory" (end-quote) and beyond it. But this is a good step forward and, to a degree, the interrelationship between all of existence is profound. If a leaf falls in a distant forest on the opposite side of the sphere called Earth, you are impacted by its impact to the ground. You are also impacted by that life form which is in a state of transition. It is the degree of that impact that becomes important and/or significant to the relationship of your sense of consciousness and/or well-being. See that?

The garden-like place has a familiarity to you because you have, indeed, been there. And to the extent that you have allowed yourself to become spiritually aware in the present, it will continue to seem familiar, as shall some certain portion of the experiences which have been and which shall be those ahead. The reason that you can remember (and, as well, certain others to varying degree) has to do with your spiritual consciousness and your purpose for being in the Earth at present. As these continue to unfold and you gain greater realization and moderate the rather harsh attitude of expectancy you have upon yourself, dear friend, the greater shall become your sense and literal expression of freedom. Do remember that no one here, nor should any entity in any realm, expect from another to the degree that imposes a limitation in the obverse sense. Remember, begin with yourself lovingly, gently, openly, and you'll find that all things will flow to you and, thus, you will become far greater than you even now strive to be, dear friend. (This given lovingly; you are being just a bit hard upon self. See?)

Turning now to the entire concept of creation, as we had wished to correlate this with the preceding questions as relate to healing, sound, light, color, we find the following given:

The benches were created through mutual agreement. In essence, they were created because they were there to be created. In other words, as there is a need in a realm which has a more unlimited nature, the need is filled by the willingness of all involved with that realm to provide for the needs of one another. So, as Peter observed and felt the sensations of aliveness from the bench, he was, in essence, feeling his own life form being reflected back to him. He was also feeling the reflected life forms or energies of the others, all of them in that realm ... including the entity Jud, who asked the question just above and others of you, as well.

Now, how can this be? Well, quite simply, in this manner: If all of you agree to a certain thing in a grouping, then to greater and lesser levels of agreement you are participants in the agreed-upon thing. From that point forward, your mutuality of consent makes you co-creators with all others in that realm. As long as you continue to contribute your willingness to be a co-creator, you are enabling the creative process to be immediate or instantaneous within the limitations of your willingness to contribute or to participate. See? This is why in groups of like-minded entities it is often stated that the Master is there, as well, that the spirit of the Christ potential is there, as well. (*Where two or more are gathered in my name, there I shall also be.*)

For the connotation here, and the literal expression is, quite simply, this: Free will, a Universal Law, provides that as you come together to co-create, you create a thought-form which is, by definition of its parameters, capable of producing within itself to the extent of your willingness. Thus, the power which is thought of as the Christ Consciousness is freed within that thought-form. Taking that to a larger scale, in Peter's garden (not seeking to minimize the potential for it being your garden, as well, dear friends), but in Peter's garden all here are dedicated to the ability to co-create in an unlimited sense. To the degree, then, that Peter is capable (not so much willing, but capable) of accepting this unlimited nature, then such things as creating purple flowers, butterflies, benches and the like, becomes a simple task. See that, then? This is what is meant by the co-creative potential.

In considering the question regarding the creation of the butterfly, we would first turn to the points as were indicated during the discourse between Peter, Zachary, Paul, that the expression of the butterfly, as such, was through the portal of joy, the accomplishment of a state of ease. And, thereafter, the expression of the butterfly, was, in essence, a recollection of similar times of peace and tranquility, near-meditative-like achievement, on Peter's part while incarnated in the Earth just previous to the present.

The expression of the butterfly is moreso an extension of Peter, albeit formed in the pattern or form of a butterfly, recognizable as such. This draws upon what could be called the collective consciousness, as such, which is aligned with or which comprises the butterfly consciousness. (These are difficult terms to express to you, for we have no appropriate terminology in your language which conveys the actuality of occurrence here. We ask your indulgence and understanding with regard to same.) And so, as it were, then, paralleling this to the comments or questions regarding *In the beginning was the Word, and the Word was with God,* ... here, then, we would not presume to infer having such a position of consciousness or oneness with God to be presumed to be speaking on God's behalf or any such of this nature. Conversely, the creative wonder of God has never terminated. And, thus, we can, through those of our associates and such, become attuned to that creative process and relate to you definitions as we believe would answer your question.

In the beginning was the thought or expression. This, then, was *with God, as God,* and therefore, in the instant that this was, as such, expressed, this expression became a form of Consciousness in the sum total of all existence. It is not like a center of the universe being the focal point of what you would consider to be God ... a light, as it were, immense and indescribable in its brilliance and scope but, nonetheless, centrally located, defined, demarcated, and such, and that this great wondrous light created a thought or came forth with the word which created. But, rather, that that Word came forth in all of existence at one time, not from the central core of light and then radiating outwardly.

Conversely, there are realms of expression that we are cognizant of where the creative process is still unfolding at the level of expression which you have defined. This is not because it has taken this amount of time, as you measure it, to reach these points, but, conversely, that these realms of consciousness have taken this amount of time to become aware. See the difference?

Thought creates first through the pattern. And as we see the pattern of wondrous beauty and intricacy as expressed by God, this then takes form moreso from the outer than from the inner. The creative power and presence is without restriction or limitation. Thus, it is the realm. If you would prefer, think of it as location. If you would prefer, think of it as the latitude and longitude of a map of eternity. The point of intersect in that sense, in eternity, defined then as the point of perspective, the interpretation of the beholders from that point of perspective determines much of the expression of that thought, contributing then in a co-creative sense to the color, to the vibration called sound, color and light. These, then, combining or, more accurately, precipitating into the formation of creation as are the dimensional consistencies or constraints of that point of latitude and longitude in eternity. See? From the perspective of the Earth, you could consider your commentary, your analogy, to be reasonably accurate... the *Word* equaling vibration or sound, to color, to light, to creation. There are some other interim steps here, for each level of expression of vibration interacts with adjacent realms of expression, creating a sort of resonance which precipitates into that expression. See?

Conversely, then, the butterfly created (quote) "by Peter" (end-quote), while it is in every essence a butterfly, has no need for the biological genetics or intricacies as are the norm in the Earth.

Think of it in this way: If you would see a butterfly in the Earth which in description appeared much like Peter's, then think of Peter's butterfly being superimposed on top of that physical butterfly. The physical form, then, having the DNA and all such intricacies of its organics as are appropriate for it to express itself, i.e., to live in the Earth and all that sort. Then think of the spirit of this butterfly lifting up above same, leaving behind the physical structure. And yet, in the spiritual form the butterfly is every bit as detailed and exact as the physical counterpart. Yet there is no need for the digestive tract or such, and so these, while they could be thought of in that sense as being present, we do not perceive them as such.

So, is this just a sort of hollowed-out or stuffed image of the original, as you consider it? To the contrary, and with a note of loving humor that would be the inverse of truth, for the physical is the stuffed version of reality, suitably so for interacting functionally within the constraints of the Earth. If the butterfly could not ingest, digest, and produce in a form which was acceptable in the Earth, it would not exist there, at least not in the detectable sense ... the accomplishment of advanced detection which has to do with the electrical pattern, the electromagnetic pattern of the physical body, in an advancement in your science and medicine which is not too far ahead, in terms of time. This accomplishment will do as much to radically change your field of medicine as the entirety of your accomplishments to date from, let's say, the last two hundred fifty Earth years. See?

Instead of injecting, instead of surgically removing, the direction will be to simply realign or retune, re-harmonize or rebalance through the electro-molecular structure at the atomic and sub-atomic level. This having to do with the constraints of the genes, the stringing mechanisms, and the electrochemical completion of same. The pattern originating then in a perfect form, deviating in accordance with the influences external, can then be brought back into harmony with the perfect pattern and, thus, eliminating the condition of dis-ease. Advancements of such a sort are visible in the Earth, even as we speak, in their preliminary forms. See?

What does that have to do with all of this? Well, think of the Christ as that expression of Consciousness which came from the Word, and that that Word, as such, exists even as we speak in and about each of you. And that is the perfect pattern which is exemplified in every cell, every molecule thereof, every sub-atomic particle thereof. And that is the pattern which is present in the butterfly. See?

More will be apparent on this in the future, but for the present we shall now conclude, thanking those who have come forward to provide information during this gathering.

May the grace and wisdom of our Father be present in

your every thought, word and deed, providing you the lamp of wisdom to guide every footstep.

For the present, then, we conclude. Fare thee well, then, for the present, dear friends.

Q&A READING #7

Continuation of Questions After Chapters 4 and 5:
CO-CREATING (V-650)
THE CRYSTAL WORKER'S REALM (V-660)

Given July 31, 1990

AL MINER/CHANNEL: *This reading is code number V-661. It is a follow-up reading on the topic of Working with Crystals as we were given that information in reading #V-660. This will be questions and answers number one relevant to that title.*

QUESTIONS SUBMITTED

#1 - Why could Zachary touch Wilbur who was of a different vibration, but Paul prevented Wilbur from touching Peter? *(From Anita in Florida)*

#2 - Any significance to the observation that Peter, Paul and Zack entered Wilbur's realm side by side? However, that they departed that realm in single file. *(From David and Leiko in Florida)*

#3 - The dear soul laboring to project his thought-form into the crystal ... Is that thought-form amplified and broadcast to the crystal to specific individuals in prayer or meditation, or into the mass-mind thought pool? Are there crystals on Earth that have been pre-programmed by entities in other realms or by entities in previous existence on Earth, or both? Does clearing a crystal wipe out these messages? (If the foregoing is so, that is.)

#4 - I understand now why we always ask for the highest and best possible source. I also understand the zeal with which some individuals feel they have received information from God, which sometimes seems erroneous to me. Of course, that may be exactly what they need at that time. *(That's from Anita in Florida.)*

#5 - The people in the realm Peter visited ... In what way did their love and desire to do good become an obsession? What process will unbind them? Will they have to reincarnate in the Earth to become unbound by or from that obsession? *(That's from Harold and Linda in Missouri.)*

#6 - When Wilbur formed a bond through the intensity of his love, just what did he do? What are some of the things we do that create bonds? *(From Marie in Washington state.)*

#7 - As I was working on these questions and re-reading the readings 650 and 660, blue-white lights lit up before my eyes on the pages I was reading. It is not the first time I have seen these little blue-white lights, and in the past I have always taken them as a sign of approval of what is taking place. And it has given me the knowledge that I am not alone. Although I cannot see them in a physical form, I know they are entities before me and wonder if this is anything like what the benevolent souls experience when they intuit the presence of Peter, Paul and Zachary. *(From Aida in Florida.)*

#8 - In 660, as Paul and Zack each take one of Peter's arms and begin to move off down the pathway, what caused Peter to feel a strangeness come over him? Is the movement that takes place during the state of balancing similar to our out-of-body experiences, in our sleep state and in other such states? *(From Aida in Florida again.)*

#8 - Peter was not allowed to touch Wilbur's hand. Reminds one of Jesus and Mary in the garden right after his resurrection. Would you please elaborate on this? *(Why was Peter not allowed to touch Wilbur? And vice-versa? That's my comment. I just noted that this question is almost identical with the very first one from Anita in Florida.)* Why the abrupt departure from that realm? *(That's from Ken in North Carolina.)*

#9 - It appears to me that Peter is somehow a guide to Wilbur and has not had the awareness yet. I found it interesting that as Zack is introducing Peter to Wilbur, Paul abruptly steps between Wilbur and Peter and says to Zack that they need to be going rather quickly. What was transpiring that that became a necessity? *(And that's from Aida in Florida. Looks like Anita with the first question, Ken here with the just-previous question and Aida ... All three of them focused on that one point, which is interesting.)*

(The next question is from Joan in Pennsylvania.)

#10 - Well, Al, the last reading, 660, blows the lid off being a do-gooder, doesn't it? I must confess to some major confusion here. Somehow, these folks in this realm visited by Peter, Zack and Paul have gotten stuck, not because of the acts of help, et cetera, but because of their perception that this is what they must do, and this is the only way. Is that correct? A form of tunnel vision, I would say. However, we all have our tunnel vision and self-limitations here in the Earth. This reading certainly points out the results of that limited thinking. How can we overcome this within ourselves so as not to get stuck in such a realm and to greatly improve our lives right here and now?

The fact that their beliefs are old accounts for their old appearance. Yet I thought the ideas introduced by the man making the crystal were all good ideas and certainly still held as useful ideals here in the Earth. Is it the fact that once those ideals were established he stopped growing from that point, and that has limited him? In other words, he just keeps teaching the same thing over and over and, even though it's still needed here, he personally needs to move on? Am I getting a handle on that? On the subject of Wilbur, can he see Zack and the others because he is getting ready to expand his limits and leave this realm, so his vibration is higher than that of the others? I am supposing that Peter will become Wilbur's guide or teacher. Correct? Wilbur isn't permitted to touch Peter. Why?

(Interesting, the similarity in this group of questions.)

The next are a group of interesting questions primarily relating to Wilbur.)

#11 - Is Wilbur's realm the exception or the rule? In other words, are more souls of Zack's consciousness or of Wilbur's in other such corresponding realms? *(From Chip in Virginia)*

#12 - Is Wilbur an earlier stage of Peter? Like revisited? *(That's from Jud in North Carolina. That's an interesting question, isn't it?)*

#13 - You stated that Wilbur was a teacher with pure intentions and wonderful qualities (V-660). And yet he was hindered from reaching higher realms because he had "formed a bond of sorts to the Earth or to another realm." Can you elaborate more on that topic? *(That's from Dorothy in California.)*

#14 - How is it that Zack was helping Wilbur? And on what? *(From Carew in Wisconsin)*

#15 - How is it that the old man could not see Peter and Paul, but Wilbur could? *(Also from Carew in Wisconsin)*

#16 - Who or which realm answers our prayers if we ask for the highest and best in the name of the Christ? Is there any advantage to seeking answers in Wilbur's realm, if it has such limited scope? *(That's from Dorothy in California.)*

I present these now before You, Father, asking as I do that You would guide us all to the very highest and best possible information that can be given. We ask a prayer of blessings for all those in need of our Voyager grouping and their friends and family and, in particular, those who have asked for our prayers. And also for all of our friends in other realms, particularly our new group of friends centered around Peter. Thank You, Father. Amen.

THE READING

LAMA SING: Yes, we have the Channel then and, as well, those references which apply to the questions, the topic, and those inquiring minds as have submitted same now before us. As we commence with this work, we would first pray in this manner:

> *Lord God, we know that Thou art ever with us in all things. And thus it is our prayer that we might herein accomplish Thy will and Thy purpose, and that these, Father, might awaken within all those who shall become aware of these works that greater oneness with thee. This then is, as well, our prayer on behalf of all those souls in all realms presently in some need and for whom there are none in joyous service or prayer. We humbly thank Thee, Father, for this opportunity of joyful service in Thy Name. Amen.*

Zachary has been involved with the entity Wilbur for some period of existence or time and thus, and through such, has attained a state of balanced harmony with Wilbur. This involvement has been initiated through the willingness of Wilbur and through mechanisms yet to be revealed (at Wilbur's request, see).

The activity involving Wilbur and Peter is different ... new and unique. To that extent, then, Peter, in his present state of consciousness, has not attained a complete state of (what you would call) balance, or perhaps better understood as having precipitated himself into a form of expression which is consistent. Therefore, any interaction between he and another realm and an entity thereof at this point could have some impact upon both Peter and Wilbur and Wilbur's realm. This, of course, is in some violation of Universal Law and, thus, Paul's action was to prevent the occurrence, whether it would have been inadvertent or not. This function was afforded to Peter and Wilbur through Paul's action, which is granted through the capacity of his being a guide.

The entry into Wilbur's realm on the part of our trio, side-by-side, is significant. Noting that the period of balance or rest was necessitated in order for Peter to acquire a state of ease in that realm, albeit he was under the protection and preservation of Zachary's spare cloak, as it were. Nonetheless, this is a normal action, not abnormal, not unique. Once Peter has gained a full state of expression and/or balance, you will note that he will move much more easily to and from other realms. That, of course, lies yet ahead.

The departure from Wilbur's realm in single file has to do with movement through what you would recognize as the *tunnel of light* (that existing beyond the Earth ... even here) and that, then, being a more basic form of movement. And, as such, Peter, you will note, was surrounded in the blue-white light which consistently provided a means of transition without influence or effect to or from any other realms. The movement into Wilbur's realm, conversely, was made through a different mechanism, that mechanism being moreso defined as a transitional movement apart from, in essence, the tunnel of light ... yet, nonetheless, the tunnel of light being present but being expressed in a different form. (Let us see if we can find an example which will explain this more clearly, more understandably. A moment, please ...)

The pathway downwards from other realms (for example, from a higher vibrational level to a lesser vibrational level) can be made more easily because of the magnitude, the breadth and depth and range of the higher levels, as compared to or opposed to those of the lower realms. So, as the movement is downward, this is made with considerably greater ease. As the movement is made in the upward sense, that is subjected to considerable constraints, not unlike Peter's passage through the varying realms or levels of color, you may recall, in our first meeting with him. Peter was already in some state of what we would call depletion and, therefore, it was determined that this would not be advisable (on the part of Zachary, and Paul, as well). That predicated their hasty departure, and the movement single-file out of that realm. See?

The dear soul laboring to project his thought-form into the crystal ... This entity is, indeed, a dear soul and, as such, you will see and hear more of him in the times ahead. But for now, we would answer your questions in this way: There are crystals which exist in the Earth which contain, in essence, a sort of record, though not in the sense of a phonograph record or a tape recording or that such, but moreso bearing the imprint of the forces that have come and gone while it was in existence. These imprints, then, are not so much so electronically imparted to the crystal. To some degree they are imprinted in the form of lines of irradiation and lines of intersect of focal planes (particularly in the case of crystals) and in other cases they are evident to a degree as part of the growth strata of the crystalline structure itself ... the latter being, of course, similar to the growth rings of woody plants or trees in the Earth (coniferous, we believe, or conifers, is your term).

Nonetheless, the crystals are not, as such, simply capable of being plugged into something and allowing you to go back and review time (though, in a manner of speaking, that would not be impossible; however, we don't see this quite expressed here in that sense). It is, rather, the resulting impact of those activities upon the striations, the cleavage, the planes, the ocular focal planes having to do with light, light refraction, and the point or juncture wherein light and sound intersect, and such as this, similar to the projection holographically, as you know of it.

In terms of the crystal's ability to sustain these patterns (in the case where the patterns actually have impacted the structure of the crystals), clearing the crystal does not wipe this out, for they are structural. But these are moreso the resulting precipitants into the Earth, not unlike the physical body; in the case where these are moreso essences as energies, clearing the crystal would have an impact upon this. Though it is doubtful that simple clearing methods would totally eradicate such, but reduce these to what would be considered a very insignificant background imprint. See?

There are instances where entities have (quote) "programmed or pre-programmed" certain crystals, and these crystals have been used for various purposes, not the least of which, in the Atlantean times, as devices and defensive and offensive weaponry. They have also been used as tools. They have been used in many other forms of expression as instruments and for healing works. The nature of the crystal, as you will recall, those of you who have heard our earlier commentary on crystals, is to function moreso as the amplifier or as a storage media, which then continues to emanate an intent, a prayer, a thought, or such. That is the primary function of the crystal that provides a valuable tool to Wilbur and his counterparts in this realm. They are seeking through this mechanism to contribute to the Earth those tenets of helpfulness, of healing, of wellbeing, of truth, and all that sort. See? They are, indeed, as such, dear souls … benevolent.

The matter of the crystals is one which has breadth and depth but, in essence, they, categorically, should be thought of as extensions of self. Their unique properties are as amplifiers to enhance and to localize or to focus or tune into specific areas or frequencies. They also, in their capacity of retention, create an echo resonance within their optical planes which are actually electro-optical and, as such, retain a base image for considerable lengths of Earth time, altering such or eradicating same only by introducing a stronger and more consistent charge, as it were, if that is an acceptable term.

It is well, always, to ask for the highest and best or to seek from God. Those who would answer thereafter, as you have asked in God's Name, cannot be less than that which is your original intent. See? If an entity is seeking just to channel information, as such, then there's lots of that available. But if they are seeking to serve God's will, then that's a different matter. But, please, do not misconstrue what has been given to you. Wilbur and his counterparts are very wonderful souls. Very loving souls. As they would contribute in answer to prayer or whatnot, as is detected from the Earth, it would be to their highest and best. Under Universal Law you would be preserved. See?

The love and desire to do good became an obsession, as such, because they believed in it so firmly, to the extent that their lives in the Earth began to exclude all other things which they thought in those times to be superfluous or to be a distraction from their chosen mission. As they continued rather zealously to attempt to deliver their message and do their work, many things which were intended to be a part of their joy, their blessing, in those sojourns in the Earth previous to their present expression, were overlooked or cast aside. As such, then, when they reached that point where they realized there is much more to spirituality, to oneness with God, than simply the tenets that they have held to so zealously, so much so in an attitude of truth and that sort ... nonetheless, there is more. They are their own limitation, not God, not those whom they serve. Their own consciousness has been limited by their intensity. Hence, it is oft-times encouraged here that you would strive to accomplish your works in the Earth in a state of joyous moderation, balancing one attitude, one activity with another. The Earth is intended to be a blessing.

There are those in the Earth in need; there are those in Earth who bear you blessings. If you deny either one, you have gained only part of the purpose for your existence in the Earth. If someone comes to you and has a need and you answer it, you have done a good work. If someone comes to you from a state of abundance and wishes to give to you a blessing, a gift, or simply an expression of love or friendship, and you grant them that opportunity, you have also done a good work in God's name. Being a channel of blessings does not mean that you are a one-way conduit from God to those in need. Allow the blessings to return to God through you, just as they return to the Earth from God. See? Don't limit.

Some will have to reincarnate in the Earth; others may not. Wilbur is one of those who appears to be at a point where he may not require reincarnation in the Earth to become less limited. Wait and see.

When Wilbur formed a bond through the intensity of his love, he did so because his ideals and purposes were the highest and best he could muster. They became all-important in his life. He allowed himself no other latitude than his attenuation to these as goals. He was loving and he was loved. But he was always seeking those in need. See? Take time for those who have received blessings to share them and let them share them with you.

The things that you might do that create bonds? Not allowing yourself joy. A dedication to a work in the Earth is indeed something of admiration here. A dedication to keep that in a state of balance is equally important and looked upon with respect and admiration from here, as well. For in order to keep an appropriate perspective and to be able to keep a complete progression for your entire being, such latitude and such breadth are important. Finitely focusing upon some singular aspect of existence in the Earth creates a narrow pathway for you to walk and a narrow realm in which to exist once you have departed from the Earth.

Do not convince yourself that you'll rest when you leave, and that you'll simply move to a state of joyful existence with all of this behind you as a stepping-stone to rise upon. You can gain as much elevation in spiritual awareness and acceptance by extending a hand of friendship to a passer-by as you can a hand of assistance to one who is in a state of disease. Joy in the moment. Joy in the hearts and minds of many.

Don't limit yourself.

The blue-white lights are, very much so, similar to what the benevolent souls experience when they intuit the presence of Peter, Paul, and Zachary. You are correct.

The feeling of strangeness experienced by Peter as they began their movement was indeed similar to that which occurs during the states you have identified ... of out-of-body experiences and/or sleep or meditative states. One aspect of this that does not correlate completely is that Peter has no physical body which he continues to sustain, so while he does not feel weariness or heaviness in the sense that you might, he uses this for an expression of balance and for allowing his consciousness to reorganize itself and to rebalance itself at a new level. Each experience is becoming a composite part of the total and, therefore, these times of *rest (as* they are called) are actually spiritually rebalancing periods, similar to the *sleep of spirit*, only in a more moderate scale, as Peter experienced upon completing passage through the colors, as you will recall them.

Once again, as we would comment, regarding Peter being prevented from touching Wilbur's hand, this is to a degree a parallel to the relationship between the Master and Mary after His resurrection. In this instance, the Master was capable of expressing Himself in all levels. However, the entities in those levels were not capable of dealing with His heightened vibration or energy and, thus, He cautioned them not to touch Him. The relationship between Wilbur and Peter is similar, though on a much smaller scale. The potential which might have occurred here is that Wilbur is seeking and is in some state of receptiveness. Peter, while he is under the protection, under the influence of Zachary's cloak, nonetheless, had he extended himself beyond that cloak to grasp, in essence, Wilbur's hand, could have somewhat depleted himself, being drawn into Wilbur's presence, and created a situation of imbalance for both. Paul, then, knowing this and interceding, prevented not only this from happening in the literal sense, but provided a buffer, an insulating factor (if you will) to prevent any further transference through Peter's openness and very significant receptiveness from allowing any opportunity of bridging this protective envelopment of Zachary's cloak. (We have greatly paraphrased something which is in the explanation of considerable complexity. In the reality of using and functioning within the cloaks, it is marvelously straightforward. We know you have comprehended this.)

The abrupt departure was for the reasons as indicated above: to allow for a time of rebalancing. Peter had sustained about his limit or level of absorption for that period of consciousness or time. This was detected simultaneously by Paul and, thus, the suggestion that they needed to depart.

Paul's responsibility, if you could call it such, is primarily to Peter, while, you will note, in this instance, Zachary is functioning to Wilbur much in the same way Paul is functioning to Peter. Zachary can interact with Wilbur because they have had periods of balance. Zachary also is well-experienced in movement throughout different realms and interacting with different entities. His spiritual consciousness or acceptance level is very stable, remarkably so, and, thus, his latitude of movement and experiencing is very significant, if not quite profound and unique.

Peter may well become a guide to Wilbur. And, of course, he has not the awareness of this as yet and is, as you will note from his past reactions, quite dumbfounded by the entire matter, stating, if you will recall, that he knew nothing, what could he give or do for Wilbur? You'll note that he won't be left empty-handed but, rather, will be provided remarkable support and assistance, and in a manner which will be consistent with that which has gone before.

It has been asked here what causes such bonds of intensity to the Earth that are similar to those which are experienced by the entities in Wilbur's realms. Note that Paul and Zachary and the others are providing Peter with a continual flow of experiences. Perhaps much to the chagrin (or perhaps that's a bit strong) ... to the impatience of some of you (with a note of loving humor). They have moved him from one focal point and/or topic to another, to another, to another. He hasn't settled in on one singular thing and become intense over it. They have kept him moving along, intentionally so. During his sleep of spirit, he balanced with all those matters as are pertinent directly to the Earth and which are relevant to emotional bonds.

You may have questioned and wondered why he has not thought more profoundly of his family, and why he hasn't experienced emotional bonds or tugs, or feelings of loss or loneliness (with the exception of the occurrence between he and Zachary, which lies ahead). This is because during his sleep of spirit much transpired. He accomplished a state of understanding and placed all of this in order within himself, so that his emotional body could be in a state of restful ease regarding these matters. No, he hasn't forgotten them. No, he hasn't given up his love for them. Not at all. You should see this ahead, as well. But they are in harmony. They are in balance. He knows, through the presence of a sense of wisdom provided by the presence of the Book of Wisdom, that he is assured of their well-being and the continuity of their existence, just as he is now aware of his own continuity. So, then, what is there to fear? For he knoweth there is no death. See?

Under no circumstances was it intended to (quote) "blow the lid off being a do-gooder" (end-quote) ... although, with a note of loving humor, such entities who would convey to others the image of being a do-gooder are not unlike those who would wear certain garments indicative of their (quote) "holiness" (end-quote) when, within their hearts and minds there is perhaps a less than desirable level of that which would be consistent with their outer garb (given lovingly, see).

It is true, you are correct ... not in terms of their acts of help, their compassion, their support, concern and love, but because these became preoccupations to them. In the example of Wilbur, *tunnel vision* is a very good term to use. Wilbur had those around him who loved him very dearly and who admired him for his kindness and charity to others. They continually made sacrifice and gave up much of that which was their rightful expectation of joy in order that Wilbur could continue and sustain his acts of (what you would call) charity and kindness to others. These entities did so willingly because they love Wilbur. They are his family. They are not in this realm with Wilbur. They are far beyond it. They are free. Wilbur is not. See the difference? Then who giveth the greater?

Look about you. In your desire to serve God and serve those in need, do not ignore those who love you, but allow their love to be reciprocated, for it is their love which supports and inspires. No one serves in God's Name alone, but through the loving compassion, prayers, and kindness of those who are about thee ... whether seen or unseen. Ever be mindful to give thanks for all that is present, in all realms.

Limited thinking is what you'd call a sticky wicket, no matter where one dwells. Limited thinking becomes habit-forming because it provides references. Most entities find that having reference points is very important to their sense of wellbeing. The only eternal reference points lies within. And that is why Peter moves within himself and his cloak sparkles and emanates the lights and such, and that is appropriate. Remember that. Limited thinking and habit ... These things can bind thee to the Earth, to a way of thinking, to a way of life, to a dis-ease. Expand your thinking. Open yourself. Not wantonly or casually, but keeping an eye on the ideal, the purpose, and the goal, allowing these to move with you, to grow as you grow. And therefrom, then, you can draw another reference point, but the difference being, these reference points are yours and under your direction. (You don't seem to have a significant problem with this at any rate, entity Joan. See? Given with a note of loving humor.)

The concept of the crystals and the ideas held by the entities are, indeed, good ideas and certainly useful ideas in the Earth. Nonetheless, their obsession with them as *the* way or *the* method and *the* tool is limiting them. It's as simple and straightforward as that. And yes (you are getting a handle on it) he personally needs to move on. Redundancy doesn't contribute much to one's progress, and at a certain point, one can lay the last brick of a foundation and need to move on to build something on it. Wilbur's at that point, and he knows it. And that's why Zachary's there and Peter has been introduced. See?

Correct perception, that their beliefs in being old account for their old appearance, to a degree. In a sense, they believe they have done their best work at the twilight of their existence and, therefore, they have moderated in their thinking into the belief that those who are of such a countenance are wise, and those who are less than this have less wisdom. This contributes in a part, as well.

Once again, yes, correct. It is probable that Peter will become an aide or a helpmeet to Wilbur, a guide (if you will) or some other expression paralleled or similar to this.

Wilbur's realm is not at all the exception, nor is it the rule. It is just one realm (given with a note of loving humor). More souls exist in the sense of their potential than in either of these realms. It is difficult to answer your question in the specific sense as you have expressed it. In the sense which you hold it in your mind and heart, you will likely go to a realm well beyond Wilbur's … if not the garden, another similar to this, but we believe to the garden. The majority of souls involved with the Earth at present seem to be approaching a state of some balanced distribution, with quantities proportionately scattered in the strata or realms connected to the Earth (about 25 to 35 percent), another 15 to 25 percent very close to same bound somewhat, another equal percentage just about at midway between Wilbur and where Peter is. The remainder lie scattered from that point to and beyond Peter's. They are in the lesser number, yes.

Wilbur is not an earlier stage of Peter, such as being revisited. However, with a note of loving humor, Wilbur is not a casual participant in this series of experiences, as you have intuited, entity Jud. He does relate to this grouping significantly, and there are past associations here which will be revealed in their good time and order. You have perceived this quite accurately. Just move the identifier over a notch or two and you'll have it fairly accurately.

Zachary is and was helping Wilbur because Wilbur reached a point in his current realm where he opened himself ... perhaps, in part, out of a sense of frustration, a small modicum of futility, a dash or seasoning of frustration and boredom, and a large helping of what we will call inadequacy or insufficiency. In other words, he suddenly realized that what he was doing seemed very limited. He began to pray. He began to seek and ask. In that moment, Zachary answered his prayer. Zachary, then, initiated the opening for Wilbur to begin the preparation to depart from his current realm. And that is what Zachary was helping Wilbur with, and is.

The correlation between Peter and Wilbur is very important. It is an opportunity which will provide for both of them and others of the grouping a significant potential for growth. They are all inter-related in a manner which will become more and more evident as we progress. But this is no different than the interrelationship or correlation between all of you in your grouping. See?

The dear soul, the old man, could not see Peter and Paul because he wasn't possessing that sight, as yet. He intuited their presence, just like the entity Aida intuited the blue-white lights. But he did not perceive this in the form. As such, then, he'll probably be next.

When you ask for the highest and best information in the name of the Christ, the information comes from the Christ. When you ask a prayer in God's Name, that prayer is answered from God. As that moves from that presence of God, of the Christ Consciousness to you, those good souls who are in that pathway and who are willing may contribute in accordance with Universal Law. It cannot detract nor modify the difference to some of you in your understanding. For example, entities in Wilbur's realm, albeit they are perceived as limited and very finite or intensely focused, nonetheless are experts in the area of crystals and the potential, the uses of them, because they have employed them as tools. They have not employed them inappropriately. Note that they are not obsessed with crystals. They are using them as tools, lovingly, but not under obsession. Their bond is with their thinking and its limited nature, not with the crystals. Crystals are wonderful tools. They have potential, latitude that can be very contributive. Conversely, if they become the focal point and usurp the presence of God in your life, then you are likened unto these in Wilbur's realm, and even moreso, for you are focused upon a thing, rather than an ideal, a concept.

Very well. We'll pause a moment here and seek further questions from the channel. A moment, please ...

Q&A READING #8

Continuation of Questions After Chapters 4 and 5:
CO-CREATING (V-650)
THE CRYSTAL WORKER'S REALM (V-660)

Given August 2, 1990

AL MINER/CHANNEL: *This reading is code number V-663. It is questions and answers #3 relating to the topical tape #V-660. The following questions have been received from the Voyagers and in this reading I'm going to delete reading all the names and locations, since there were so many people that had submitted the same or similar questions. I'd be spending a great deal of time just reading names after all the questions. I'm sure you'll all recognize your questions, and so I hope this is acceptable to you.*

The first series of questions, as I mentioned in the cover letter for the last mailing, have to do primarily with the cloak ... the spiritual cloak. It would appear that there's a great deal of interest in this particular aspect of the readings, and I will admit to sharing that interest. It seems to have a particularly unique impact on movement and so forth, and so without further comment from me, here are the questions.

QUESTIONS SUBMITTED

#1 - With regard to the spiritual cloak, feelings and emotions affecting the cloak ... what is the balancing process, and is there any similarity to the chakra system as we know it here in the Earth?

#2 - Please, more information regarding the additional cloak for Peter from Zachary. Also, Peter's feelings of strangeness and some comments on the blue-white color. *(One person wrote, "sounds like a fine diamond.")* And also comments about the feelings related by Peter regarding it feeling warm, comfortable, as though it were having a melodious sound, his feeling at peace ... and then ultimately feeling a bit sleepy. Was he approaching his level of acceptance at that point?

(Another question about the state of balancing time:)
#3 - Why was Zachary apparently sleepy after giving the or his cloak to Peter?

(Next, there were several people who asked about the cloak:)
#4 - The process of brushing the cloak: its significance: What does this do, actually, and any further information about that.

(Several people asked about):
#5 - The significance of Zack's comment to Peter, "Keep the cloak as long as you want it." Is there a particular ramification to that comment?

#6 - What was the function of Zachary's cloak? Does it possess magical powers, in effect? Is it for protection? Does it change his vibrations? Or does it change vibrations, period?

(With regard to Peter's cloak, once again:)
#7 - "Sparkles and crackles as he turns inwardly to balance himself." Please explain this further and how best to apply this balance or balancing principle while we are in physical body in the Earth.

#8 - As Peter was concerned with his spiritual aura (cloak) lighting up and interrupting those around him, can this occur in the Earth?

#9 - Each time Peter experiences an emotion or is processing new information, his robe gives off sound and light. You said before that emotion is the "stuff" we build with. Am I right in surmising that this is an energy Peter is manifesting and the same happens in Earth? Emotion equals energy, which is then transformed into mass, a la Einstein? Likewise, each thought which evinces an awakening, which produces a state of wonder or satisfaction, which I think could be classified as emotion, is also building. If not something physical, then building a vehicle (body) capable of sustaining higher vibrations. The higher the awareness, the purer the vibration? And is that being balanced, being able to experience and control emotion i.e. one's creation? Is one of the differences between Peter and his friends (at this point in his progress) the fact that they are in control of this emission of sound and light from their cloak? They emit them and use them at their own will ... whereas, with Peter, and most of us on Earth, this is happening mostly because of the prompting of external circumstance.

(Next are several questions dealing with the crystals mentioned in Wilbur's realm.)
#10 - Are thought-forms amplified through crystals only from that realm?

#11 - Crystals are amplifiers?

#12 - I have a crystal given to me, which has a lot of triangle shapes etched on it. Christina Raphael in her book on crystals says that these triangles are record-keepers and are symbols that information is stored in the crystal. If this is true, how is it best to retrieve the information, and in what forms may the information come?

#13 - V-660 seems to be saying that crystals have a limited ability to aid our communication. Is there any situation in which they could be especially helpful? If so, when and how to use them, and how best to select one?

#14 - Peter seemed to create his butterfly unconsciously. In other words, his unconscious process brought about its creation. This implies that we need to clear up our unconscious process so it won't create things we don't want. Do you have any comment?

I'll conclude with the questions at this point.

And now I submit them prayerfully and humbly to You, Father, asking as I do that You would guide us to the very highest and best possible information that can be given. As always, we are deeply thankful, Father, for Your presence and guidance and for the presence and efforts of those loving souls who are serving on other realms to help us along the way. We thank you all, and we thank You, Father. Amen.

THE READING

LAMA SING: Yes, we have the Channel then and, as well, those references which apply to the questions, the inquiring minds behind same, that of the grouping now gathered, and the intents and purposes of this work as it is now set before us. As we commence herein, we first pray:

Lord God, we know that Thou art ever with us in this and all such works. Thus, it is our prayer that we might herein accomplish Thy will and Thy purpose. Contributing, further, in Thy name this prayer on behalf of all souls in all realms who are presently in some need and for whom there are none in joyous prayer. We humbly thank Thee, Father, for this opportunity of joyous service in Thy name. Amen.

Consider firstly, dear friends, that the cloak might be thought of in terms of its counterpart as the aura or auric field which surrounds your physical body in the Earth. Once beyond the realm of the Earth, where certain constrictions or limitations are imposed due to the mass-mind thought and agreement to same, the aura becomes visible, largely in the form of what we have called the cloak.

In the sense that one would interpret the word or term *cloak* in the Earth, it does, in fact, in many realms, appear very much as though it were, in fact, a cloak woven of fabric or of some structure, conforming and/or adorning the physical body or the reflected form of the entity in their respective realm. See? The cloak has much to do with the accomplishments and the level of acceptance of the entity or entities who are perceived within same.

In the case of Peter, his cloak would appear different to you than those of Paul and Zachary, the female entities, Wilbur, and those who are his colleagues in that realm. The difference, then, as it is detectable visually and harmonically through sound and through other methods of sensory perception, has to do with the, generally speaking, level of acceptance of the entity and their point of progression. As an entity such as Peter moves in the transitional sense from a finite incarnation to a more infinite incarnation or existence (the latter being the more appropriate, with a note of loving humor), they begin a process thereafter, once arriving at their chosen level of consciousness, of stabilizing themselves. That includes, then, the balancing with previous influences, both from the just-previous incarnation and the summation of influences from their collective past as you measure time in the Earth. Then the process of this balancing, as it were, is reflected in the aura or, in this case, the cloak.

As such, then, perceiving the cloak upon an entity enables the perceiver to identify the position of the entity possessing the cloak in question, and provides very valuable information about how to deal with ... or in the case of such as Zachary, Paul, and the female entities, how to guide, how to assist, how to help those who are before them. As an adjunct to this in the perceptory sense, there is the ability to perceive on levels which have naught to do with the sensory perceptive mechanisms as you know them and are identified with them in the Earth, i.e., sight, sound, smell, taste, touch. The intuitive portion of self upon transition becomes another sense. The communicative ability of the intuitive at these levels would be much paralleled to what you would consider a transmission of thought, the ability to perceive thought-forms and the ability beyond this to communicate in thought-form.

Then, returning to the cloak itself, this (as the garment worn by all souls in such realms as are applicable to the explanation given) becomes, generally speaking, a consistent measure of the viability of that soul and that realm within which they are experiencing. By *viability* we mean the capacity of the entity to make movement to accomplish certain objectives and/or works and the capacity of the entity for transitory movement, and such, to and from other realms.

And so, then, feelings and emotions, as they might be thought of affecting or being represented in the cloak, are very significant. For example, as Peter reaches a point of some, we'll call it, saturation of experience (you might call it being overwhelmed, startled, surprised, or whatnot), he has been given the awareness that by turning inward he can accomplish a state of balance with this. One of the indicators, outwardly, of reaching this point of saturation is the sparkling, crackling sounds, the dancing movement, staccato-like in nature, of light and color across his cloak, at which point he knows, as do the others observing same, to take a moment for inward reflection and balance.

The comparative situation in the Earth, or a parallel situation, might be defined in the following manner: When you in the Earth are overwhelmed or startled or taken-aback by a situation, or perhaps confronted with something which seems insoluble, pattern yourself after Peter. Take a moment and turn inward. As you do, you'll find a sense of tranquility, calm, and peace will take place within you, particularly so if you have developed an affirmation or prayer which identifies a place (mentally and spiritually speaking) within your being, your mind, which is your garden-place in the Earth … a sanctuary, a place of calm and wisdom. This, then, would be very similar to what Peter experiences in this sense.

While others outwardly might see this as you having paused for just several moments, several Earth seconds, you, through practice and becoming adept at this, can expand that time inordinately in comparison to the several seconds the observer might detect. You have only but to experiment with this to understand the breadth and depth of what we speak here. Remembering that you are in command of your own destiny, and as you command from the inner and as you move into the inner self, you are not subject to the constraints imposed upon the outer. Therefore, under Universal Law you are capable of escaping the measure of time in the Earth.

Thus, several Earth seconds can be turned into minutes, even hours, in terms of the gain of balance, peace, tranquility and guidance, that you can garner by so doing. See?

There are certain similarities between the effect of the cloak and its outer reactions to stimuli to that of the chakras or the chakridic system in the Earth. As a continuum of this train of thought, the glandular system also correlates rather nicely to same. Both, then, correlate in terms of the colors, as indicated by Peter's initial journey through them to reach these realms. And the colors themselves correlate to tonal qualities, generally speaking, moving from the lower, slower oscillations (that would be lower tones) to the higher, more excited vibrational frequencies, but where they reach the point of becoming harmonics. See?

Zachary provided the cloak for Peter because it was a necessary part of his being able to journey with Zachary and Paul to Wilbur's realm. Peter's condition was, and to a degree still is, sufficiently unstable so as to prevent him from moving into another realm, such as Wilbur's, without being a disruptive force. Being mindful of Universal Law, Peter's guides then preserved him from this and the subsequent potential responsibility under Universal Law called karma that might have resulted, were he to have ventured there without this state of balance preserving him. So Zachary's cloak was and is a mechanism which provides for continuity, reflecting inwardly, preserving Peter, reflecting outwardly, preserving wherever Peter is or was and those within such realms. Essentially, Peter, while he has Zachary's cloak on him, is capable of a very vast degree of movement which will come forth in the future, we are quite certain, as we follow them further.

Zachary did not literally make another cloak. His comment about having a spare, so to say, was the extension of his own consciousness, spiritually speaking, to Peter. In effect, he formed a cloak from his own will and from Peter's willingness to receive it. The realm in which they exist is conducive to such creation and, thereby, did not hamper, impede or prevent this from occurring. The action, then, created an extension between Zachary and Peter and also between these two and Paul, for you will note Paul sustained a consistency with that vibration also, with the blue-white consistent color. Therefore, then, all were in harmony with one another and moved as an integral unit, essentially, into Wilbur's realm, and also out of it. But Zachary's cloak does not prevent Peter from exercising free will. Therefore, had Peter extended his hand to Wilbur, he would have had that right, but since he knew not the ramifications of so doing, Paul acted to prevent an error and a responsibility as the result of same because of a lack of knowledge. By taking Peter to Wilbur's realm, Zachary and Paul were and are responsible and involved. Therefore, they have that right, you see, to act on behalf of and in accordance with Universal Law.

The essence of Zachary's robe is the essence of Zachary. Zachary is profoundly accomplished in terms of spiritual acceptance, even beyond that which you perceive and anticipate as we evaluate your previous questions and admiration of his abilities. Then, those qualities as were defined by Peter ... the warmth, the comfortable feeling, the peaceful feeling, the melodious-like feeling ... all of these are qualities of Zachary. In effect, Peter was describing Zachary's essence, albeit in limited forms of expression but the best he knew at that point.

The feeling of sleepiness was, indeed, due to Peter reaching a point of some transition, for the placement of Zachary's cloak upon Peter did and continues to create considerable opportunity for Peter to grow, to accelerate in his spiritual acceptance much faster than he would be able were he not to be in possession of Zachary's cloak. It's sort of like an entity stumbling about in a darkened room in the Earth and a friend handing them a light. With the light, they can see where they are going and accomplish their objective quite easily. If they had not the light, they would continue to stumble for an indeterminate amount of time. Zachary's gift of the cloak to Peter is like giving that entity in the darkened room a light, spiritually speaking. See? The sense of fatigue, then, was ... how can we define this to you ... not imposed by Zachary, not mandated by Paul and Zachary, but anticipated, known. For this created an environment of what you might consider rarified atmosphere, spiritually speaking. And as such, then, Peter required this period of time for balance to adjust to same. During that period of adjustment, as Zachary indicated, a feeling of a bit of weariness was due to the connection between he and Peter through the bridge between them existing because of the cloak. Do you see this, then? Zachary actually wasn't sleepy or tired and, actually, in the literal sense, neither was Peter. Only feeling the need to rebalance within himself.

As Zachary brushes the cloak, it accomplishes several-fold things. It renews and recharges, in a manner of speaking, the bond between he and Peter. It also stimulates and activates what we would call the envelopment around Peter to a heightened potential. In other words, you could consider that Zachary is like a builder inspecting a vehicle which he has constructed, making last-minute adjustments and attunements before that vehicle is used for a good journey. See? And as such, then, this accomplishes several-fold objectives, as just indicated.

It also has an impact of a process similar to what you know in the Earth as magnetic healing. Each time Zachary does this, you will note that there is a transference of a certain level of energy or consciousness which is very supportive and very neutral, very pure. You'll note also that when Zachary fidgets or fusses with his own robe, that this, too, is due to the connective link, in essence, between Peter and Zachary and between Zachary and others. Peter is not the only one who is being, in a sense, loved by Zachary ... tutored, guided, protected, preserved. He has others. When you note this, these may be times when they are in a moment of need, and Zachary's actions are providing for them, to meet their need. This is a bit more involved than these words can convey to you, but at least now you will understand just a bit more what's transpiring here.

Zachary's offer to Peter to "keep the cloak as long as you want it" is a comment given under Universal Law, once again. As you would pray for another who has not requested same, but you know to be in need, you would offer your prayer open-handedly to them, not forcibly. Would you not? You would pray for the highest and best for them and make your offering before them, that they might choose if they will, and if they do not, you would not infringe upon that right. In the clarity of Zachary's vision, he knows that by making this statement to Peter, and Peter then accepting the offer, that a bond has been strengthened here. And the latitude between them for growth, for movement, and for Zachary to be able to help Peter, has been expanded significantly.

It may seem like a small comment, a small action, and of little significance. We can assure you that in these realms the actions, the words, the activities, are rarely, if ever, idle. They have purpose, they have meaning, and they are always joyful. They are never intended to be burdensome nor to be that which would limit. Conversely, they are always offered in the spirit of a heart which is joyfully seeking to uplift and to free those who are offered or given of such blessings. See?

Zachary's cloak functioned (perhaps we could concur with you) in a magical sort of way, in the sense that it is like a flying carpet (with a note of loving humor) enabling him to traverse many different realms swiftly and easily. It does provide protection to Peter and to those who are in realms where Peter might travel. It does change his vibrations, moreso in the sense of stabilizing them, balancing them, and making them passive. That's an important term here, and you'll see, again and again, that a state of moderation, harmony, and passivity ... These are important qualities for guides, for teachers, and for those who serve, of which, of course, a number of you have surmised, much to your credit, we should note. But Zachary is preparing Peter (and, as well, Paul is assisting significantly,) to become or to be offered the opportunity to be a guide. See?

It is possible for your aura to light up and interrupt those around you in the Earth, most assuredly. Often, entities may come and go into a group of other entities, and without speaking, without any sensory (in the physical interpretation of same), influence get the attention of those in that room, in that gathering. And this is through the influence of the aura, the cloak. In some instances in the Earth, an entity's aura may precede them, as they are moving, about by many meters, which, of course, can be felt by some entities quickly, and by others less consciously but, nonetheless, felt.

When an entity is emotionally jostled in the Earth, their aura reacts in one of several ways, generally speaking. Very often it closes down around the entity, becomes dense and intense, and is in close proximity to their physical perimeter (that being their physical body). In other instances, there may be sharp, shooting lines of intense color radiating out from the aura like light shining through holes of a fabric covering a bright lamp. See? So the answer to the question is yes, that can occur in the Earth.

Control of the emission of this sound and light from the cloak is very important, and Zachary, Paul, and the female entities are in control of such. The ability to control them is important and is mandatory to be in the positions that they are. Peter, conversely, is not expected to control his, for he is in a state of transition, as we indicated above. Those of you in the Earth are prompted by external circumstance and by your internal reaction to same. Again, if you learn to turn inward and balance with that, in a moment or two you'll be able to control your spiritual cloak, your energy, as the result. The moreso you work with this, the more rapidly does it come under your control. It expands or multiplies upon itself in a ratio proportionate to your effort. See? Your emotion creates an energy which moves outward from your cloak. The greater your emotional reaction, the more your cloak will snap, sparkle, crackle, and will have lights dancing about it, and may emit fingers of light from it, as we indicated above.

Generally speaking, then, the higher the awareness, the purer the vibration or the capacity to harmonize and to be neutral or passive, yielding to the influences of the realm in which one might be, but not submitting to them. In other words, sustaining an inner countenance of balance in accordance with your own spirituality, but confining that to the perimeter of your cloak ... emulating, then, as in terms of the radiation of your thought and energy from and upon the cloak those of the primary influences of the realm in which you exist. See? So, in essence, then, we believe that this narrative and information in regard to the cloak should be revealing to you and, prayerfully, answer the questions as you have presented them, and some which you have not. Each thought, each deed, each emotional thought-form that is created and experienced by you, potentially becomes another fiber of your cloak. The way you deal with these determines what that shall be and the pattern thereof. Do you see this then?

Wilbur's realm is not the only one wherein thought-forms can be or are amplified through crystals. Crystals are, as such, a potential amplifier and, to a degree, a retaining device for thought-forms. As such, then, as one becomes knowledgeable with and of these as extensions of or instruments of their intent, they can be utilized to a considerable degree to accomplish a variety of good works ... among these are those which are involved with healing, with prayer, with the building and transmission of thought-forms, and other such activities similar to but not limited to these.

In the instance of the crystal given to you, Christine, we would encourage you to think of this not so much so in and of itself as a record-keeper, but moreso as a catalyst, a means by which you can use this as a focal point to move yourself to that information as you would seek. While we do find there is some indication of support for the hypotheses indicated here by Christine R., we would not totally subscribe to that in the physical sense. For that implies, as such, a certain degree of what you would call magical power to the crystal. And while the crystal or crystalline form of structure in the Earth does have many and varied unique properties, these are (humbly given) not magical. They are not powerful in and of themselves. But using the unlimited power of God and the awareness of this, entities and the forces under Universal Law can, indeed, make use of these as a media or medium of such activity. See?

If you are seeking to gain information, then gain it between yourself directly with God. If you use the crystal, then do not become absorbed in each facet of the stone itself, but rather the literal depiction of what the stone represents, the crystal. It represents the force of nature, a created object which has come to be because of God's will and grace. As the crystal has been and is subjected to the forces in the Earth, these cause deviations in the lines of electromagnetic transmission or planes of same, and also to the lines of cleavage, of fracture, of refraction, and the photo-chromatic properties of the elemental structure of the crystal itself.

And so, in what forms may the information come? Probably in that form which you are most willing to accept. If you believe, and you believe that these in the triangular etchings or layered forms would be more accurate (wouldn't it, for your crystal?) are indeed a mechanism of recordkeeping, then you will obtain that information via same. The truth is, the information is available to you with or without the crystal, dependent upon your faith. If you use the crystal, that does not mean you are limited in faith. It means only that that is the direction you have focused your faith upon at this point. There are many, many beautiful souls who do use crystals for fine and wonderful works in God's name. One could do worse than to emulate same.

Crystals do not, in that sense, have a limited ability to aid your communication. They are very broad in their spectrum of functioning as tools or extensions of self in those capacities. There are crystals in the Earth which yet retain properties which were stimulated ... or perhaps the term best given is *imbued*, within them over 200,000 Earth years ago, just as purely and strongly as the day these properties were placed within them.

If you seek to use the crystals, then we'd recommend that you make reference to our earlier comments and such about them, and then, if there is sufficient desire among you, if the Channel agrees, we can assist you with specifics on these, their properties and such. But not as an integral part of this work ... as an aside to it, a peripheral project or such as you would seek it. We'll leave that to your decisions and the Channel's.

The method for selecting the crystal we've spoken on previously, as well. The best of all ways is to reach a state of inner attunement before attempting to select the crystal. Once attained, the crystal should emulate with you in a sense of simpatico. There should be a feeling of mutuality, an essence passing between you and it or they. Those who are practiced in such, or who have opened themselves as channels of blessing, are perhaps most familiar with this process. But all of you can accomplish this in and of yourselves, if you simply dedicate some of your effort and time to that work. If you don't wish to, then have one of those who can see and hear choose it for you. See?

The creation of the butterfly did involve the attainment of an unlimited or unrestricted consciousness. In the realm in which Peter exists, the unconscious and conscious are much closer as one. The super-consciousness is also much closer ... that often referred to as the God-Consciousness by some. And therefore, as these continue to move ever closer towards a point of merging somewhere off in (what you'd call) the distance, Peter's capacity to create will improve, along with that movement.

The implication that you need to clear up your unconscious process is a very good and astute observation. It can and does create things you don't want. Usually these are not perceptible, but they can be. What they do tend to manifest, however, are blocks or diffusions, dispersions of your primary flow of energy which is otherwise directed towards a particular objective. The unconscious can draw off sufficient of that primary energy so that by the time it reaches your primary thought-form objective it has (to coin your own words) insufficient *prayer power units* (remember that? ... given with a note of loving humor). So we might now turn about the table on you, lovingly, and state that you need to have sufficient creative power units. (See? If you think of the acronym, you'll find humor in it.)

Your process of following along through the pattern of movement, as you are of recent times experience, should enable you to do this. As you reach the varying levels and literally, figuratively, and symbolically, unburden yourself, or yourselves, you will reach a state of pure Consciousness ultimately. That state of pure Consciousness is extremely dynamic. Once it is attained, it would be difficult to un-attain it. And so it is, perhaps moreso likened unto the development of this as an ideal, do you see; for as one reaches a point of some awareness of this *potential* (as it might be called) this is transforming, in terms of the consciousness of self in the Earth. It becomes, then, increasingly difficult to prevent this Consciousness from returning to the Earth with you. Do you see the nature of what we speak here?

While the creative process involved in the manifestation of the butterfly seems at this point to be casual or random or by chance or simply a by-product of some other work and of no significant import, you should see in future that there is some significance to the manifestation of this particular element, or the butterfly. It will become a part of future works in a unique and perhaps humorous way.

Now, then, as we turn to some of the other questions unexpressed above ... The topics of this project were chosen, as we stated, to promote some understanding which shall extend beyond the current incarnation, making the way just that much moreso passable for you as you move beyond it and into other realms. The meaning behind this commentary is as follows: This information has been, is, and shall be offered to you in the knowledge that your consciousness will absorb varying degrees of what has been given. As such, then, this becomes a part of what we shall call your total being. Then, as you move from the Earth, whether through the portal called death or through other means, as it is in accordance with your will, or as there is the need, this information will be available to you, should you choose to use it.

As you consider that now in the Earth, think of yourself as being in the position of Peter, for, indeed, you will likely be there once again. Having this knowledge available to you in your own consciousness, then, provides you the opportunity to move forward very rapidly into a position of your highest possibly attainable consciousness. See?

In the case of yourself, entity Rudy, and many others of you (indeed, all of you, should you choose) you might well employ this information while yet in physical form this incarnation in the Earth. Then, dependent upon those activities, events, and such as are standing before the Earth, you might contribute these to others who are not incarnated in the Earth at present, or who shall take form in the Earth in those coming times. In this way, then, the information is made available to help prepare the way. See?

Everyone has a (quote) "soul name" (end-quote) as implied in your question about same. However, at the level of the soul itself, this is not expressed finitely as a name but, rather, is expressed in the form of a collage of vibrations or energies, not unlike a symphonic passage. The further one moves from that level of expression, the moreso does that collage of energy or vibration manifest itself in differing ways. At some points, it is expressed as color and light; at others it is expressed as sound and color and light; in yet others it is detectable moreso visually or sensually through the outer expression of the soul called the cloak, the spiritual cloak; and in the Earth, as such, through the aura.

The name, then, as it is used (for example, for yourselves in the Earth) is your individual identifier. However, others may bear the same identifier or name. In realms beyond the Earth, the uniqueness of the spiritual cloak, or the other expressions as we gave them above, is such that the individuality cannot be confused. Do you see?

There are instances where the cloak may appear to be similar, if not identical. These are those cases wherein visiting entities have chosen to manifest themselves in that form for the purpose of participating in activities or observing in lesser realms. Conversely, this cannot occur as souls move under the guidance, primarily, of entities from such realms or higher, as they would move into higher or more rarified realms. See? So, in effect, the expression of the soul name in its primary form does not vary. The manifestation of it does. Therefore, it changes as they progress to and from varying levels of vibration. See?

Not all souls experience activities in other realms, as depicted by those of your planetary expressions, though any soul may partake of same or be, as such, a visitor in same, if they are of sufficient awareness to enable themselves such a movement. They are used much in the form of experiences or expressions in the Earth (also known as incarnations): for the purpose of contributing to the growth of the individual and group soul consciousness. They are also used (referring to others, such as Venus, Mars, Pluto, Saturn and such) for the purpose of rapid balancing on a particular tenet, trait or aspect, and/or for the preparation for works which are to follow which are greatly contributed to by such preparatory sojourns in these other realms.

In a manner of speaking, Peter's current primary realm or home realm, called the Garden, is not unlike those. Each realm of expression could be thought of, in a manner of speaking, as preparatory for the next, could it not?

The oversoul, as such, is likened unto the Book of Wisdom. The oversoul is the completeness of the soul's consciousness. It is unique in the sense that it can detach itself from the soul residence. Well, we'll explain it this way, if you'll understand and accept that we are using examples and colloquial terms, and that these are not precisely literal, see: Assume that the soul lived in a certain place. Perhaps we could call it Philadelphia (given with a note of loving humor, where love is so brotherly and abundant ... at times), and suppose the soul had a friend who lived in Chicago, and another who lived in Wiesbaden. Rather than taking the tram or the airplane, they could dispatch a portion of their consciousness, which we'll call the oversoul, to visit. Now, the friends or relatives in Chicago and Wiesbaden are actually expressions of the soul itself, and the oversoul is visiting them to assist or to do some work which might be in need or is lagging behind schedule, or something of that sort. Do you see? So the oversoul is moreso likened unto the complete consciousness of the being. The oversoul is, perhaps, the closest approximation of definition of the Book of Wisdom, as it has been identified above. (That should certainly raise even more questions, we should think, given with a note of loving humor.)

The question was asked, "Is there a significance to the detailed description of action in relating the experiences of Peter," and further, that "much seemed extraneous to the points being made." The detail has been given because that's what's occurring. In other words, we are attempting to convey to you information in specific, detailed form, with precise and concise examples, in order that these as thought-forms will be complete and live on in your soul memory for the reasons we indicated to entity Rudy's question above. If we merely provide you concise statements, as we have often in past projects, we have discovered through observation and participation with you that these are ofttimes difficult to apply and to understand, since the application is complex and difficult in your realm.

It was determined here, then, that by exemplifying this to you through the experiences of the entity Peter, that this would be more meaningful. It is intended, further, that as these experiences continue, that you will have the opportunity to participate in a more active sense, rather than merely observing and questioning, as you are at present. And so that is the purpose for the detailed description. We ask your forgiveness if it appears to you to be excessive. Conversely, there are many among your grouping who, even as we speak, wish we'd give more detailed explanation on nearly every single point (given with a note of loving humor, and we might add here for your further humor, lovingly, the Channel is among that number.)

There are, indeed, other portals through which one might enter and depart the Earth, other than that which you call death. There are those who have used these ... perhaps noteworthy so would be the Master in several incarnations. Particularly noteworthy is that of His expression called Melchiz-edek. It is possible, and it has been accomplished frequently by those of Eastern study and application to do so at will. The activity called astral projection, some forms of meditation, and the process of sleep are all variations upon these other portals.

There is a question regarding (quote) "Is Lama Sing's accent a carryover from the past ... perhaps a past incarnation in the Earth? And might we know where?" The accent, as it might be detected in the Earth is dependent upon the influ-ence of that information here regarding the sources respond-ing to same, their level of consciousness, and the group or groupings which are involved in same.

Also, as a part of this, we find given here previous incar-nations of the Channel itself, this Channel, and primarily those wherein the greater spiritual awareness has been at-tained in the past. Here in this grouping there are counterparts to the Channel and this applies among them ... the derivation, then, having to do with several Eastern incarnations and also those among the English Isles; these being moreso distant in terms of your current Earth time measure, the most recent of which occurring some 800 Earth years after the Master en-tered the Earth as the man called Jesus. We trust that is suffi-cient in answer to that inquiry.

The question was asked, "Since entities go through vary-ing incarnations and obviously are called by name in each of them, at least in the Earth, how is it decided what name to speak of them or call them?" Presuming that the question is meant in regard to what name would we call them, we would call them that name which is the summation of their highest spiritual consciousness at the point in which we are interact-ing with them. In the case of Peter, Peter was not his name in the Earth. It is his name at present because he is at a point of considerable transition and, thus, his spirituality is most reflected by that incarnation wherein he was called Peter... that simple, that straightforward. See?

The question was asked, "What realm is Tobar's[5] home base?" That is a difficult question to answer, because Tobar is not limited, in that sense, to a home base. (He's not just dwelling in Philadelphia.) Tobar moves about and has interaction with many different realms. Tobar is primarily among the group known or identified here as the Elders, and, as such, he's frequently present among these works. So, therefore, his home base would be considered that of the realm of the Elders, which is well beyond the realm in which Peter is now experiencing. See?

The question was asked, "In what year did the entity Peter die?" Well, Peter, of course, in the terminology of the Earth, passed through the portal called death (of course, he is very much alive) but, as such, passed through that portal in your current Earth year [1990], Earth month January-February ... make that Earth months; the process involved, the latter portion of same, the earlier portion of the latter.

Interestingly, another entity asked how best to use the information and/or knowledge and to retain it, and also expressed gratitude for the (quote) "excellent detailed descriptions of everything" (end-quote). See what we meant, entity Linda?

So, we would again turn to this: Whatever you experience becomes a part of you. The degree to which this is actively a part of you in the now, in the current consciousness, is dependent upon how much you use it. Using it does not mean that you go forth and do a certain work daily with it; but, rather, that it becomes a part of or incorporated into your

---

[5] Tobar – "The Stones of Tobar" was a project Al Miner conducted with the Voyagers in 1989, just prior to the Peter Project.

way of thinking and your way of living. It is that type of use that we are referring to. If you wish to keep knowledge, if you wish to retain it, then use it, so that it can become wisdom. Wisdom is eternal. The best of all ways to use knowledge is to share it or manifest good works that become the example, that others would see same and, as such, emulate it and support it. If two of you agree, it becomes a viable thought-form in existence under Universal Law in the realm in which the agreement is made. See?

Then, dear friends, we will next turn to Peter once again, and importantly so. For many of the questions which you have asked here of recent times will also be asked by Peter and will be exemplified in new experiences. It is our prayer and our belief that these will exemplify to you (much more than our responses here) the answer to the questions you have expressed and many of those which you have not.

In the interim, then, we encourage you in your prayer and in your meditations to focus now upon these entities. Why not experiment on your own, individually and as a grouping, with perceiving Peter, Zachary, Paul, the female entities, Wilbur, and such, in your meditations and in your prayers? And when you visit them, leave a loving prayer and see what transpires. See what happens in the future in the experiences of Peter, if you do. Those of you who have and use crystals, why not think of Wilbur and his grouping and send them a thought-form of prayer and of unlimited joy? There are reasons for our suggesting this, as many of you have come to understand when we so do. It's your choice, but make it joyful, not as a mandate. See?

We pray now in God's Name on behalf of all of you who are in need and who have expressed unto this, our Channel, and others a desire for prayer:

*We ask of Thee, Father, to awaken those bless-
ings and that abundance as is their rightful heritage.
And we thank Thee, Father, for answering this prayer. Amen.*

Until next we meet, then, may the light and blessings of
our Father's grace ever be a lamp to illuminate your footsteps. Fare thee well, then, for the present, dear friends.

Q&A READING #9

Questions After Chapter 6:
UNDERSTANDING THE CLOAK (V-710)

Given September 10, 1990

AL MINER/CHANNEL: *This reading is code number V-711. It is questions and answers #1 for Voyager Project #7, and the questions that I am about to present will basically relate to our opening reading, V-710, which dealt with the cloak and then also the visit with Wilbur and friends.*

I'll turn now directly to the questions.

QUESTIONS SUBMITTED

#1 - Is Zachary capable of incarnating in the Earth without using the birth cycle?

#2 - Up until now we have been referring to the realms involved as Wilbur's Realm and Peter's Garden. What would these realms be called if Wilbur wasn't there (in his realm) and Peter wasn't in the Garden? In other words, how is it appropriate to refer to these two realms from your point of view? *(Both of those questions are from Dave in Maryland)*

#3 - Why does Peter meet both male and female entities? I've heard that male and female bodies were part of the involvement with the Earth life only.

#4 - Why hasn't anyone that Peter encountered talked about praying to God, or praying for the benefit of other souls?

#5 - Will Peter ever see his wife and family again? Will they know each other at that time?

#6 - At one point, Peter tells Zack that he did not hear him approach. How does Zack approach? On foot? Why does he not move about another way besides what we know of as Earthbound or Earthly walking?

(And finally, also from Dave in Maryland)
#7 - Wilbur has made a lot of progress. How long or how much Earth time has he been in his current location or in this place *(which we, as Dave points out, now call Wilbur's realm)* in order to make this progress?
(Thanks for those really great questions, Dave.)

#8 - Lama Sing, you talked about there being a "perfect pattern" within us, and that if we could get in touch with that, we could be healed. Would you tell us more about this and how to get in touch with that perfect pattern within? *(And that excellent question is from Joan in Pennsylvania.)*

#9- What power is released through laughter? Our power over the situation? Please explain this? *(And that's from Harold and Linda in Missouri, and certainly refers to a really dynamic topic in terms of its potential.)*

(Also from Harold and Linda)
#10 - Do our thoughts, conscious or unconscious, affect other realms, just as Peter's unconscious creation of the butterfly influenced Wilbur? If so, how does this work?

(The next question that I am going to present here deals with a little book that Joan in Pennsylvania has been working on for several years. She has sent me a copy of the draft of the book, and it's absolutely delightful. It's the story of the principal character who is called Cap Caterpillar, who ultimately becomes a butterfly. It's just delightful, and I certainly

look forward to Joan getting it published. Joan's question is, and I can understand why she says this ...)

#11 - I just have to ask if my little book about Cap and his becoming a butterfly has anything at all to do with what's going on with Peter, Zack and Paul. Or was this all just a coincidence?

(Another question from Joan)
#12 - Is the dinshah research and work as found, for example, in the book "Let There Be Light" a correct method? *(Joan points out in a letter to me that perhaps, if it is, it could save us a lot of work in readings and such to define and associate colors with different dis-eases and such. And thank you for pointing those out, Joan.)*

#13 - In August I had a dream about my mother in which I carried her up some stairs. She departed from the Earth almost exactly four years earlier. Is this some of the work that we are now doing in other realms? The dream was pretty vivid. *(And that's from Gisela in Arizona.)*

(Next I have sort of a question and a bit of a report from my good friend Jud in North Carolina, and he writes)
#14 - While working late recently, I asked for help. I heard Zachary say, "No need to worry." I was amused and felt much better immediately. The next day I found out that there really was no need to worry. Then at work a day later, I heard a jingle-jangle sound which made me smile as I thought of Zack and Company. Please convey my thanks to Zachary and the guides and everyone who answered my call. At yet another time, I tried to think of Peter's garden-like place while I was in a time of considerable stress. If you would, please tell the other Voyagers that it works. *(Again, that's from Jud in North Carolina, and we thank you for that report, Jud, and invite Lama Sing, et al, to offer us any comments that they might have on what you've experienced.)*

And so now, Father, we present these questions prayerfully to You, asking as we do that You might guide all of us to the highest and best information that You would know and see to be beneficial as relates to the questions I've just given and, perhaps, any other questions that may have been in the hearts and minds of the Voyagers, that didn't manage to make it into my hands before this reading. I would ask also for special prayers and blessings for all those people who have communicated to me their needs for prayer, for healing, and other spiritual assistance, and ask that in the name of the Master, the Christ, that those prayers now be answered. We thank You, Father, and all those loving souls in all the realms that lie between we and You, for their dedicated and loving service. Amen.

READINGS SUBMITTED

LAMA SING: Yes, we have the Channel then and, as well, those references which apply to the grouping, those questions as indicated above, and the ideal, purpose and goal of same. As we commence with this work, we shall first pray in this manner:

Lord God, we know that Thou art ever with us. We know, as well, that within Thy house there are many messengers who shall, by their works, their intent, ever convey Thy will and purpose. Being mindful of these, we pray now, Father, that Thou would guide us through same, that we shall accomplish Thy will and purpose herein. We pray further on behalf of all those souls in all realms who are presently in some need and for whom there are none in joyous prayer. We humbly thank Thee, Father, for this opportunity of joyous service in Thy name. Amen.

The relationship between the Universal Forces and that of the consciousness of the entity called Zachary is sufficient so as to enable the entity to move from these realms into such as finite expressions, which could be thought of as the Earth and elsewhere.

Although the entity Zachary has many aspects to his awareness, we do not find, as such, that there would be the need in that sense of the question for him to actually incarnate. Because of the purposes (such as the ideal, purpose, and goal) of Zachary's works, there is by way of the mechanisms now in place sufficient means by which he can accomplish those works without adopting a physical form in the Earth.

Also (speaking to another aspect of the question which underlies your asking it), any soul who reaches a point of, we'll call it, self-acceptance to the degree that each one shall come to know that God is expressed within and about them, such souls can then become as unlimited, for the nature of God's unlimited and infinite nature is then adopted as their own. Thereafter, such works as you have exemplified in your question, that being incarnating in the Earth without using the birth cycle, are of no great difficulty. Nonetheless, Universal Law would be fully conformed to, and that activity would not be participated in or predicated were there not sufficient need for so doing. And so, again, we would turn to our comment just above: There are those mechanisms in place which are sufficient so as to enable Zachary to accomplish his intent in God's name. See?

It would be difficult to identify to you, just so, a certain name or title to a realm of consciousness that would be, in terms of a name, significant to you while in the Earth. But for sake of reference, consider the following as reference points, with the hope here that such will provide you with a perspective as much as, perhaps, the benefit of a singular name:

The Garden is, as such, referred to here as The Garden, not just Peter's Garden, for it is a place of expression for many souls, a great number. Also, the realm which is colloquially or loosely called Wilbur's Realm is also a realm inhabited by many other souls of unique and beautiful nature. These two realms, then, if they were thought of in a linear sense, moving outward from the Earth as the center of concentric circles, might be thought of as approximately seven levels beyond the veil of darkness, which divides the Earth plane and the next major realm, as it could be called.

Some of you who will recognize that, then, as being adjacent to the next veil in terms of thinking of the Earth as the first level or realm (which is not accurate, actually), would then perceive this as being adjacent to yet the next realm beyond, which could be defined and is defined by many philosophies as also containing seven individualized realms. See?

To directly answer your question, we refer to Peter's garden-like realm quite simply as The Garden. You will discover in future that some entities may refer to this by different terms, and yet each will find that it is one and the same place when explored to any depth.

Wilbur's Realm is rather colloquially and lovingly titled here as The Crystal Workers Realm. It's not just precisely that, but we find joy in thinking of it as such, for the beauty and love which is focused in that particular regard seems to emanate from it, and we find joy in so doing ... referring to it by that name, see. There is some basis in fact for substantiation of these names, as well.

Remember that you are experiencing the entire unfolding of Peter's consciousness or the building of his awareness pretty much from Peter's perspective. In other words, much of what we are relating to you is without paraphrasing it ... the recitation of a literal dialogue and the reporting of literal experiences. You could conclude from this then, that so being, the experiences are particularly (in a term) *tailored* to Peter and the appropriate combination of experiences and activities that are beneficial and productive to Peter.

Nonetheless, there is universality to this, in the sense that these experiences are very productive for all of your grouping as well, and others like you. The justification for that lies in the fact that you are seeking, and that you are striving to become, what we shall call, the master of your own will. And as such, rightfully then, much of your purposes, individually and collectively as a grouping, have been carefully considered as these relate to or correlate to the position and stature and purposes of Peter. In fact, you could think of Peter as one of your grouping. Do you see? Only, as such, off on a journey in an other realm. See? Therefore, as one would conclude, Peter has certain expectations. He has certain ... how do you call them, thought-forms of acceptance.

You see, dear friends, when you depart from the Earth

you do not necessarily abandon all of what you consider to be valid or real. To an extent, some of this remains, and until you become unlimited to the degree that such references are no longer important for the balance and well-being of your completeness, these are used. There is no set criterion in that sense, in these particular realms at least, that mandate this or that must be, and this or that cannot be. To the contrary, the breadth and depth of compassion and love in these realms is sufficient so as to embrace, among all who are sufficiently aware to dwell therein, any thought-form as is purposeful to any other entity who is present therein. See?

So, therefore, the expression in the form of a physical body, which is in fact not actually physical at any rate, would logically and appropriately be in the fashion after its own kind in the Earth ... that being male and/or female. Beyond these realms, there are other forms of expression which are neither male nor female, but more pure in the completeness of the soul's expression.

The Garden, you see, is not the ultimate destination. Although it may appear, from the perspective of what's been involved and your own consciousness and references, to be likened unto an idyllic realm, there are realms beyond, and beyond those yet others, wherein the expression of an entity is thought of to be even more pure and even more unlimited

So the answer to your question, then: Peter perceives male and female entities because that is basically acceptable to Peter. Male and female bodies are not an integral part of the function of the entities here as in the sense of the Earth but, largely, some of the last vestiges of continuity as relate to the Earth. And as such, then, to the degree of these being relevant and productive to the entities involved, such is quite acceptable here.

Although you have not heard, in the literal sense of verbiage, encouragement and references to entities praying to God or for the benefit of other souls, we would note emphatically here, much of the experiences which you are observing through our conveying them to you (and through some of your own observations to greater and lesser degrees) are expressions of living prayer.

In other words, you might think for a moment or two that Peter, Paul, Zachary, Wilbur, David, and all the others, are actually living in a state of real prayer. They are functioning within a presence which is no different than that which you create when you pray in the Earth. Another way of stating this to you is that they are functioning within the power of prayer itself. See? It would be well to make reference to the earlier works performed with your grouping on that topic[6]. There is much involved there which would illuminate more of this, we should think. If questions remain on this topic, it's well worth further exploration, and we would welcome it here.

Peter will see his just-previous wife and family again, and indeed they will know each other at that time. In a manner of speaking, Peter has (quote) "seen them" (end-quote) during times of his spiritual rest and re-balancing. During such times, the soul is not idle but is very much active. A moderate parallel could be drawn to your dream state, though here in these realms and/or those wherein Peter now is experiencing called The Garden, the spiritual sleep dream-state is much more productive, real. It is an activity of correlation, foundationally structuring and strengthening the soul. It is a time wherein soul records are available to the entity, which would, of course, include the just-previous incarnation. See?

Zachary does not actually approach on foot (with a note of loving humor) and he does not actually move about through the means of (quote) "Earthbound walking" (end-quote) ... using your terms. But he projects the image of so

---

[6] Earlier works on the topic refers to the "Prayer Project" by Al Miner/Lama Sing with the Voyagers, a rather extensive work begun in 1988.

doing because it is accepted. You will note, if you observe carefully, that this is not walking at all, but rather an assemblage of activities which portray the essence of movement through the form called walking. Sooner or later, Peter will discover that he can't perceive his own feet. When he does, you'll perhaps have more of an answer to this question.

There is no need to walk here, in the sense of the laws of physics of the Earth. Movement is by intent or will. The appearance of walking simply provides continuity for those souls who are of recent transition or birth into their current realm. See?

Wilbur's tenure in his current realm is perhaps the equivalent of fourteen Earth years. While that might seem like a considerable length of Earth time, it is actually not here in terms of activities of souls, comparatively speaking. Some souls, as we have observed them, have been in their current locale for two to four hundred Earth years. There are some others who have been in their current realm since the Master walked upon the Earth as the man called Jesus. Therefore, Wilbur's duration or tenure in his current realm is naught but the twinkling of an eye here. See? His progress is actually quite rapid. But you'll see more of this, too, we should think, as Zachary involves Wilbur much more in Peter's forthcoming works as a part of his soul's growth.

There is a perfect pattern within all souls, and that pattern is one and the same in that instant as God's Consciousness perceived thee. This we find given us from those realms wherein those called *the Elders* keep the records. And as such then, do we find that this information bears with it a certain degree of light. What this means to you is not intentionally cryptic.

We'll attempt to convey it to you in these terms: The perfect pattern is always there within and about you. Think of a light having had layer after layer of a garment or veil or curtain-like material placed over it. If you think of these as fears, doubts, habits, karma, and so forth, these are those that need to be removed in order for the perfect pattern to emerge.

It's not as complicated a task as that might seem to indicate. Through the mind focused in meditation and prayer, you can pass through all these just as we observed Peter passing through the colors or layers (also parallel to these as we've just given them). So the procedure is not to ignore what's found in meditation and/or prayer, but to frontally deal with it … recognizing its presence, then setting it aside, giving it a place of confirmation in your mind. Taking the next and doing the same, until there are no more and you are within the presence of the perfect pattern. Thereof, you will find the light we spoke of, and it can pass through, as you have made a portal … mechanisms, like we spoke of that Zachary uses to accomplish his work. See?

Curiously, the next question also has to do with this. Laughter is like releasing that light and allowing it to come forth into the Earth, into your daily life. You therefore gain primal power over that or any situation. Laughter is liberating to the power of the soul. Laughter dispels fear, anger, animosity, hatred. Laughter comes forth as a music of the soul. Take any grouping of entities who are hostile to one another, get them to laugh together several times, thereafter and ever henceforth they will look upon one another quite differently. If you do not believe that, experiment with it. It is pure and simple truth.

Laughter is one of the greatest powers you have for healing. Many healings that we have observed and have participated in, as involved the Earth or other realms, have had the final vestige of the dis-ease eradicated through the power of healing which is expressed in the form of laughter. Never take yourself too seriously, for that just closes the portal, boxing up laughter. Laughter is joy; God is joy unlimited. Laughter and joy, then, can be thought of as unifying self to God's

Word. Remember, in the beginning was the Word. The power that the Master used so often was joy. The Word of God is borne on the wings of joyous laughter, lovingly.

Peter's conscious creations and unconscious creations have impacts differently upon the realms in which he is now existing because of the functioning of what we will call Universal Law. Where entities of like mind have created an array of thought-forms which are supported by them, then this becomes the primordial law, a.k.a. (in your Earthly colloquial terms, given with a note of loving humor) laws of physics for that realm. Therefore, so as you apply your thoughts, conscious or unconscious, in accordance with the laws of physics, you could influence other realms. But where your thoughts, for example, conscious or unconscious, are not in accordance with the laws of adjacent realms, those laws or thought-forms will act as a filtration device or as a reflective covering or cloak, and your thoughts will have no impact whatsoever upon those entities. They will pass through that realm as though they were merely a gentle breeze.

If those entities wish to focus upon those thoughts, they can of course, since we are presuming your question relates to those realms above and beyond yours, as opposed to beneath yours. Realms beneath yours are, in fact, impacted by every thought, conscious and/or unconscious. Those above cannot be influenced in that sense. See? That should raise some other questions, we should think (with a note of loving humor).

All things that are expressed in Universal Consciousness are always available to all entities. If one allows themselves sufficient perception and anoints themselves (in a manner of speaking) with the power of their own creativity, which is merely done by claiming it, then you can perceive such as a Cap Caterpillar and many others in terms of variations and whatnot, as would correlate to the events as they are transpiring here. Is this a coincidence? Not at all. To a degree, you might state that your works involving Cap Caterpillar are very much in accord with what we are giving here. You have allowed your spirit, your creative consciousness that is within, to associate with that same power or thought-form (speaking in the primary sense) so that your creative self brought this forth, certainly, through your own interpretation of that consciousness. And that interpretation became Cap. You could say, to answer your question directly, that Cap came from the same realm as Wilbur's butterfly. (Now that should answer the question for you straightaway, we should think, given with a note of loving humor.)

The nature of that work as is called dinshah is sufficiently justified in what they have documented. And to the degree that one associates, in that sense, certain colors and spectrum reflections to and correlated with certain types of dis-eases, this can be a valuable asset, and indeed would be thought of here in that perspective as being (quote) "a correct method" (end-quote).

However, the nature of each entity's vibrations is unique. And as such, then, taking a certain collage of colors and stereotyping them just so, by that we mean specifically and rigidly, this can be somewhat misleading. Therefore, one should always follow the inner guidance ... that direct communication between self and the perfect pattern within, which is God, and follow that (using these as such as are found outside of self as guidelines, as mileposts along the way, see).

Both are good. Use the best that you have, but always follow that which is within. Just because another entity has experienced this or that and has found it to be good, do not cling to that, that this becomes then a barrier to your own uniqueness. That by no means minimizes the beautiful and productive works which are represented therein. We would find these to be beneficial, indeed.

The dream as is spoken of is, precisely so, one of the

types of works that you and others like you do very often in other realms. While in the dream state each entity performs many works, as well as gaining many experiences and receiving guidance and knowledge and such.

Your activity interacting with your mother was directly productive to her movement to a higher realm of consciousness. The significance of moving to the next realm of consciousness is, in her case, the benefit of regaining the prowess of youth. In her current realm, she will actually feel as though she is in the corresponding age of the mid-twenties, or thereabouts, to mid-thirties of her just previous incarnation. In other words, she's going to feel quite good. And as such, then, you have made a significant contribution. How, you might ask, and why? Because there is a connective link between you, a bond of light. See?

Calling upon those in other realms to assist you in time of need is, indeed, a great honor to those in these realms. To be recognized and to be permitted the opportunity to serve in God's name is one of the highest and best goals sought after by entities here. As you permit yourselves to tune to that potential, you are giving a great gift.

Therefore, it is we who thank thee, entity Jud, for the opportunity of joyous participation with you while you are in the Earth.

And so, for the present, we shall pause and invite the Channel to submit additional questions.

Fare thee well for the present, then, dear friends.

Q&A READING #10

Continuation of Questions After Chapter 6: UNDERSTANDING THE CLOAK (V-710)

Given September 10, 1990

AL MINER/CHANNEL: *This reading is code number V-712. Interestingly, the questions all relate primarily to the cloak, and I must admit that I was surprised that there were this many questions that I hadn't thought about relevant to the cloak. And I guess it points out that there are probably many more. And if there are, I hope all of you will be sure to send them in, because I think this is a very fascinating and, perhaps, potentially a very powerful topic.*

The first question is:

QUESTIONS SUBMITTED

#1 - During pregnancy, does the incoming soul's cloak merge with the pregnant woman's cloak? Would post partum depression in part be due to some sort of cloak separation, which occurs between mother and child at birth?

#2 - Do groups that pray together create a group cloak? Do children learning in a classroom together create a group cloak? Do individuals suffering together in a concentration camp create a group cloak? Or is the cloak something only highly aware entities can create? Or do we all create cloaks whether or not we are aware of them? Can the cloak inadvertently be used for negative as well as for positive purposes? Could we Voyagers learn to use the cloak in prayer to lessen the crisis in the Middle East? Would you elaborate on this if it is appropriate? Thank you.

(And those questions are from Nancy in North Carolina. And they're excellent, and I thank you for submitting them.)

(Next, Ken, also in North Carolina, writes:)
#3 - In our group we worked with the cloak the last time we met. We had our guides create a cloak for each of us and tried some experiments. Here are some questions based on the things we tried. When we were praying for a friend who has been going through disruptive family and financial problems, someone suggested that we create a cloak for her, almost as if she could benefit from a cosmic blanket to help insulate her. We created this, asking for the highest and best. Do you have any comments? I hope that this is not an interference with her.

(Question 2, also from Ken:)
#4 - One person asked us to tune in to someone we didn't know, and I couldn't get anything. I felt as if the cloak made me not as sensitive to tuning in to another person's vibration. I took it off and had the sensation that I was still partially insulated and couldn't get anything. It was interesting that no one else could get anything either. This is a bit unusual for our group. As I write this, I am wondering whether the cloaks were insulating us from vibrations that we shouldn't have attuned to, or were keeping us from infringement on someone else's psychic space. Do you have any comments?

(Third, he writes:)
#5 - I have noticed that praying for my own cloak makes it feel brighter, warmer, and I have a floating sensation. A feeling Peter has described on several occasions. It is almost as if the cloak traps the prayer energy next to me. Do you have any further suggestions on working with this?

(Finally, he writes:)
#6 - We asked our guides to create cloaks for us. If we went up to Jesus and asked Him to create a cloak, would it be a different cloak because Jesus, a different entity, created it? Or would it be essentially the same cloak because it was created with the highest and best intent for

us? *(He wrote in parentheses:)* This question is trying to distinguish whether many different cloaks might be created for one individual by different helpers because of the helpers' unique vibrations, or whether they would create essentially the same cloak because it is based on what is highest and best for the recipient. *(He closes with:)* Thank you, Al and Lama Sing.

And so now, Father, we present these questions once again prayerfully to You, asking that You would guide us to the highest and best, and we ask all of this in Your name, Father, and we thank You. Amen.

THE READING

LAMA SING: Yes, we have the Channel, then.

And we invoke the power and presence of our just-previous prayer and affirmation.

There are several factors involved in what you call the *post partum blues/depression*. But most assuredly, to a degree, there is involved the function of *cloak separation* (as you have called it) as a contributing factor to this. This is exemplified in that which you have been given in the experiences that Peter had in Wilbur's realm, which you noted, wherein Zachary walked away from him and he felt what you might parallel to post partum depression.

The function that occurs here is that the soul energy, the spiritual force that is the soul, conceived *in utero* (we believe is your term), must therefore become a part of the mother as the vehicle. But moving a step or two backwards in time ... The actual functioning of conception is the combined action of merging the spiritual force of the father and the mother and the child or children into oneness. This occurs not only in the physical sense through the activities called sexual activities, but also through the spiritual union or merging in accordance with the purposes of the (quote) "incoming soul" (end-quote) and those of the parents, and the circumstances and situation as prevails within the Earth and in and about the potential lifetime as is about to be experienced. If you will recall, this has much to do with the entity Judith's decisions as we reviewed them with you previously.[7]

Other activities which have to do with this are the building of what we would call an energy field which will become,

---

[7] Judith – The Voyagers were introduced to "Judith" in an Al Miner/Lama Sing project given in 1989 titled "The Nature of Children" at the point in which she was deciding whether or not to reincarnate, and if so, to which of several possibilities that would offer her the greatest possibilities for service and for personal growth.

in essence, the aura in which the entity will live, much likened unto the cloak. See? And as this parting takes place, the birth, the connection between the mother and the newly born child, as you call it, is ... (searching for a term, a moment please) ... expanded. The expansion of this could be thought of as two somewhat smaller spheres of luminosity existing within a mutual larger sphere of light. This could be paralleled to the cloak but it's actually the life-force energy. Now, in the sense of the spiritual perspective of this entire matter, where the terminology *cloak* could be appropriately applied, a similar activity occurs. But different in the sense that the life-force is not involved, as it is expressed finitely, physically, or in the three-dimensional sense. See?

To answer your question then again, clearly ... Yes, there is an involvement that deals with cloak separation. But be mindful that the cloak is that which is created by the spiritual accomplishments and acceptance of the entity and/or entities involved. And not to be confused with, in essence, the aura or the life-force. Though they are correlated, they are distinctly different in terms of their function and the relationship to the eternal nature of the entity.

The best way to convey this to you is that if you leave the Earth, whether through astral projection, meditation, dream, or the portal called death, you do not take the aura, as such, with you. You do take the cloak. The conversion of the life-force, previously expressed in the form of the aura, takes place upon the passage through the veil of darkness.

And the experiences that Peter had moving through the colors were, in fact, that transition. His movement into the spiritual sleep at the terminus of the experience with the colors was the actual (we might call it) birth of Peter into his new realms ... paralleled directly and succinctly, in opposite direction of course, to birth in the Earth. The same process is experienced moving into the Earth as Peter experienced it moving out of the Earth. If you wish to know more about this, then ask and perhaps we can have Zachary prepare an observation or some such of such an experience. We'll leave that for your decisions there among your grouping. See?

If you are referring in terms of your questions to entities who are in the Earth, the answer is no... Groups that pray together do not create a group cloak. They create a group thought-form. The cloak is much more personal. It is not the type of thing that you would extend to envelop, in essence, an entire grouping. An entire grouping can have the same general vibratory frequencies and such as characteristics of their cloak, and indeed there must be equality in that sense, in order to function in harmony in a specific realm, that is, intended for their level of spiritual acceptance. Groups that pray together create a group power or dynamic, which is in the form of a thought.

Prayer is a living thought, a living power. It comes from the spirit but it is not, as such, a cloak. When a group prays together, their auras and their cloaks, individually speaking, may take on a luminosity, an essence, which creates the appearance of oneness. The aura is much more supple, much more malleable, much more under your control, individually and as a group. The cloak is not. There must be certain very defined criterion in existence for you to accomplish what is defined in the questions you have presented.

Children learning in a classroom together create a state of ease and receptivity to a greater or lesser degree. That learning process, then, is also a thought-form or what we would call a realm of consciousness within a realm of consciousness. In other words, children are not bound by the rigidity of thought-forms as are found among most adults in the Earth. Children have sustained, to greater and lesser degrees based on individuals and age levels, some capacity to control far more broadly the realm in which they exist, your Earth specifically. And therefore, they can create and co-create much more dynamically, much more responsively, than a similar group of adult entities doing the same things or paralleling that activity.

The exception is, of course, as with prayer groups, meditational groups, study groups, and such, who have come together knowingly to break down such barriers, and through continued group effort have and continue to do so. This is why, or one of the reasons why, it is continually encouraged here to gather together to do common works and have common goals and purposes together.

Individuals suffering together in a concentration camp create group karma ... *karma* being the *opportunity*. Their cloaks, individually, may represent aspects of that, and collectively, as an entire concentration camp, would surely show some signs of similarity, for the emotional experiences would be very much alike, and a certain quantity of reactions would predicate results in the spiritual cloaks rather uniformly. Nonetheless, some of the entities therein will have greater or lesser spiritual acceptance upon the point of being incarcerated. And therefore, their reactions will be different and distinct from that of the general.

The cloak is not something only highly aware entities can create, in the sense that everyone has a cloak, a spiritual garment that is, in a manner of speaking, the outwardly perceived envelopment which protects and preserves their individuality. The highly aware, spiritually accepting entity usually is that one who is capable of knowingly extending their own cloak, their own spiritual consciousness, so as to be able to (quote) "create" another, or to *clone* (in your terms) a second or third or fourth cloak.

What needs to be considered here is that to sustain a second cloak apart from self and at a distance in terms of different levels of consciousness requires some degree of consciousness, some continual flow of spiritual energy, to do. It's likened unto projecting a light from a torch or flashlight, as you call it in your current terms. If you look at the point where the light is focused, perhaps upon a distant wall or something in the darkness, it is the battery in the torch that continues to generate, through the laws predominant in your realm, the lumens which are then concentrated and reflected and projected outward, activating particles and molecules and such, to create the spot of light off on the wall in the distance.

Zachary's cloak, given to Peter, represents a projection of his spiritual light to Peter. If the torch battery is weakened, then the spot of light weakens. Were Zachary's spiritual acceptance to weaken, then the potentiality afforded through the gift of Zachary's cloak to Peter would also weaken. That should, we think, answer many of the questions which have been presented above, but we'll continue on, nonetheless.

You all create cloaks, whether you know that or not. You create your own. Each loving thought creates a bit of light. Each action of kindness creates another. A moment of doubt slows the weaving of that thread in the cloak. A moment of fear, of anger, of hostility, weaves yet a different pattern and color, just the same. When you have the ability to deal with such influences and to approach such challenges and are able to endure them, keeping a mindful eye upon the Law and steadfastly sustaining a spiritual state of balance, because of this then you are capable of controlling the development of your own spirituality, and thusly you are controlling the power of your cloak. See?

You could learn as Voyagers, as a grouping, to use the cloak in prayer to lessen the crisis in the Middle East. You begin with self:

"Lord, let it begin with me, now, here. Let that which I have achieved in Thy Name which is good and contributive flow now from me in Thy Name unto these who are in this troubled land." But that's not your cloak, see; that's your own spirituality.

No, we do not recommend that you attempt to learn to use your cloak, in the sense that your question implies it, as an envelopment to cast around the Middle East. There are ramifications here which haven't been explored which would be potentially disruptive to you, possibly imbalancing. We do not recommend this approach. But be mindful that Universal Law always works for you in the form of God's grace and His love. It is your intent that governs the result. Therefore, as you are intending to do good, you can receive no less than this. Therefore, you are not to be, in the direct sense, harmed as the result of your effort. Even though logically, and in accordance with the Laws of Action and Reaction, that portal is open, the Law of Grace preserves you because of your intent. You cannot receive less than you have given, and you have given in the ideal of building peace, love, and harmony to dissipate hostility. See?

If you attempt, dear friend (with a note of loving humor), to create a cloak for the friend who was going through disruptive experiences in the Earth, you may, in fact, be involving yourself with the karma involved there. Why? Because of this: Your cloak is you. If you collectively as a group build a collage of thought, of spiritual energy, which is to say yourselves, individually and collectively as a group, then you are placing yourselves or an extension thereof, like the beam of light, in that situation.

If you feel particularly adventuresome, then take the chance, knowing that if you sustain that with an attitude of righteousness, prayer, faith, and no ulterior purpose, you cannot receive less than what you are giving. But a watchword here is, be certain that you are capable of doing those things (given with a note of loving humor).

The better choice is to use the power of prayer. This is directing the pure flow of God-Consciousness to that situation. If you do so, you have given the very best. Imparting or building a cloak, if you think of it in terms of a cloak which is formed of prayer power and not of your own essence, then you might be on safe footing; but if you project this as your own spirituality, individually and then collectively, that's a bit of shaky ground (given with a note of loving humor).

No, you could not interfere with her. The only karma you would have involved for yourselves would have been on the periphery, not on the individual sense. And, again, your intent was pure. Therefore, no interference could occur. See? It's not as complex as it sounds. More will come along in the next several meetings with Peter and Company and make this clearer.

To a degree, you are correct, entity Kendall. Your cloak is a preserving mechanism, a filter, that which will enable you to endure basically, no matter what. As such then, reaching out to attune to another entity's vibrations can, in effect, be impacted by the presence of the cloak. Even though you removed it, in the sense of your action, its effect still predicated a blockage or filtering. Why? Quite straightforward: The cloak preserves the energy, the spiritual balance. Even though your cloak was, in essence, opened, your aura then took upon itself the same functions. Remember our earlier comments paralleling the cloak and the aura in their function, particularly as relates to the Earth. See?

The function of you praying for your own cloak would, indeed, produce the results that you speak of. The cloak, in essence, is as much activated by that function or activity as it is confining or trapping or reflecting the prayer energy back to you ... (although both are true, see). What you are doing, looking at this from another perspective, is quite simply this: You are energizing your cloak, which in turn energizes your aura, which in turn energizes you, through the chakras, the glandular centers, and so forth.

If you went to the Master and requested Him to create a cloak that you might wear, an immense spectrum of differentiation would be involved, dependent upon the realm or realms in which you existed or found yourself expressed in when so doing. Your degree or level of spiritual acceptance has much to do with this. In essence, to answer your direct aspect of question, different cloaks would not be created by different individuals to the extent of this. If you were being served by those from realms beyond yours, in the sense of greater spirituality, this could occur. But the function of the cloak can never be any less than your own spirituality, or else it will not remain on you. See? So therefore, it has to do with the degrees of spirituality which are involved. See?

Well, there are going to be more opportunities to discuss this further, and we know that there will be greater detailed questions on this. For the present, then, we shall leave it at this.

As we do, we join with you in joyous prayer: *for those souls involved in the Middle East and all of the Earth, that none should be overlooked and no prayer should go unanswered. We pray this in our Father's Name. And we thank Thee, Father, and each of thee, dear friends, for these joyous works together.*

May the grace and blessings of our Father's wisdom ever be that lamp which guides your footsteps. Fare thee well, then, for the present, dear friends.

Q&A READING #11

Continuation of Questions After Chapter 7:
THE UNIVERSE WITHIN (V-720)

Given October 5, 1990

AL MINER/CHANNEL: *This reading is Code Number V-721. It's the second in a series of questions and answers for Voyager Project #7. These questions have to do primarily with tape number V-720. The questions are as follows:*

QUESTIONS SUBMITTED

#1 - Peter didn't know the mechanism that answered the prayer to Wilbur. It would be nice to know that, and also to know the one that gets a prayer answered. *(That's from Victor in Virginia.)*

#2 - Every time one of us in the Earth says a prayer, does some soul in the crystal workers' realm hear it and always respond? How many souls are in existence in the crystal workers' realm? *(From Dave in Maryland.)*

#3 - How do we distinguish guidance from habit, fear, our own will, et cetera? And what does it mean to "function within the power of prayer"? as indicated in reading 711, I think. *(And that's from Harold and Linda in Missouri.)*

#4 - Could we perhaps set a group date for prayer and light to be centered on the Middle East and all the Earth's leaders? *(That request is from Anita in Florida, and I have no doubt that it is echoed by all of us. So, we'll see what we get.)*

#5 - It is so interesting that Lama Sing made the comment, "We are learning to master our will" because in the past couple of weeks that issue of Free Will and God's Will has been bothering me a lot. That old time religion of submitting your will to God's Will in all things seems to conflict with the New Age thinking that suggests we create our own reality through the use of God's gift to us of free will. Frankly, I have a lot of confusion on this. Perhaps we only have true free will once we have mastered our will. Please explain, Lama Sing. Thank you. *(Joan in Pennsylvania.)*

#6 - How best can we exercise the concept of "first by will and then by action?" *(And that's from Victor in Virginia.)*

(The next question really isn't a question, but I thought it was profound or significant, or both. So I've included it here. In the midst of the text of her letter to me, she wrote this:)
#7 - Of course, I am enjoying Peter's adventures. I have the feeling there is much more information under the surface and that these readings need a very thorough study or studying. I think it is similar to our own lives. It seems we are existing and operating on more levels than one, even simultaneously, as we go through our day-to-day affairs here. When an act or thought is accomplished here, it has reverberations. *(And that bit of profound thinking is from Anita in Florida. And I would appreciate any comment there might be in regard to that.)*

#8 - I'm fascinated by humor, its use, importance and healing properties, the last of which I've certainly experienced. Were references to and examples of humor taken out of the original Christian scriptures, as were some of the other spiritual truths, such as references to reincarnation? Are there ways in which we can enhance our own awareness of and use of humor in our daily lives? *(That is from Lynne in North Carolina.)*

#9 - During a recent time of struggle (opportunity?), I was unexpectedly given a medal by someone I barely knew, and the medal was from Medjugorje *(I'm sure I'm not pronouncing that correctly, but you'll probably all recognize it ...)* where apparitions of the Virgin Mary appear. I have worn the medal every day and slept with it under my pillow since I was given it. When I got up on Saturday, September 8, after our seven days of prayer, the medal was gone. I literally tore the bedroom apart, even took the box springs off the bed. (Another plus, Al. I got the room house-cleaned!) But I couldn't find it. I *know* it was under my pillow because I remember waking up and feeling it there during the night. So somehow, even though I was a bit upset, I knew it would come back to me. And, Al, today it did. Last night I had jokingly said, "Okay, St. Anthony, how about finding my medal?"

Today I decided to put my summer handbag away, and I was cleaning it out, and there in the change purse were three dimes. But when I took them out, one of the dimes was my medal! Boy, did I gasp. Naturally, I'm more than curious about how and why did this happen and where did it go, etc., etc. *If* you feel it has some relevance to our project, I would greatly appreciate it if you would ask Lama Sing about it. *(And that's from Joan in Pennsylvania. Well, Joan, the only way for me to find out if it has relevance, I guess, is to ask it. And so I did. I think we've all experienced little examples of what, I guess, could loosely be called tricks or pranks or poltergeists, or however you want to view it. So, maybe the answer will be interesting to all of us, if just from only that perspective.)*

(Next:)
#10 - I was wondering if Peter and Paul are the Peter and Paul from Jesus' time in the Earth. *(And that's from Joan in Pennsylvania. I believe that's been answered, but in case not clearly or you didn't hear it or maybe others didn't hear it, we'll ask it again.)*

(Also from Joan:)
#11 - Was the "cloud" that people saw Jesus ascending into really one of the tunnels between realms? No one asked how come David could see and talk to Peter on their second visit, when he couldn't see them on their first visit. *(That was also from Joan. She had some great questions this time. Took some of my own!)*

#12 - What is the highest realm that Paul and Zachary are capable of existing in? What is a name for that realm or realms? *(And that's from Dave in Maryland.)*

#13 - One realm of expression and level of consciousness are quite similar. When we rise to a higher level of consciousness, why is it that upon getting back, the same old chains shackle us and the same old limitations seem to bind us? *(And that's from Victor in Virginia.)*

#14 - My questions concern the "movement from one realm of expression, one level of consciousness to another." While sitting here at my desk, do other realms of consciousness exist in the *same time and space* as I do? Are they aware of me in my realm? Am I in my realm visible to them? Are there, perhaps, some realms that may exist here that are as oblivious to me as I am to them? Would it be desirable for me to be able to move from one realm to another while I am still living in my physical body? Are the veils of separation put there as a challenge for us to overcome? *(Now, that's an interesting thought, isn't it?)* If so, could you give me some practical techniques for doing so? *(And that's from Barry in California, and at the end of that letter he wrote, "Al, because the Lama Sing grouping can observe me, I must assume that they exist unseen in my realm. Nevertheless, if you can use these questions, I would like to hear Lama Sing's response." So would I, Barry, and so here they are.)*

#15 - Peter observes that David's realm is lacking in color and brilliance due to the focus of their attention by their choice. I also find it to be so here. I see so many devoting all their attention to the works of the Father; and as they do, the brilliance and what seems to be the very bare necessities suffer. A call, a prayer, just doesn't seem to remedy the situation. And, quite frankly, it becomes quite unsettling. Is this also our choice, or is there a better way? *(And that's from Victor in Virginia. A really astute, really cutting and profound question, Victor. I appreciate you taking the time to send it in. It's something that I have also seen many times, as have probably most of us.)*

#16 - Are our guides with us at all times, or do they have other projects, as well? Paul seems to be with Peter all of the ... *(Excuse me for laughing. I got the mental picture after that question of sort of a Guide Friday Corporation up there in the sky—you know, or a Hertz Rent-a-Guide. No one ever said I didn't have a strange sense of humor. I like that question, as you can tell, Harold and Linda. Thanks for sending it. Let me repeat it.)* Are our guides with us at all times, or do they have other projects, as well? Paul seems to be with Peter all of the time, but Zachary comes and goes.

#17 - Are our guides different entities at different times, or at different event cycles of our lives? *(That's from Harold and Linda in Missouri, as was the just-previous question that struck my funny bone.)*

#19 - How do we communicate with our guides? Can we request the specific help at any time of Zachary or any of the Lama Sing group? How do we know who to ask? Are there specialists, as seems to be indicated by the reference to different soul groupings? How do they respond if they're not assigned to us? *(And both of those, or all of those little questions are again from Harold and Linda. Great questions. Thanks.)*

(Now, here comes the one that also tickles me. And it's from Lynne in North Carolina; and Lynne's the one who asked the question about humor up at ... sort of up at the top of these questions. And so, Lynne, you've got a great sense of humor, 'cause this really tickles me. See how it strikes you.)

#20 - If one of us wanted to "borrow" Zachary's cloak, could he or she? *(Well, I don't hear anyone laughing, so I guess it's just me, Lynne ... you and me, Lynne.)* If not, does each of us have a parallel guide or similar relationship with an entity in the other dimensions whose cloak is available to us, e.g. to enhance travel to other realms, to balance? Zack loaned the cloak to Peter. Is Christ's cloak, mantle, or thought-pattern our cloak? And is this the closest we have to the Book of

Knowledge? How best might we attain that or attempt to accomplish that, if that is so?

(Now, next, I'm going to apologize for making some paper-shuffling noise here, but I've got some lengthy correspondence here that I just ... It didn't seem practical to retype it all. This is based on a letter I received from Lois in Florida, but it's also based on, you'll recall, some comments and questions, great ones, I got from Ken and Nancy in North Carolina in, I believe it was, 711. And a fascinating phone call I had with Cathy in Missouri. And it has to do with the cloak. You guessed that, right? Lois sent me a letter telling me about an experience she had, and it was dealing with something that was in meditation or out of body, and it had to do with her interaction with two people she met during that, and that she used the cloak to resolve certain problems. I wrote her back and asked her if she could elaborate on it, and based on her first letter and the comments I got from Cathy and the questions from Ken and Nancy in North Carolina, really kind of startled me because I had, up to that point, not had a very strong ... Well, let me restate that. I had always thought of the cloak in a different way, and much more personal than just being able to, you know, sort of share it, which is, in part, why Lynne's question tickled me so. And I want to read a paragraph from the letter that I wrote back to Lois, asking her for more information, because it's kind of pertinent to what she's going to say in her subsequent letters back to me. Got all that?)

#21 - At this point I have the mental image of a "celestial cloakroom" (pun intended) wherein row upon row of infinitely beautiful spiritual garments are hung. I next see a group of less than spiritually elevated entities enter and casually choose from these precious garments whatever strikes their fancy for whatever motivation they might have in the moment. Deep within me I hear a voice crying out, "Sacrilege, blasphemy, they know not what they do!"

(And so I went on to state to her that I was really impressed with the discovery of this attitude towards the cloak and the possibility of that attitude carrying over into other things. So, now, turning back to Lois, she wrote in a follow-up letter:)

In my previous experiences I was always able to communicate by various methods with whoever was in need, even if they were unable to see me. *(As a bit of background, they had been working with healing from higher realms, moving into an altered state and asking for opportunities to be of service to others. And that's what she's talking about, where she's coming from with this.)*

In the last experience *(she goes on to say)*, I was unable to communicate with a young woman who was filled with such grief and sadness. It was as if she were surrounded by a wall of intense emotion ... or of a different realm? I couldn't penetrate the wall. This was new for me, and while I was observing her and wondering what to do, I thought of placing a cloak of light around her. It was immediately transforming. In answer to your question, Al, regarding whether or not I "made it," I can only say that as soon as the thought occurred to me, I was able to place it about her, mentally. It seemed more *created* than *called forth*. It was also another one of those "Aha!" experiences wherein I later ask myself why I never thought of that before *(which is about what I said to her, as well)*, since the answer was so blatantly apparent and simple. Fortunately, those who are helping us along have a great sense of humor *(I'll emphasize and go along with that, Lois)* and don't seem to mind my groping around in the light (!) while looking for the answer. *(Great play on words.)*

So, regarding the cloak: Is it part of my energy I transferred to her, a la Zachary, or something I checked out of the "celestial cloakroom," a la Miner, for her to wear? Is it the same as prayer and I was in a position to see the effects? Or all or none of the above?

(So, then, she wrote me a little note which I just received today. Thanks, Lois. And she wrote:)

After I sent the last letter off to you, per your request, I realized I had failed to give you "the rest of the story." I'm including it here, since it dealt with the cloak and may provide more information.

The second entity I encountered in the healing session I previously described to you was a young man, I think in the Earth plane, who was extremely distressed. Since I had such a good result with using the cloak with the first entity, I "placed" the cloak around him and, intuitively, began gently stroking it. This had a soothing effect upon the entity, who became quite peaceful. End of story.

Well! And so we go on with more questions about the cloak. For your information, I'm going to try to pull all of this together on the cloak and see what we've got and possibly we'll do a little follow-up on that at some point along the way here. But I'll let you know.

And so, Father, we prayerfully submit these questions now to You, asking as we do that You would guide us to the very highest and best possible information that can be given. As always, we ask special prayers of blessing for all the joyous workers in your realm and for the continued patience and good humor of them and You, Father. And special blessings for all those in need in the Earth during these trying times in the Middle East. And last but not least, prayers of thanks and blessings to all of the members of Peter's group and each and every one of the Voyagers. Thank You, Father. Amen.

THE READING

LAMA SING: Yes, we have the Channel then and, as well, those references which apply to the topic, those questions now before us, the inquiring minds and, collectively, that grouping as has come before us to join together in this work. As we commence herein, we first pray in the following manner.

Lord God, we know that Thou art ever with us in all things and in all thoughts. And thus, it is our prayer that we might herein accomplish Thy Will and purpose in the knowledge that so as we do, Father, there shall be the greater manifestation of Thy presence and Thy joy. We pray on behalf of all those souls in all realms who are presently in some need and for whom there are none in joyous prayer. We humbly thank Thee, Father, for this opportunity of joyous service in Thy name. Amen.

The relationship between self and the Universal Forces is one which is important, in terms of the mechanism that enabled the accomplishment of Wilbur's prayer to be answered. In essence, then, more will be coming forth in times ahead regarding this, to be sure. But to answer your question, the mechanism is one which does not require the conscious attunement of an entity to a request which comes forth from a realm which is in the sense of a linear depiction, in other words, striations or levels ... comes from beneath them. So then, Peter, dwelling in a realm less limited than Wilbur (in this situation, at least) was actually functioning in his realm and on all realms beneath that.

To answer the next question before it arrives (with a note of loving humor) ... To a degree, he functions on realms above his, as well. But to an extent, this is more limited to a degree of functioning that interacts with that realm, providing wisdom more or less back downwards to him. While the mechanism in place for the transference or participation in prayer works to realms beneath is direct and is, in a sense, more capable of producing a manifestation after its kind. In other words, it precipitates into moreso of substance. See?

The mechanism to get a prayer answered is complex in the sense of defining it to you here briefly, but utterly simplistic, on the other hand. The beauty of its lack of complexity is quite simply stated in these several phrases: The power of effective prayer that will get an answer is directly dependent upon the need, the belief of the person in prayer, and the willingness of the recipient or target of that intended prayer. All of these forces are conditioned by, of course, Universal Law, and must function within them in order to be effective. And that, then, is the overview of the answer to the question in its second part.

Each time one of you in the Earth states a prayer, some soul in some realm hears it, and will answer to the degree that it is appropriate. Again, prayer is free-flowing, not encumbered by the presence of other realms and other entities. It is immediately heard and known before you can verbalize or express it. That knowledge and awareness, of course, is in the presence of God. When the prayer is complete in the sense that God's answer is instantaneous, the matter becomes one somewhat paralleling the mechanisms indicated in the first question above ... or rather, the answer to it.

As the answer moves back to you ... the response to the prayer ... the activity is one somewhat of passing through varying levels or filters or *veils* (in the terminology of the Channel) which then might be, each one, met by an entity or group of entities whose soul intent and purpose is that of a benevolent intent to enable that prayer to make itself manifested in your realm. So they are, in essence, aiding the passage of that prayer through what could be called the thought-forms of your own consciousness. The lesser are your limitations, the greater is the probability of that prayer reaching you in the form of an answer, concisely and specifically to your need ... or *better*. (The latter comment intended to clarify here that there are ofttimes those prayers which aren't the wisest of all.) The answer, then, comes from the throne of infinite wisdom, which is God, and therefore is perfect. See?

So, to the extent that a soul in the Crystal Workers' Realm might become conscious of a request for prayer as it moves to God and the answer passing in return to you ... (This is greatly paraphrased, it's not precisely like this.) God is within, see? And we do not wish to create an illusion here that seems to imply that God is distant, that you are on one end of the universe and God another. That's simply not the case. God is everywhere, in all things. All is of God and is God, including you and the crystal workers. See?

But to continue on ... The crystal workers, then, can respond in accordance with their ability, their level of acceptance, and such. The same criteria that apply to you, apply to them. Then they can answer. We hope that's of some assistance. But specifically to state concise answers, no, not always does some soul in the Crystal Workers' Realm hear it and always respond. But always there is the opportunity for them to hear it, and almost always the opportunity to respond. In fact, we could state they can always respond to the extent of their own spirituality.

The number of souls in the Crystal Workers' Realm ... This is a very difficult question to answer. It requires that we define a particular point in reference, which would equate to or summarize to, in your terminology, a certain point in your time measure. Souls do come and go here, and none are bound to this realm save by their own choices or their own dedication to work which might carry them to this realm. There are many souls in motion who pass through realms, as well. And it would be difficult to define in a specific sense the answer you are looking for. In general terms (to answer it in the type of nomenclature you are seeking) 423,179 souls … plus or minus several thousand. See? Does that seem like a great number to you in the Earth? Not at all. The population of only an average-sized town, village or city, isn't it? This isn't any different here. See?

Emotions are clearly definable. They have a native resilience and an impact upon the body. Distinguishing guidance from emotion (that is, emotional response to a certain need or question) should be capable of being discerned easily. Learn to perceive the changes in your body, based upon external emotional stimuli. Carry a mental notebook, and the next time you feel a sudden surge of an emotion, based upon an event or some such, jot a note mentally on that notebook of how it feels. You'll quickly develop a sort of schedule or guideline that can be used thereafter as a template to detect when something that is felt is, in fact, of the emotional level.

Emotion tends to have an impact upon the cellular formation of the body through the neurological system. Since it interacts with the mind and, as such then, deals with both levels of the consciousness as are called the subconscious and the (not counting the conscious) and the super-conscious or collective consciousness. These, then, are interactive and, as such, tend to predicate after their own kind a response which is a part of a memory. So, most of the time an emotion should carry with it a memory, an image, a pattern. If that's of your own nature, you should be able to detect that.

Your will is a part of the quest for guidance. Therefore, as such, your will should also create a triggering response mechanism which is capable of being denoted at the physical or physiological level. The differentiation here, then, might be the focal point at about the solar plexi center of the body, for some. For others, it might have to do with body temperature, circulation, or total neurological activity or lack of activity instantaneously. These might be in the form of a sudden rush, a sudden passing of warmth or chill as relates to the solar plexi. It would be so beneficial to you if the Channel would relate some of these things directly.

Nonetheless, here, within the body, consider it somewhat likened unto a magnetic directional meter. When there is the out-flowing from the solar plexi and a feeling of exuberance or a rush of wellness, that is guidance. When there is impact to the solar plexi that is more pulsating, likened unto the circulatory or the body pulse, this is generally thought of, then, as the others, see ... the *others* being habit, fear, your will, emotions, and such.

Functioning within the power of prayer is living a life of joyful prayer. In other words, when one is in a state of joyous prayer there is generally to be found thereafter, a period of elation or bliss. When one attains that state wherein they are in a mindset which is continually in prayer or acknowledging prayer, that is functioning within the power of prayer, living within it.

There are variations here, and some of them are probably going to seem remarkable, stupendous, and such exclamatory comments as those to be used with the discovery of the power of prayer. You'll find more of this, to be sure, not only in the examples as we observe Peter, but we believe and it is our prayer that you will experience some of these yourselves as we continue on. See?

We would encourage and support, always, group prayer, for whatever work, and particularly as one might attempt to envelop the world leaders and the Middle East in a raiment of loving prayer.

We'd give two dates here. October the 21st and October 31st. The first is intentional for the purpose of aligning with certain phases, lunar and otherwise; and the second is an opportunity for you to work within power, to transform power and to align it in accordance with the power of prayer. It's a good time for all of you to test and strengthen your group authority, for you are functioning in God's name. Then, do so, October 31st. You have the power. Claim that power as will be available to you. Are these certain special dates? They are as special as you believe them to be. *We* believe them to be special. Do you? We believe your group to be special. Now do it, be it. See?

Mastering the will is not, as such, likened unto the lion tamer with a chair and … the other thing, uh … the whip, for the will is not your enemy, an opponent. If it were, it would surely be the winner in a contest.

You are your will. Mastering yourself is simply giving credence, importance, to your knowledge, to your desire, and to your ideal. Mastering it is an issue that becomes, as such, then, subjective to the situation and the environment, to the extent that these are interactive with your belief.

The Master dwelled within the Earth, but knew Himself to be eternal and knew that the Earth, as such, was only a place for Him to function in His Father's Name and to do works which were and are in accordance with His will. Therefore, He could function in accordance to the full potential of His will without being subjectively limited by the overriding thought or thought-forms that were involved and are involved with others.

There is no difference between submitting your will to God's will in all things, versus claiming your own free will and being responsible for your reality. For your will and God's will are one. The difference here is very slight.

Look at it this way: If that old-timey religion claims that you must submit your will to God, are they not already stating that you have command of your will? If they are stating that, then, and you can command your will to be one with God, then where do you draw the power for such commands? From whence cometh the authority for you to command in such a manner, if not to affirm that God's will is already within yours, affording you the authority to command. See?

Don't let this confuse you. Don't even let it be an issue. Most of those who state "Submit your will to God's will" state it and perform a ceremony, and then go about their life doing what they want anyway, thereafter claiming it's God's will (given with a note of loving humor). Not all, but many.

The only way you can truly claim power is to not have a personal need for it. If you have a personal need, a limitation, that in and of itself blocks you from obtaining the fullness of God's power. God's power given to you is unlimited. If you have a need that is personal, a goal, an addition, a predilection, a bond, then that very thing limits the full potential of God's will, His gift to you.

Power is unto itself universal. It is supportive to existence. When existence is confined, defined, and as such therefore to be considered limited, the power therein is limited within the structure of the observer and the participant. See?

Exercising the concept of free will is your right. Therefore, you must first exercise that right with conviction, in other words, just as above, so that your will is unlimited. And then you must act. And the action must be secondary only to the conviction of your will. If you act within the conviction of your will, you cannot fail.

Example: An entity stands upon the edge of the rooftop of a 40-story building and wills himself to be capable of leaping from the building and floating gently to the Earth. Can he do that? Well, yes, he can. But he must be capable in his own will of subjugating all the other laws or other wills, singular and mass-mind thought, in order that he can (quote) "suspend" (end quote) their effect upon him sufficient so that he might defy the *laws*, as such, of gravity, of physics, and all those sorts, that will enable him to float to the Earth. What's to stop him from floating upwards instead of downwards? See?

When an act or thought is accomplished in the Earth, it does have reverberations. There is indeed, entity Anita, far more within the heavens and Earth of the universe in which you dwell that is worthy of some reflection. But there is no need for you to intensely or deeply study the information as has been given here previously and shall be given yet ahead. Hold it gently, lovingly, in thy mind, in thy heart. These are but seeds. The greater fruits will come thereafter. If you labor too diligently to grasp, to seek out just this or that hidden meaning, you might miss the passage of the greater glory which is yet to come. We are honored that you consider the information in such a way, but hold true to your own guidance. Pass the thoughts through your mind. Listen for a resonance within your spirit. Study in that way, but not intensely. For these are intended to awaken within you a much greater power. See? Ours, as such, as the passage of the information are not worthy of standing before the true beauty – which exists within – save only as His humblest of all servants. See?

Humor has the healing property because it allows the energies to flow outward. In most cases when there are conditions of dis-ease, the energies are bound or attracted or drawn within the body through varying mechanisms ... this, almost likened unto comparison to magnetic fields, those magnetic fields, then, considered in the sense of the glandular centers, the seven major and their subordinate centers. These centers, then, become charged, polarized, and might have the wrong direction or the wrong flow. Or the gauss, just simply the magnetic potential, is off.

And so then, laughter causes the flow of the greatest potential within you to sort of electrify or neutralize and balance all of these centers. Dis-ease cannot remain resident within the body when the centers are being charged and balanced in that way. That's just one physiological explanation for the benefit of humor. See?

The potentials for humor have always been present all about you. It is the eye of the beholder ... the heart and mind that sees, hears, and acts upon them. And so it follows logically, of course, that the Master's humor was well-known, that His love for merriment and joy was resplendent. His delight in the presence of little children bears witness to this, for their greatest pastime is, was, and always shall be to find mirth and joy. Therefore has He stated unto you to, *Be as these.* See? Some things were removed, yes, from the works. But these were known by the Master, and those who have eyes to see and ears to hear in the spiritual sense shall find the presence of the joyous aspects of the Master's spirit within those works, even yet.

The best way to use humor in daily life is to look at everything through the eye of humor. No matter how desperate, no matter how dismal, look for some humor in it. Learn to laugh about the events and the finiteness of them, for you are eternal. You have the power to find joy in all things, even when they may seem from your finite perspective to be very burdensome. There is as much power for healing in a good dose of humor as there is in a dosage of medicine ten times its weight. See?

The example of the lost medal is an example which can occur very often when entities pass across the bridge or transcend the veil, wherein such things as movement and all manner of other activities become possible, second nature, or idle. That is to say that they are no longer impossible. And thus, it is well for one moving about in other realms and passing through these to look upon themselves as having a newly released potential.

No, you didn't actually cause it to dissipate and then reform elsewhere. But something did. It wasn't us. It wasn't Zachary. And it certainly wasn't Peter (given with a note of loving humor).

What took place? Movement. It was actually moved. And the result of that movement was intentional. Your higher self was, to a degree, a part of that. But the eternal force of light, which is the perfect pattern for all, was involved here, as well. For that symbol and that force are a part of the medal, are they not?

What was to be learned? That's what's important: Don't place your faith in a thing. The power of the medal has already been given to you. If you continue to use it in the sense of being just a focal point, then you are missing the point of the entire matter. But if you see it as representative of that power, then that is well. You could go outside and gather up a pebble and put it under your pillow, and that's a symbol, an emblem of God, is it not? (Keep the medal; that's not our meaning, see.)

Peter and Paul are not the Peter and Paul from the Biblical renown or historically famous in that regard. Peter and Paul, however, are known to the Master and have been with the Master.

We should state that the cloud that the entities saw the Master ascending into actually was, as such, just as you have described. But a bit different in this sense: that the Master, in His position of ultimate acceptance of His oneness with God, was capable as well of sufficient authority so as to transcend the finite, or limitations of Earthly laws.

Therefore, his transcendence could be, as such, controlled by him and in alignment, or in allegiance to and with, those forces of God. In this case, yes, likened unto, as such, the tunnels between realms, but much of this action predicated from other realms in honor of the Master and to welcome His return to the true consciousness. See?

David could see Peter in the second visit because Peter was now ready, balanced, able. Zachary's cloak upon Peter enabled that to transpire more or less automatically. The level to which Zachary's power, as such, as a guide or as a mentor to Peter, is very significant. And as such, then, his attunement also to David and Wilbur is thereby passed on to Peter by the presence of his cloak. And that's what enabled it ... the preparation, rather, of Peter and not David.

Paul and Zachary are capable of reaching very high levels or realms. The key word here is *capable*. The realms of their full potential are unlimited. Indeed, they are capable of reaching what you would know as the Godhead or the center of God-Consciousness in all of existence. They do not, we believe, at the moment fully know that they have that potential at present. They know of it as a potential, and understand that they shall reach that point, but they in their own consciousness haven't dwelled on it sufficient to recognize it, as best we can see them in the present.

In terms of their capability as they do affirm same (in other words, capability, having the capacity to) their realms of higher consciousness would be several full realms of existence beyond the current and beyond that. In other words, if you consider there to be, for example, seven major veils, and within which there are again seven sub-veils, and within those yet other points of demarcation, Zachary is capable of reaching into the sixth major level. (Paul has asked that we not answer for him in that regard.)

The question that you have asked, Victor, is one which we have often, in turn, asked of entities in the Earth: Why do you resume old habits and old limitations once you have entered into these and other realms and know them to be, as such, merely thought-forms, garments of non-physical substance, that are familiar and, thus, comfortable?

So the answer to your question is a question in return. Will you not discontinue that habit? It is your choice, you see. Familiarity, comfort ... the familiar is often warm. The unknown may bear different reactory stimuli to you. And that's not just to you, entity Victor. That's to most entities.

Good question. Follow it up with a good effort. See? (Given with a note of loving humor.)

Other realms of existence may, indeed, occupy the same time and space as yours. In your astrophysics and nuclear physics, this is becoming evident. You are noting the presence of not only what's called matter, but anti-matter. You are noting the presence of a sidereal time-reference, which has to do with the paralleled images in the positive-negative reflection of what could be called substance.

For example: When you look into a single-dimension object, such as a looking-glass or mirror, you see a reflection which appears, as you look into it, to have depth. And yet, if you step to the side of the mirror, you will see that it may only be an inch or less in the American measure in thickness. So, where does the depth and the dimension come from? Reaching out your hand to reach through to something reflected in the mirror, you strike the surface of the glass.

So, then, think of this in this way: While the looking-glass can reflect to you what is in your realm, you are seeing only one-half of that dimension, in the potentiality of it. The other half of that dimension lies beyond the capacity of your current ability to see or perceive. If you add a second level of dimension to the looking-glass, then you will begin to be capable of perceiving that you have not only length but breadth, height and depth. Each of these being discovered as you add yet other dimensions. See?

If you look at a polarized magnetic bar, one end being positive, the other negative (as you define these), you may gather some ferrous oxide or iron filings and see which end they are attracted to. They will then adopt the same polarity as that end. But what you do not perceive is all things strive for balance. And therefore, the opposite end has as its field of magnetism the inverse of the ferric oxide, or ferrous oxide, particles. In another dimension, then, in the same time and space as yours, the other end has the particles surrounding it.

Sound abstract? Not really. Your, as you call them, sciences will advance very rapidly in the next ten to twelve Earth years, so that in twenty Earth years your current science will seem very historic. See?

There is no real need for you to make the effort of striving to move from one realm to the other in the sense of a parallel or co-existing realm. You are visible in your realm because you are conforming to the major thought-forms or laws of that realm. They are conforming to theirs. And, thus, each is visible in their own. Were you on a much higher level of spiritual expression, it would be possible at some point that you could perceive one another and still dwell in the same time and space. The matter becomes so abstract in our method of expressing it to you that it may begin to sound absurd, and that would not be our intent here.

The visibility of one realm to another has to do with the vibratory frequency. For example, we can and do have the potential to observe your realm to certain degrees. But when we observe your realm, we do not observe you as you are or as you see yourself in your own mind and in your own optical perception. We see you as you are. You do not look to us as you are to you. You look to us as you are actually. And therefore, it is the extremely valuable contact between realms of the functioning of such as a channel that enables the vision to take on the properties of perception in the expression of the realm, the native expression of that realm. And so the functioning with and through this Channel enables our perspective to be in the same vein as the Channel's and yours and everyone else in your realm. See? That should be considerably revealing to you.

Movement, then, for you, in terms of from your realm to another, should have a purpose. If it is idly done, then there is no meaning, and the full capacity of your potential then does not align itself with that. This does not mean that the purpose must be something emphasized dramatically. It can simply be a purpose of satisfying your own curiosity, or a desire to help or to explore. Those are good purposes. But if you think you must, then don't. But if you want to, then do. See the difference?

The example here might be given of the entity Kendall, if he will forgive us for drawing him into this. He goes forth often for the purpose of exploration and service, to broaden his own consciousness, and to contribute to the consciousness of others, including his mate, his group, and such others as he knows he shall meet further down life's pathway. Those are good purposes. And thus he is welcomed, the way is made passable, and he himself breaks down many of the barriers of limitation that would otherwise be present for others who don't have that conviction to the strength that he does.

In the case of another entity, the entity Lois does the same thing but does it in a different direction, for the most part (though this is changing). The entity who is known to you as Jud who has been here previously does neither of these but simply falls back upon his memories and follows them as though they were a pathway and moves very easily. We could go on here and name just about every one of the Voyagers, but we believe the example is now clear. See?

If there is a call, a prayer, and it is properly expressed, it does answer the need. It does remedy the situation. Entities are generally in the position they are in because of choices. Not necessarily, then, does it follow that you shouldn't do anything to assist them if you can, for those are *your* choices, as well. And, as given, one enters the kingdom of our Father, more oft than not, on the arm or arms of those whom they have served. See?

Then let it be said that as an entity denies the existence of the physical body in favor of (quote) "our Father's works" (end quote), they are denying one of our Father's most precious temples, are they not? For wherein in the Earth does

God truly dwell? You may construct a building, a temple, a chapel, a great shrine, but God does not dwell in there. That is stone, mortar, wood, and as such. But the instant an entity passes through the portal and goes within, therein too does God dwell.

If you seek to do our Father's works, then tend to your own temple as you do them, for it is well-loved by God else He wouldn't be therein. Do the best you know to do and keep a balance. This we have oft given here. Do not ignore the physical, the mental, the emotional needs, for though thou art eternal, the body is the temple of your current dwelling and focus. Let it be the best tool of your soul that it might be.

God would bring to you abundance, but you must act in accordance with Universal Law to seek it out. If you are continually in a deep state of reverence and prayer, that is well, if it fulfills and brings to you your every need. But if you are lacking, it is because you aren't acting with authority. God giveth you the power, His power. It's your choice to use it or to set it aside.

We concur with your observation. It's unsettling here, too. Given with a note of loving humor, but a strong tone of seriousness. The temple of thine own heart is also the temple of God's light. Tend it, mend it, heal it, nurture it, treat it well. See? Do you believe that your Father would have you do less? Do you believe that your Father is doing less? Spirituality begins within self and is expressed outwardly as the example. If you are attempting to teach abundance, then demonstrate abundance. If you are attempting to teach wellness, then demonstrate wellness. If you are complete, then demonstrate your completeness.

Now then, the opposite side of that verbal or literary coin is quite simply this: Ofttimes we might find one in need along life's way as the opportunity. And as you see this, friend Victor, it is well that you have given and served as you have, for that is your opportunity and their blessing to you, albeit they may not know it as such. No longer lament, no longer deny, but reach out. Look at the talents here, the abilities. Use them. Don't focus and dwell upon the past. Go forward. Take these abilities, these talents, and these blessings from God, and share them. And thereof, in the sharing, will come your just reward. And the entity we are speaking of won't lack or want again. That is lovingly given. See?

Certain guides are with you at all times. They may or may not have other projects. There are no hard and fast rules here. There are no limitations. God's kingdom is unlimited. God's workers are unlimited. Paul has chosen, Zachary has chosen, as has Peter. But make no mistake Zachary is present at all times with Peter, even though he's not seen. He knows of every moment.

Now we have approached again here the question of dimensions. Zachary can see Peter at all times. He has a connection with Peter. Knows every thought, every concern. And, thus, you have noted, he appears just at the right time, with just the right answer. See? Your guides do the same.

Your guides may differ in the sense of your growth. As you grow, the guides also share in that growth. As you become limited, however, the guides do not. But they will work all the harder to help you become unlimited. Guides may change, come and go and such. But there is generally one (or more) primary guide/s who remain with you from the time of entry (actually, before) until the time of departure and, as in the case with Paul here, well after. See?

You may request the help of Zachary or our grouping, if you wish. But we would rather, very sincerely, that you always direct your prayer to God. That way, the highest and best will come to you. If that includes us, know that we will answer. If you wish to ask us for assistance in a matter, we will always respond as we are permitted. If there are others that we believe can better serve you, we will ask them to do so, and we will stand aside.

It's not a question of entities being, as such, *assigned* to you or being *specialized*. It has to do with the degree of spirituality of the entities involved and the parallel degree or need of the request. That's breaking it down into the most simplistic mechanical terms we can.

You could borrow Zachary's cloak. He's a charitable fellow, that one. And most assuredly, he'd probably loan it to you. However, you wouldn't want it unless you were prepared to wear it. See? It might be like you having a size 6 or 7 foot and asking someone for a pair of size 12 or 13 shoes. Wouldn't fit very well.

If you want the power associated with same, that's a different matter. And we'll get into that very shortly here, we should think.

Each of you has a guide capable of providing you with the same service as Zachary did to Peter. In other dimensions, the cloak would function no different than Zachary's. It depends upon you more than the cloak. If you are prepared, then the cloak will work for you. If you aren't prepared, then the cloak won't. That's Universal Law preserving you. You wouldn't be allowed to enter into excessive heat unless you were wearing a protective suit, such as a fire-fighter, if you had a good chief watching over you, would you?

Well, you have the best of all chiefs ... God. And so you are given that to suit the need. And where you are not fully prepared to meet a certain environ, Universal Law gently prevents you from entering therein. If a guide determines that you would be benefited by so doing, they can raise the vibrations of the cloak to the point where you could pass through for that specific purpose. You could not dwell therein inordinately. And that would only be temporal and probably very briefly so. See?

What could be called the mantle of the Christ, or the cloak or the spiritual garment of the Master, this is, in fact, as such: the pattern, the perfect pattern, that might be searched for, sought after by all of you because it is the example, perhaps the pattern from which your own garments might be woven, that will guide you in every step, in every activity, all throughout your life. So it is (to the degree that we might respond to your question) yes, this is the goal, the pattern to be emulated.

With regard to its proximity to the Book of Knowledge, there's a difference here, and that will begin to become more evident as we proceed with Peter. Thus, we'll bow to that impending discussion, hoping it will answer your question more fully. If not, inquire here further.

The best way to attain the Christ cloak is to live your life in the pattern of it. In other words, the more you believe and act in accordance with a certain thought-form, the moreso does it become your thought-form. Live within the pattern. Live, act, and function that way, and that gives you claim to it. It becomes, in effect, yours. You are weaving your cloak, changing its colors, its patterns, with every thought, every deed, every action you perform. See? Again, more will be forthcoming on this.

With regard to the entity Lois ... In effect, you have transferred your energy, your spiritual and life force energies, to another entity. The exemplification of transferring a cloak, as such, as we see it, wasn't really your spiritual cloak, but something which you have learned to accept as such, and so it functions much in the same manner. Again, we ask your forgiveness, but this will come forward just ahead.

It is, as such, similar to prayer. The cloak is somewhat of a by-product of prayer and living in a state of joyful prayer.

Well, we'd say loosely, *all of the above* (but not some).

(Given with a note of loving humor, see?)

We're going to conclude at this point, for the following reasons: Firstly, we wouldn't want you groping any further in the light. We'd rather give you some clear, concise answers and not blind you with a barrage of verbosity, but provide, in the example, clarity.

Which returns us to our comment to each of you: Ever strive to be the example of what you believe. You'll do more and better works that way than you could ever imagine.

(There is a sort of cloakroom, and we don't mind here if you borrow cloaks from it. We do ask that you return them, however, in equal or better condition. And on that note of very loving humor, we shall now conclude.)

May the grace and blessings of our Father's wisdom ever be that lamp which guides your footsteps.

Fare thee well, then, for the present, dear friends.

Q&A READING #12

Continuation of Questions After Chapter 8:
SPIRITUAL ACCEPTANCE (V-730)

Given October 26, 1990

AL MINER/CHANNEL: This reading is code number V-731. It is Questions and Answers #3, based upon the opening or topical readings we have received to date, ending with V-730 on Voyager Project #7. The questions we have this evening are again excellent, and are a bit more varied than we perhaps have had in the past, which makes the information (I believe, I hope) even more exciting.

QUESTIONS SUBMITTED

(And so, the first several questions have been submitted by Larry and Mary Alice in Louisiana.)
#1 - While following Peter as he made the transition from the Earth plane to the realm where the Garden is located, and where he met Paul and Zack and the other entities, as I understand his situation at that time, he was not aware of where he was or what was truly taking place. What bothers me is, if Peter has had numerous incarnations in and out of the Earth plane, surely he must have had similar experiences as he is now having. If so, why does he not remember them? Why is this experience so new and strange to him? Those memories of past incarnations would be very helpful in assisting him to adjust to his new realm, would they not? Lama Sing, please enlighten me (us) on this topic. *(Thanks, Larry and Mary Alice. They wrote further:)* If an entity has had one hundred incarnations in the Earth, then we can assume that that entity has also experienced ninety-nine transitions to other realms, right? It seems to me there is a lot of experience here to call upon.

#2 - There were four entities (Zack, Paul, and two females, plus others) assisting with Peter's awakening. Considering the millions of souls who have departed the Earth plane, for example in the last fifty years, how many spiritual beings like Zack and Paul, et cetera, are required in assisting these souls to adjust to their new realms? This could be a real mindboggler for me with my finite mind. I wonder if the information in the Urantia book, with their millions and millions of divas, light beings, et cetera, applies to this question.

(Next, several questions from Jud in North Carolina:)
#3 - Concerning the relationship to the Universal Forces, a topic of great interest to me, and all of us, I'm sure. While Peter was seated in the building, I had the impression that the long table, chairs, et cetera, was like a council of the "Elders" meeting that was taking place in the Garden. I was praying that Peter be accepted. I looked upon the entity standing at the end of the table with Peter's book as representing our Creator, or the Christ. This is probably way off, or is it? I also seemed to be present, near Zack's position. Was I there in spirit, or was I seeing through the Lama Sing group eyes?

#4 - The beautiful lightness that surrounded the three prior to their meeting with the entity in the building, this light was of and from God and it balanced with each of the three? Or a better way to say this was that they and the light became one? Is this correct? This same light made up, or was, the man with the book. Would you comment on this, please, Lama Sing?

#5 - Some, if not all of you, may sense I feel like the movie character "E.T." in that I want to go home. Yet I want to stay in the Earth also. So I want to walk in both worlds. All in all, I want to know our Father's will and purpose and to accomplish it.

(Jud, I'm sure that we can all echo those sentiments, from time to time at least.)

(Next is a really great question from my friend and fellow

Voyager, Rick, in Georgia. Little town called Atlanta.)
#6 - I've noticed that Peter is "awake" for ninety minutes and "resting for a month." If we here in Earth worked like this, we would need to sleep for twenty-one years. *(Doesn't sound all that bad sometimes. How about twenty-one days?)* Makes me wonder what it ... *(forgive my comments here. This question tickles me, Rick.) Makes me wonder what it looks like in The Garden with sleeping bodies all over the place. (You have to join with me as I visualize Rick's question here, and I can hardly wait to hear the answer to that.)*

(Next, some questions from Ken and Nancy in North Carolina, and, here again, they're going to stretch us a little bit and make us think, and I think bring out some good information as the result. They write:)
#7 - Here are some questions on the reading about Peter's dream. I would like to call the realm that Peter experiences the "realm of laughter". *(I might interject here and point out that Ken has gained a great reputation as coming up with a lot of acronyms for us and real catchy phrases. You might remember "prayer power units" and things like that. Those came from Ken, in case you didn't remember. Going on ...)* This sounds like an important place for balancing the soul. For example, when Peter starts getting drawn into emotional experiences during the "dream" Paul takes him there *(and I'm sure he's referring to the realm of laughter)* and he loses the sticky sensation. Would you comment more on this realm? On laughter? On the re-balancing that seems to occur?

#8 - My wife Nancy, had a dream when we were first met that we were two lights tumbling through space, laughing. Is this coming from the same realm? *(Again, I refer you to the "realm of laughter.")* Could you comment on how to recognize this realm?

#9 - When Paul looked into Peter's eyes and Peter was able to re-experience the realms of light, how did Paul do that? He was asked twice during the reading but didn't answer in words. *(So, Lama Sing, what*

Ken and Nancy and all the rest of us echo is, "How about an answer in words?" Thanks.)

(Finally, Ken and Nancy write:)
#10 - Peter, Paul and Zachary seem to be enjoying themselves so much. Are they beyond sorrow?

(The next composite of questions are from Phyllis and Jill. Jill, you might recall, is the one who is carrying the youngest Voyager. You remember? She's expecting a baby. In fact it may even be here as we speak. The questions, I considered them carefully for a moment or two, thinking that they might be too personal, but then I reconsidered from the perspective that I think they might provide us some answers which are very revealing. So, with that note in mind, here are their questions:)

#11 - What are this soul's preparation and instruction for coming into the Earth? From which realm is this soul coming from? Are there any symbols or tools given to the soul that can help him to consciously remember his purposes for coming into the Earth? I imagine he's "packing his bag" and attending his going-away party. Are all the Voyagers invited? (With a note of loving humor.)

#12 - When this is the last lifetime on this realm, Earth, we're told the soul first goes to Arcturus (that being the transitional point). Then into what realm or system does the soul go after that? And please comment about those realms and what creative works are accomplished there.

#13 - When Peter was experiencing the emotion of seeing his family photo, did his family sense his presence? I have heard many family members say they dreamed or heard a voice, et cetera, from their loved one who had passed over, giving them a sense of relief or reassurance all was well with them.

So, I'll conclude with the questions here and submit them

prayerfully to You, Father, asking that You would guide us to the highest and best information that can be given. We thank You very much, Father, and each of the Voyagers and all those souls who are a part of this work. Amen.

THE READING

LAMA SING: Yes, we have the Channel then and, as well, those references which apply to the questions, the topics, the individuals, and the purposes as are now before us. As we commence herein, we pray first in this manner:

Lord God, we know that Thou art ever with us in all things, these works and all of existence. Therefore, we seek through this prayer to acknowledge and thereafter accept Your presence, that this shall become as a lamp to guide us unto Thy wisdom, Thy grace, love and compassion. We pray on behalf of all those souls in all realms who have presently lost their way and have no one to walk before them bearing Your light. As ever, in humbleness and joy for the opportunity to be of service in Thy name, we are most humbly grateful, Father. Amen.

These are most excellent questions. It is our prayer that the information in response to them is worthy of being present with them.

The purposes for which Peter is sojourning at present are somewhat different in terms of the general, or the *norm* (as you would call it), for souls who are in the transitional stage.

Therefore, the full and complete knowledge of all previous incarnations and all previous experiences would not be significantly beneficial to this particular work. You might consider this, dear friends Larry and Mary Alice, as to be an incarnation of sorts. However, it is not in physical body but in the evolving spiritual body.

Peter is embarked upon a purposeful work to recover a significant portion of his awareness. Therefore, the measure of knowledge in the conscious sense of all those previous experiences would be, perhaps, self-defeating, too scattering, to be of particular benefit here.

Note that he can recall here and there various things, and also note that some new experiences and/or discoveries are met with remarkable ease. In these and other instances, the full complement of all past experiences are available to him in their end product. They are not necessary to be available in the conscious sense in their detail. That would be too deterring to the purpose at hand. They are, however, fully available to him in the productive sense as summarial information and knowledge, and he is discovering this bit by bit as he is able to absorb same and incorporate it into his total being.

In the normal sense (that is, with those who are transitioning from the Earth in the general), entities do review and have some knowledge of all past experiences. For the most part, however, they reach a point where they begin to re-focus their attention and their progressive growth upon the next logical or chosen objective. At that point, the detail of those experiences begins to merge itself into a productive resource, and thereof they can draw as they are willing or have the need, productively. See?

For example: How many Earth years have you lived? Count them and multiply them by the number of segments in that Earth year. (You call them Earth days). Each of those days begins and ends as though it were a miniature lifetime. And where you are now, if you multiply 365 times the number of Earth years sojourned to date, that would be an impressive number of lifetimes, would it not? And yet, if you were to be flooded with the memory vividly of each of those in this very moment, would you not just a whit be overwhelmed? Emotionally, mentally, and so forth? And so, you are not. But rather, you are enriched by the wisdom that you have gained collectively, and that is summarized into varying references upon which your subconscious and super-conscious draw. See? This analogy, we hope, is the very best to clarify our point here.

One hundred incarnations and 99 transitions is an understatement (lovingly given, and with a note of loving humor). For that presumes that nothing happens between lives, which is not the case. There are, in fact, a numeric value of (in the sense of a multiplier exponentially derived) greater numbers interceding the Earth incarnations that take place in other realms. For example, an entity might enter the Earth, and that's a transition from one realm to another; have the Earth incarnation; make a second transition out of it. See? That's three movements or experiences. Make a third transition into yet another realm from the point of awakening from the Earth; have an experience; move to yet another realm; have another experience; and so forth, culminating anywhere from one to, on an average, 15 or 20 marked experiences. And then return to the Earth.

So, even though it would seem that we are supporting your case here (given with a note of loving humor), be mindful of our analogy above. Just in the current past 365 Earth days, would you like to have all those thoughts and memories in your head at one time? See?

We know the intent of your question, and the answer is that Peter is available to that information. That is, he can move into it if he wishes. And often, when he moves into his state of spiritual sleep, he does move into that consciousness and draws or learns from all that, just as you do in the dream state. See?

If you consider one cell in your body and you give it a name, and you find another and you name that, and two more and you name those, and perhaps you call them Zachary, Paul, and Betty and Joan, because you have identified these entities, it gives the appearance of some sense of singularness or even importance beyond that which is appropriate for the remaining cells in your body. Just as well, then, Zachary, Paul, and the two female entities are emphasized in these works, but they would be among the first to emphasize to you that they are no greater nor lesser than any other soul. That's the first point here, see? It has to do only with their acceptance, their stature.

Again turning to the cells of your body, many cells die in your body every approximate 28 Earth days or so. In fact, over a span of an Earth year, your body has rebuilt itself, in some cases many times, in other cases only a few.

So, the answer to your question is: You are cells of the living body called Earth. Because some cells have been replaced by others, some cells have departed. Again, this depends upon the focus. If you have several billions of cells or entities in the Earth, then you must have an equivalent number elsewhere for all the souls who have ever dwelled therein. Among those there are an equal number, as in the example of Peter's experiences, of Zachary's, Paul's, and the two female entities' as are associated with Peter in the present, see?

And so, therefore, consider that you are dancing on the head of a pin (as the colloquial term in the Earth is given). And in the universe there is an infinite number of pins upon which others are dancing. So many so, dear friends, that the number would escape your comprehension. But the point is here, quite simply, the question is asked from the perspective of limitation, and God is unlimited. The perspective is asked also from the physical perspective, while the spiritual has no bonds, no boundaries, no limitations.

We can assure you that, among those souls who are active, (that is, involved in incarnations) there are sufficient there involved that there are some Zacharys and Pauls and female entities who are having to wait for those to work for or work with. We are grateful for your questions and hope that these answers clarify a different perspective.

If each of you were to now accept your spiritual nature, there would be more than enough Zacharys, Pauls, and the others, to go around and have a sizeable number left over. Don't fall prey to numbers, to limitations, and to the expectations as are solely perceived from the Earth. You are the Child of an unlimited Father. Always remember that. The Master can appear to 20 at one time as easily as he can to one. This is no significant matter for Him to accomplish. See? Zachary exists in multiple levels. This is why you find Zachary very seldom present on a consistent basis. (This may change shortly because of the nature of the work given to Peter, if he accepts it.)

But for now, understand that once you reach your level of spirituality in a fuller sense, it is not complex for you to be present in multiple realms, in multiple expressions, simultaneously. Time is the illusion of a linear, singular movement from the Earth. And yet, time exists all throughout eternity. What happens when that singular, straight-line measure of time meets itself? Does it repeat, or does it spiral inward, upward, or what? See? Do not your laws of physics state that it must eventually meet itself? See?

The Urantia material, as we see it (lovingly and humbly given here), is a perspective of consciousness and existence. And from that perspective we could concur with the general theme of same. The individual expressions are dependent upon that perspective and have much to do with the thought-forms constructed of such a nomenclature of belief. See? So, in that sense, yes, it could apply to the question.

You are correct, entity Jud, in the assessment of the experience. You could consider that the entity, as such, was and is the expression of God ... in a form. See? We won't at this time identify the uniqueness of that form in the expression of a name or definition, but only confirm to you that that was and is an appropriate conclusion. The council was, in fact, the purpose of the locale and the environment, and you should come to find that Peter will meet, actually meet, with that council and some very significant works which may well involve our grouping, including yourselves, in the future. This, again, is dependent upon Peter's choices (they are his right of free will) and the activities of Wilbur and David and others you have yet to meet. So, have a cheer in your heart for the correct assessment. See?

With regard to your presence, this is not ... How can we identify it to you, dear friend? Rather in the form of a question, we are advised, than a statement: Is this so inconceivable, for you to be actually present, standing there with Peter, Zachary, Paul, and this being of light? Not at all from where we are. And, of course, you are aided here in seeing or perceiving through the activities of this grouping gathered to assist you. For this we have given as our pledge, our promise to you in the past. So both are correct. Then, believe unto the one with which you are comfortable, knowing them both to be entirely possible for you. See?

That light you spoke of is, in fact, from the Source, which is God. The closer Peter, Zachary, and Paul and others get to that Source, the more predominant and frequent shall that light be present, until such time as they, one or more, pass through a transition of sorts which will be indicated clearly in their potential and upon the effects of their total spirituality, which will be evident in their cloak. But, in essence, that statement you made is correct. The light is not necessarily made up of the man with the book, but present because he is present. See?

While all of you may wish to (quote) "go home" as with this *ET*, be mindful that wherever you are in your consciousness can and should be *Home*. For when you create your home therein, you can bring into that home the full complement of your soul's consciousness.

And that is one of the purposes for sojourning in the Earth. As you have chosen to be in the Earth, you have chosen to do a work therein ... in part, for self; in part, for others;

in part, for the contribution of illuminating that realm of consciousness to its fullest potential. A little here, a little there, one by one, then the groups, then the masses, then whole countries, continents and, hopefully, ultimately, the Earth and the spheres which are adjacent to same.

When all have that light within their house, their temple, then the work is completed as relates to the Earth. See?

If you want to walk in both worlds, that's always available to you. But be mindful that it is difficult to bring the consciousness of one world into another and remain acceptable to the general masses (given with a note of loving humor). You'll need lots of that light to preserve yourself under their questioning and/or criticism, or worse. See? (Given with a note of loving humor.)

Entity Rick, consider for a moment these several things in answer to your excellent question: You are measuring time, tick-tock, or you are measuring time electronically, vibrationally. And as you measure time, you might consider that from point A to point B is a certain span of incremental demarcations. Supposing that you were capable of moving at a right angle from point A at a speed which would pass beyond that known as sound, light, atomic particle movement, or any other such measurement that you know of at present. And that this movement could be so swift and so complete that before you could think of the destination completely, you would find yourself there, irrespective of distance. See? In other words, complete, instantaneous movement.

Then, how would you measure, in terms of linear time, that distance between point A and your parallel movement to what we'll now call point C? Then, supposing that you move back from point C to point A, and when you reach point A again, you find that only an Earth minute has transpired. And yet, you have traveled perhaps trillions or quintillions of miles, as you measure those in the Earth. All the while, the other souls in the Earth are moving forward in a linear sense. You have moved perpendicular to that.

Now, if you turn the point A-C so that it's flat, so that you have C to A as your horizontal and A to B as the vertical, and now you are experiencing on the C to A line (or A to C line, whichever suits you), how would you measure your experiences along that route? You can't measure them based upon the increments of A-B because they are moving in a different reference point. See? They are moving in the sense of what you will call three-dimensional conscious time. The A-C line moves beyond the laws of physics into other laws, other expressions.

And supposing for a moment you wish to slow down that travel ... but not actually slow it down; you are not going to slow the movement, but you're going to examine it in small increments. In other words, divide the A-C line into, let's say, 20 demarcations. And as you take each of those demarcations and explore it methodically, you would be experiencing it, would you not? And you would be experiencing it finitely. Once you had moved from segment one all the way to 20, which is point C, and back down or over to point A, you might say that you have had 20 years, could you not? Or 20 months or 20 days or hours or minutes. It would be arbitrary, and if you all agreed upon it, that would become the rule, the dictum, the reality.

Now, let's flip this right angle over again so that point A-B are again on the horizontal. Now, would you mind explaining to all the other entities who are traveling from A to B how it is that you lived 20 years in the span of a minute on their scale? See? Quantum physics? Ethero-magnetic computations? Well, whatever you'd use, you'd better be good, or they'll give you one of those garments that lace up the back (with a note of loving humor).

Another way of stating this to you is this: Nearly each and every Earth day you stop your activity and you lay your body to rest. Once you fall into what you call sleep, how long does it seem that time has passed until you awaken? Where is your gradient of measuring time? Some mornings we believe you would state that you would awaken feeling that only minutes had passed, wishing that there had been many more such minutes. Other times, the evening slumber seems to have dragged on and on, and you thought it might never end. Is it not relevant, then, to one's consciousness and perspective, this thing you call time?

If you picture, finally (as an example for this excellent question) a pyramid, a "V" which is inverted over you in the Earth, and that from a point somewhere out in time-space the cone-like top or apex of this "V" gradually tapers until it reaches a finite point. From that finite point back to the Earth, you can consider that time is expanded and slowed and defined. The closer you get to that finite point, the more accelerated and instantaneous is consciousness, until you reach a certain point where a second and now inverted pyramid begins to form. And it expands out into the universe, into infinity, where once again finite expression becomes the watchword. But when you get to the other side of that finite point, it is with the full complement of your spiritual potential, and on the other side of that point you might consider therein liveth God. See?

Peter is progressing towards that finite point. Thus, an hour's time with Peter might be the equivalent of many Earth days or months of your time, because it is expanded as you approach Earth and condensed or compacted or accelerated as you approach Peter.

It is true, there are certain experiences and activities which Peter is having that you are not hearing about. And there are a number of these ...

[tape turned over]

... will rest or spiritual sleep. He is not idle, any more than you are when you are in your sleep state in Earth. See? If we haven't answered that to your satisfaction or completeness, do inquire further.

With a note of loving humor, we would well accept the title (*handle*, as Zachary would call it) of (quote) "the Realm of Laughter" (end quote) and we thank thee [Kendall] for christening it as such.

This is an important place for the balancing of the soul and, indeed, a place of significance for each of you to find healing. The place of laughter, the *Realm of Laughter*, is a healing realm. Its purpose is to provide you with a freedom, a healing effect from those things which might otherwise limit. It is a solvent to the sticky substance called emotion. It is a component capable of providing a final ingredient to dissolve the glue which binds entities to the Wheel of Karma. It is the finger of God expressed in a moment of grace, to rub out doubt, to brush away tears of sorrow, remorse, sadness, or guilt. The Realm of Laughter is present within all, through Universal Law. The Realm of Laughter is the pure flow of energy from God which is identified as grace, forgiveness.

This as a realm is available to all of you. It is available to you in the Earth plane within you, albeit perhaps not to the full potential as it is now available to Peter. The greater is the number of a grouping of souls who gather together for the purpose of laughter, the greater is the potential of that which is God's grace. Follow that? This is, as you have discerned, a very important point, one which your grouping (referring to Kendall and Nancy) can experiment with to very good purpose... and also, by the way, make you all feel very good. There is as much power of healing in joyous laughter as in a good shelf saturated with medication. And we'll stand by that statement, unequivocally ... regardless of the dis-ease and regardless of the medication. It's true. Try it.

Peter's dream ... Well, then, here we have an example which helps somewhat to explain both the entity Rick's and Larry and Mary Alice's questions, sort of in a composite way: Paul is able, because of the bond between him and Peter, to experience what Peter experiences. And conversely, then, because God's Law is perfect, Peter can experience what Paul experiences. Because of Paul's level of balance, spiritually, his love for Peter and for God, and his dedication to service, and his attained spirituality thereof, Paul is capable of giving back to Peter what Peter has given to him.

Now, the best example we can give you in the Earth would be the following: Supposing that someone who has dedicated themselves in the Earth to developing their vocal ability, and in one moment of one Earth day they decide to sing a wondrous song. Once that song is sung, it's gone, isn't it? Unless they share it with someone. Then the memory of that song remains, in effect, tape-recorded, etched into the memory of all of those who have heard it. Then, very much like a tape-recorder, they may think back to that moment, close their eyes, and re-live it, actually re-hearing the sounds, the variation in tone, the expressions, the gestures. Just as though they had, in a manner of speaking, video-taped it (using your Earth terminology) within themselves.

When you reach that point of spiritual acceptance that you become unlimited to the point where you know that thought-forms and experiences are eternal, it is simply a matter of re-presenting that thought-form. Once the thought-form is accepted by those involved, both or all parties can move into the thought-form and continue on experiencing it and expanding it, which is precisely what Paul did. Once Peter and Paul experienced that, it was a very simple matter to add Zachary, and will be an even simpler matter to add others ... perhaps, let's say, such as Wilbur. See the point? That's how he did it. See?

This is a realm which has potential equal to that of anything we have given to you in past ... prayer, meditation, focal images, mantras, anything. Laughter unleashes the bonds of limitation from the pureness of your spirit. Joy flows through you. Joy is wellness, completeness. And therefore, it brings, after its own kind, healing. Dis-ease cannot exist in pure joy, laughter. And so then, appropriately so, the Realm of Laughter is every bit as potential as you have surmised.

You are correct. This is coming from the same realm (with regard to your mate's dream). Souls do tumble through space, laughing. And it is indicative of the bond between you and the level of shared joys that you have attained in past. It is also indicative of the level of your spiritual acceptance.

For example, you do not remember, as such, nor did her dream indicate, that you were on some lush shore, a tropical isle, basking in the sunlight, did you? Instead, you were the symbols, the true expression of that joy which is symbolized, or perhaps finitely presented, by the tropical isle shore. That is an expression of joy, of fulfillment, of ease. You reduced that to its purer form because you were less limited. Very simple. To recognize the Realm is to know the joy and the flowing that takes place within you. See? You should hear more on this as we continue. If you don't, ask further if you wish.

We'd like to give you this addendum: As Peter, Paul, and Zachary are experiencing in the realms of light, the realms of living light, the Realm of Laughter, they are doing so not only because it is joyful but because it is purposeful for Peter. And therefore, because it is purposeful for Peter, it is purposeful for them all, because they are joined together through the wondrous bond of friendship. And therefore, as Peter grows through these experiences, you may note from time to time that within the realms of light Peter may discover a fibril, a thread, a bit of different light that is the focal point of many past experiences which are now reduced down to this singular little spot of light, like a thread or a hair. And that is its proper perspective in Peter's cloak, his spiritual cloak.

This little fibril of light, then, represents something he has yet to meet and balance with. Once he does, it will become transformed into a better state, a more complete and harmonious state, and his level of spiritual acceptance will rise just that much more.

So you will note, very wisely and very significantly, Paul and Zachary introduced Peter to a portion of his own wisdom wherein he discovered some of his own remaining emotional bonds which were and are yet, to a degree, limiting to him.

If he wishes to become of greater service, and if he is indeed to assume the mantle of light which is called that of a guide, a teacher, he must be capable of enduring similar emotions as might be experienced or expressed by those whom he is seeking to serve, without faltering, without hesitating, and without being drawn into that and thereby losing sight of what he has gained.

And so as the entity Larry has asked, here, then, a spot of tiny red fibril represents the cumulative experiences of many lifetimes of emotion. In that instant, he felt the impact of all of those. And Paul and Zachary helped him to meet it and to understand it and now to use it as a lamp of wisdom if and when he shall meet this same energy on the part of one of those whom he might serve in Earth or elsewhere. See? If it's not clear, you'll need to ask. See?

Are Peter, Paul and Zachary beyond sorrow? In a manner of speaking, they can be if they *want* to be. And when it's necessary for them to enter into some further productive works of growth for themselves or any other, they can do so. But when they are in the Realm of Laughter, as your question is truly asking, they are beyond sorrow. Sorrow cannot exist in the realm of laughter. So you are correct. Good work. See?

A soul about to enter the Earth encounters many things and many considerations. We would recommend that you ask of the Channel for those earlier works in the previous project having to do with the entity called Judith (having to do with the topic on children[8]) and that will clarify your questions, we believe, quite nicely, and give you the answers and more to what you are seeking. See?

Going away parties, as such, from this realm to yours or to another, are not necessarily cause for celebration here, in the sense that you would think of it in the Earth. But they are cause for times of rejoicing in the sense that there is the knowledge that the soul will grow and much will be gained. They are times of preparation, of bonding, of completing relationships that these might endure and be helpful to that soul as they are moving along the pathway of their current incarnation. Each soul is given those symbols, those signets, those opportunities, those talents and blessings, as are most contributive toward the completion of their intended works. See?

We cannot at present identify the specific questions for you, for we don't have those specific records here before us. Those would need to be requested in order to answer that. And we see that they are, so we'll turn to your ... (that is, that they are going to be requested), so we'll turn next to your subsequent questions:

The realm which is identified as Arcturus, or the *pole star* as some think of it, is generally thought of as demarcating that point in time and consciousness ... not just in the physical dimension, now mind you, but in more ... as being similar to that point of finiteness we indicated in our comments above, where the pyramid reaches that point, and then on the other side there is the mirror reverse of this, as an inverted pyramid.

On the other side of that point, those souls, then, begin to

---

[8] Project: The Nature of Children (given in 1989) – Al Miner had asked Lama Sing for a list of potential projects, this topic being one of them. Once the group engaged in this project, it was discovered that this wasn't intended to be about children per se at all, but about appreciating and setting free within self the very nature of the child within.

experience in the more complete sense of their potential, first here and there, little by little, then broader and broader, until such they are moving outwardly towards the infinite expanse of what you would presume to be the base line of that pyramid. See? And that's the activity there. The form or manner or shape which is involved is literally infinite and might mirror or pattern itself after other realms, indeed even those such as Earth, and such similar as this.

It is possible for some of those souls to return through that portal and to work in this side of that concentrated point of light. When such do, they are often thought of as masters, avatars, and such as this, beings of light, or such as the Elders. The Elders are identified as those who dwell in and about that point of intersect between realms, between the points of transition from that which is called these expressions and those beyond. (We've probably raised more questions than we've answered, with a note of loving humor, but we do find that this should answer that question, to some extent.)

Creative realms, you see, are dependent upon the creator, are they not? Where two or more agree upon a certain thought-form, then they are creating. If two of you decide to create a new sport, a new game, you'll discuss it, you'll decide upon the tools, if any, to be present, you'll decide upon the rules, the demarcation points, the conditions, you'll decide upon the order, you'll structure the measuring stick or point structure or accomplishment measurement, and you'll then embark about playing it, won't you, in terms of the game?

And if you involve three or four or five entities in that game, then it becomes, for that space of consciousness or time, the reality of those five entities. And so long as you uphold the thought-form of that game, it is your shared reality. Then it is in these realms beyond Arcturus similar to this with the exception that the creativeness is unlimited and instantaneous. And that's why it's so important to reach the full culmination of your spiritual acceptance before passing through that point, for if you did not you couldn't pass through it. It's as simple as that. Because if you were to pass through it (let's say because a momentary breakdown of that structure which would prevent it) you couldn't endure in that realm because you would still be fragmentally limited, and you would be playing in a game with others, partners and so forth, who are totally unlimited. The instant the others agree upon some course of action or activity to which you have even the most minute limitation, you would cease to be a part of their experience. And there you'd be, drifting alone. See? You would ultimately be drawn back to the point of light, and you would pass through it, back down to that level in the upward pyramid which focuses upon your Earth as a part of the pyramidal structure, and you'd move downwards in that pyramid to the level at which you would be the equal of the others therein. See? Follow that?

Now, to the questions, the last ones stated above, with regard to ... we believe it was Patty? The relationship between souls as they form bonds in any realm is an eternal one. And therefore, when Peter viewed the photograph of his family that impacted his family, indeed. The degree to which the impact was felt or known was and is dependent upon several factors, one of those being (and the first one) the intensity of the thought-form or thought-forms in which they were involved in that moment. For the density or intensity of a thought-form in which one is functioning acts more or less as a filtration device. Understanding that Peter's thoughts and emotions are coming from a different structure of existence, they would therefore be different and also would not blend or complement a random thought-form of intensity. As a matter of course, much of Peter's feelings and presence would be reflected off that. Therefore, you can deduce, rather logically we should think, that when an entity is in the sleep state, they are generally not involved in any intense thought-form.

They are not participating in shared activities with other entities whose intensity of thought or emotion might inadvertently block Peter's emanations. And so therefore, Peter's presence can much more easily and more fully be detected and/or felt during sleep, in what you call the dream state, than in the wake state.

And so it is that most entities in the Earth should find that loved ones who are beyond the Earth now will most frequently and vividly appear during their sleep state.

Perhaps second and/or third almost equally in this in terms of receptivity would follow times of being alone, of idleness, of relaxation and/or rest, where the mind is freed from needs or demands in the sense of communication with others, where the body or the hands may be busied about some task which is replicated often and so has become more or less automatic, so that the conscious mind is freed to be very receptive.

Or, a direct parallel to this, equally in its receptive state, is meditation.

Next, we would find prayer, where an entity has uttered a prayer and is dwelling in the holy silence and may therein or thereof perceive the entity.

Fourth, the entity may be literally seen in a moment of subtle relaxation or receptiveness, again following somewhat the criterion given above. The entity may be actually seen, in the sense of perceiving the image of the entity, as the entity revisits and/or moves about a familiar environ of the just-previous incarnation. In other words, had a family member been present when Peter was there in the place of his familiarity, they might have perceived him. And Peter might have perceived them. See?

Peter will ultimately learn how to perceive entities in other realms. And ultimately and perhaps finally, perceive them in the Earth. That will be a major step forward in the growth of Peter's spirituality and will be an indicator of his final stages of preparation to function as a mentor, a guide, a teacher, a helpmeet, to others who are yet in the Earth.

This is attainable by Peter. And this is a part of the work which the entity of light and Paul and Zachary and all the others are attempting to contribute to ... some knowingly, some as their primary work; others subtly, and as secondary or tertiary works, as you might rank them.

But what will happen here should, perhaps, in some ways, come to be a revelation to each of you. The activities with David and Wilbur have only just begun, and the activities of teaching another, guiding another, will ofttimes (indeed more oft than not) educate the teacher moreso than the student or pupil. See?

In other words, Peter isn't fully aware of how much he does know. Peter isn't prepared to know what he knows, to actualize or realize his own knowledge. But he's getting there, step by step. See?

We should like to take these next several Earth minutes to comment in a broader sense, and we thank thee for this opportunity:

Peter, as you know, has moved from experience to experience. In some instances we have relayed to you in very specific detail some of the finite events, almost to the point where you may have wondered why we would bother with such ... that these might seem trivial to you, and that the greater information and benefit could be gained by you by hearing the overviews and moving swiftly to the experiences and the explanations of them, more or less removing the personal-ness from the experiences shared by Peter, Paul, Zachary, and the others. But we have intentionally left these in and will continue to do so, because we know certain things about you in the Earth, about ourselves, and about all souls and you can learn from this, as well.

If you want to take any action, if you want to accomplish any work in the Earth or anywhere, look for the keys which are pivotal to accomplishing that work. What singular point in the Earth can make the difference between accomplishing a certain objective and not accomplishing it? We hear a number of thoughts, a number of responses, and offer our own:

Does not emotion have one of the most powerful effects on anything and everything that you do? Yes, we know there are other motivating factors. But feeling good/feeling bad, feeling joyful/feeling sad, feeling happy/feeling angry, feeling remorse/feeling sympathetic, feeling warm/feeling cold, feeling sweet/feeling sour, feeling dry/feeling wet. We are attempting to give you the feeling of being there with Peter, with Zachary, with Paul. We are attempting to convey to you the essence of each of these beautiful souls by identifying to you the composite of their being, the accomplishments of all of their sojourns, as they have been now concentrated into their personalized and finite perspectives as Peter, Paul and Zachary.

And if you would, after concluding with this meeting, wander over and step in front of a looking-glass and see who you are. See what temple you're living in. And just for a moment, don't think about what you feel or believe that you are. Look at the image you see. Then close your eyes and see if that's who you find living inside the body. And if you don't feel a difference, then we haven't effectively conveyed to you the intent of this last few Earth minutes of commentary.

You could take a garment and cover your body and you'd look different. You could take your clothing off and you'd look different again. You could paint half your body green and the other half red, and you'd look humorously different. You could speckle your body with small, glued-on swatches of fabric until you looked something like a multicolored bush. You could part your hair this way or that, you could color one cheek red and the other pink or yellow or white. You could do all manner of things that would change your appearance, and the first entity who would see you would react to that. Wouldn't they?

Some of them might cause them to be startled, others might cause them to laugh, and others would cause yet different emotions. But the real you that is within is never known by an entity in the Earth (unless they can see spiritually) until you speak and act. True?

Then that which is the outer is capable of instantaneous change, simply by any of the actions (or others) as we have just given. But the true you, the real, eternal, wondrous being that you are, is only known when you look at the detail of what's inside, what's in the heart.

What's in the mind? What are the desires? What's the color of that thought? How smooth is the angle in that creative work done by your hand? How does the verbiage of a letter you have written grasp the heart? How has an action or deed you have performed helped another? What about that prayer of loving kindness to the entity you saw huddled in a corner last week along the street? What about this and that?

You see, you are what's within. And the specifics of that are the specifics we are giving you in the experiences between our trio. They are these experiences.

The Garden is the outward manifestation of their cumulative resource in the spiritual sense. It is also the manifestation of the cumulative resources of many other souls, including yourselves. Peter's garden is your garden. As you would choose to be there, to support it, and to find joy in it, then it is yours. It is like the entity who passes through the ever-narrowing upright pyramid into the focal point of light and emerges on the other side. If you can dwell in and about that level of consciousness, of spirituality, and sustain all that takes place therein, then you can claim it as your own. But only when you can do so, can you therein dwell. See?

Then look into your day's activities and see the color, the light, the excellence of the works and deeds of yourself and others. And then you'll know them. But if you see them one-half green and the other half red, know that you're looking at the illusion, the outer casement; that what you're looking for, that what will have meaning to you throughout eternity, can only be found within and in the demonstrated examples and actions of what that inner self is.

Joy to you all, and our blessings and continued prayer for each of your needs.

We are grateful to Thee, Father, for this opportunity of humble service, thanking all those who have come forward herein, and asking humbly that we might ever be worthy, Father, to continue in this service now and throughout eternity, in the wondrous company of these, our brethren in the Earth.

May the grace and blessings of our Father's wisdom ever be that lamp which illuminates your pathway.

Fare thee well, then, for the present, dear friends.

Q&A READING #13

Continuation of Questions After Chapter 8:
SPIRITUAL ACCEPTANCE (V-720)

Given December 5, 1990

AL MINER/CHANNEL: *This reading is code number V-732. It is Questions and Answers #4, the next in the series of questions and answers for Voyager Project #7. The questions that I am about to read for this reading are quite varied, but very interesting, and again show the broad and deep level of thinking and perspective that we collectively bring together here. And I think, as always, that's one of the very strong benefits of working together in a group. I know I certainly enjoy the questions that come in, and they certainly contribute a great deal to my total perspective, and I hope they do the same for you.*

QUESTIONS SUBMITTED

(The first question is from Gisela and Guenther in Arizona.)
#1 - I'm wondering if we will remember Peter's experiences when we pass to the other side and be that much more aware and can utilize this information, or would it be like we would have to experience it for ourselves?

(Next, from Dorothy in California:)
#2 - In V-710, Peter paused for a moment of introspection and something inside him told him that now was not the time to reach back into his consciousness to recall past experiences. Please explain Peter's inner consciousness or inner guidance more fully. How can we learn to follow our inner guidance more fully and more proficiently?

(Next, from Marie in Washington State:)
#3 - What is the difference between reincarnation and illusion? Isn't reincarnation somewhat of an illusion? *(Interesting.)*

#4 - Lama Sing used the phrase "prayers properly expressed." What constitutes the proper expression of prayer? Please elaborate. *(And that's from Harold and Linda in Missouri, and I'd be very surprised, Harold and Linda, if you didn't get a reference to the extensive material we received in the Prayer project.)*

(Next, from Dave in Maryland:)
#5 - In the Earth when one thinks of dying, it seems to be a natural thing to look forward to experiencing the opportunity of meeting your parents or others who were close to you in the Earth. Why hasn't Peter inquired about his Earth parents or grandparents? Why hasn't he met anyone from the Earth? This seems a little disturbing to us in the Earth.

(Next, Dave wrote:)
#6 - If Peter had died in an "accident" simultaneously with another person on the Earth, would they have noticed each other as they started to go through the colors, or would they be separated immediately, with no contact? Please make comparisons between two people, such as husband and wife, two close friends, two close strangers, and two "enemies." *(Well, that ought to be real interesting, Dave. Thank you for those questions.)*

(Next, from Joan in Pennsylvania:)
#7 - In V-420, page 15, Peter said to the radiant being with the Book of Wisdom: "If everyone doesn't get to experience this, I would like to know what others do experience and what makes the difference in terms of deciding who experiences what and where." From the other materials I am given, I am going to assume the difference is an entity's "spiritual acceptance." If so, please explain how one gains spiritual acceptance. If we came from the Oneness, we must have had spiritual acceptance at one time. Did we lose it accidentally, or on purpose? In the

Earth, people believe in struggle, and so it seems that we struggle through physical, financial, and relationship difficulties to "find God" and have some peace and spiritual acceptance. There should be an easier way. Is there?

#8 - Another difficulty comes along when you really begin to feel like a child of God, and your ego starts chastising you for arrogance and lack of humility, et cetera. What are your suggestions for dealing with this? *(And that's from Joan in Pennsylvania, and also we had some similar questions submitted from Gisela in Arizona, addressing that same issue.)*

(Next, from Ken and Nancy in North Carolina:)
#9 - You state that choices predicate talents. Would you please elaborate on this?

(Next, from David and Leiko, and I think I've pronounced that right this time, Leiko:)
#10 - Regarding polarity and/or balance, please explain further why the second female expression was necessary to the first female expression who was holding the "Book."

(Also from them:)
#11 - Regarding Peter's last Earth incarnation, please tell us the purpose and function of that incarnation. What was his mission?

(Finally, from David and Leiko:)
#12 - In V-710, you make the ending comment, "There is a Zachary, a Peter, a Paul, a David and a Wilbur in each of you." That seems to be a comment with much potential. Please open the door and tell us more. We recently hosted a guest from South America and had much to share with him during his 11-day visit. Is this experience an example of part of the understanding we are to derive from this comment?

(Here's an interesting question from Harold and Linda in Missouri:)

#13 - At times Lama Sing seems to be addressing someone directly. Example given, on side 2 of the tape, he's explaining about entities encountering the minutest limitation in another realm, and immediately returning to their own realm. He then states, "See? Good" ... as though he'd questioned the Voyager who had posed the query and received a response. Is Lama Sing in direct communication with our souls or minds during a reading, so that he's getting feedback as he speaks, even though we aren't consciously aware of the reading being done? Or is this just a rhetorical comment? *(Gosh, I hope it's not, don't you?)*

(Next, from Dorothy in California:)
#14 - In the overall historical perspective of mankind, what connection does Zachary, Paul, Peter and Company have with the people who lived at the time of Tobar and present-day Voyagers? Is it possible for us to live more than one life simultaneously?

(Also from Dorothy:)
#15 - What would you suggest would be the best way for like-minded groups such as the Voyagers to change the overall thought patterns of the Earth from one of separateness (for example: limitation, disease, fear and doubt) to one of unification? And again, the example being willingness to grow, to be whole, to be at a point where all are a part of the sum total of all existence. Is it possible to co-create such an idea with God and yet not violate Universal Law which preserves the right of others' free will? How would this affect Earthbound souls, the Sea of Faces, and unseen forces or realms beneath or above us? *(That's a fascinating question.)*

#16 - Peter's lesson was anticipated by Lama Sing as potentially having a striking effect on Peter. When the lessons came, they seemed so slight that I didn't recognize them at first. It seems that Peter is presented with events that shake him up a bit. For example, when Peter observes that his friends can disagree with each other, this shakes him up a bit. He is again shaken up when he learns that his friends are not all-knowing. Zachary and Paul then have to work a bit to get Peter back open to the light. So the lesson seems to be that when we get shaken up and, by habit, fear, or guilt, closed to the light or to new learning, that we not stay closed. Is this right? Aside from the lesson about not looking down on Wilbur for his choice of realms, was this the major lesson? Would you please elaborate on this? *(And that's from Ken and Nancy in North Carolina.)*

#17 - In order to obtain the best-possible healing environment for Reuben, which tape would be best for him to begin with? *(That's from Elizabeth in Texas, and I'm including it here with the hope that we might have some similar successes that we did with Jimmy[9], you may recall, in an earlier project.)*

Those are the extent of the questions that I am going to submit for this reading, and we now present them to You, Father, asking humbly that You would guide us to the very highest and best possible information that can be given. I would again ask for special prayers for all of the Voyagers, and I thank You, Father. Amen.

---

[9] Jimmy – A man for whom a prayer work was done by the group during the Prayer Project in 1988.

THE READING

LAMA SING: Yes, we have the Channel, then, and, as well, those references which apply to the questions, the grouping, and the intents and purposes as are gathered within same. As we commence, let us first join together in this humble prayer.

> *Lord God, we know that Thou art ever with us, every one. And thus, it is our prayer that we might herein accomplish Thy will and Thy purpose, as same shall contribute to the enlightenment of each of these inquiring minds as indicated above and as the collective grouping. And it is in their names that we pray on behalf of all souls in all realms who are presently in some need and for whom there are none in joyous prayer. We humbly thank Thee, Father, for this opportunity of joyful service in Thy name and for the presence of those souls who have come forth to respond to the inquiries as given. Amen.*

The relationship between self and the Universal Forces is one which is unlimited. Therefore, it depends upon one's extent of acceptance of that unlimited nature, the degree then to which they shall recall, in detail or generally, previous experiences. Thus, knowing about Peter's experiences has and shall continue to contribute significantly to each of you.

Whether you have employed these in your daily life as philosophies, or experimented with them, or what not, they do, you see, remain resident within your overall consciousness. And therefore they are a part of the foundation upon which you shall build once you depart from the Earth plane, and indeed in fact you are building upon at this very moment. You will probably experience some of these things yourselves, each of you likely different facets, for the purpose of completing the essence of your being, so to say, in the manner which suits you as an individual. But, generally, the answer to your question (the first above) is that you will be more aware and will most assuredly utilize this information. Of this, we have no doubt. See?

The center of consciousness within Peter which guided him as in the question above, is also present within each of you. The deeper one moves within that light within, the more profound it becomes.

The question then becomes one of bringing that consciousness back to the forefront of your awareness when you are in any expression, be that physical or nonphysical by the standards of the Earth. Peter is less encumbered. Therefore, it is easier for him to bring that awareness to his current consciousness.

In the Earth plane, this may be a bit more difficult because you are conditioned, first of all, by the mass-mind thought, then by the collective thoughts of that grouping of souls with whom you interact on a more personal level. Then, and perhaps more importantly, by your own thoughts, habits, doubts, fears, and what not.

Learning to deal with these, then, will enable you to follow your inner guidance more fully and more proficiently. It's a question of casting off shackles or blinds, removing veils (with a note of loving humor), than it is to learn something. You are attempting to regain something that you already have. The barriers between you and that consciousness are those as we have given them. The procedures for removal of these are many and varied and would be uniquely individual in many cases.

However, you will recall, dear friend, we have given a number of these in the past. Specifically, those dealing with habits as found in the project on Universal Law. It would be good to review this and to make this, to a degree, a daily companion of a sort. See?

Perspective is the gauge by which one can measure what's called illusion and reality, for reality becomes such by bringing it into self and making meaningful use of it. Reality (in the sense of the three-dimensional in the Earth) is thought to be physical matter, while the reality therein exists because of the agreed-upon laws ... both those at the spiritual level and those in the physical (as the laws of physics). Nonetheless, these are all subject to the Law Universal. Therefore, Universal Law states quite clearly that wherever a grouping of souls agree upon a certain thing, then that thing has, as their right, an assurance of existence.

So, *reality*, you see, depends upon, as such, at least somewhat, the degree to which one can gather and strengthen the power of thought and/or prayer, and allow that thought-form to become a reality.

Reincarnation and illusion *are* somewhat the same, for the true existence is nonphysical and is unlimited. Reincarnation, such as into the Earth or other realms, is the intentional choice of movement on the part of a soul into a realm of more finite or limited definition, for the value to be obtained, presumably, from the experiences therein. Ofttime, motivating factors here are surely those of karma and such.

But the answer to your question is, specifically, yes: Reincarnation is somewhat of an illusion, to the extent that it is not eternal. The differentiation, perhaps, in a clearer term of reality and illusion is its continuum of existence. From here, we would see reality as that which endures and remains which is eternal. Those things which are the steps along the pathway towards the attainment of reality are reincarnative paths, often. See? It's our prayer that's of some assistance.

The Channel is correct in his presumption that we would make reference to the project on Prayer. There is, very definitely, much good information there that was shared between many of you.

But to answer the question directly: Properly expressed prayers are those which are expressed by you (for example) praying for another entity but not praying in a limited sense ... praying in an unlimited way, where you would ask for the highest and best in accordance with God's will and that entity's needs and/or purposes. To pray specifically for an entity to have their foot stop hurting may be responded to directly, and the foot will stop hurting, only to find that several days later down the pathway of life the shoulder or elbow may start aching. The reason for this is, quite simply and probably clearly to you, dear friends, is that the root cause has not been addressed.

By directing prayer to God in His infinite wisdom, that becomes an energy, or a light if you will, for the subject to work with to find the underlying cause. And that's what's important here. See? There is much more on this in the project, as the Channel indicated. See?

When one considers the relationship between self and parents or grandparents or mate or friends, or even enemies, for that matter, we are certain that a high degree of energy will be generated. That energy will be, dear friend David, of a considerable emotional content ... some of the most powerful energy that one has to deal with. And make a note of that. It's a very important point. See?

But consider for a moment, David, that you have existed previous to this lifetime, and previous to that and previous to that. Let us presume for a moment that you have had 24 previous lifetimes in the Earth. Upon the departure from this lifetime, then, to meet and greet old friends, family members, which of those 24 sets of parents and grandparents would be the more important to you? Because you have just recently departed the current lifetime, for the example here, as you are called the entity David, you would think from your current perspective of being (quote) "alive in the Earth" (end quote) that these parents would be the most important, and of course they are. But once you depart the Earth, you will remember the importance, the joy, the love, the compassion shared with these other 24 sets of parents and friends, brothers and sisters. You may also remember an enemy here or there (with a note of loving humor).

Peter has reviewed all of this in his records. It hasn't been indicated here in great detail because, perhaps by an error on our part, we had presumed that you know of such things in the Earth. Essentially, all souls pass through what we would call a strata or level of remembering. This is very close to the Earth, and it has much to do with the veil of separateness between the Earth and other realms.

You will often be met by those entities, parents, friends, and such, who have departed the Earth previous to you (providing they haven't returned or gone elsewhere), and they will as such be recognized. And love and compassion will be shared between you in the presence and guidance of your guides, who may also be one or more of these ... the parents or whatnot.

But for the purpose of answering your question, it is our prayer that you do not allow this to unsettle you or disturb you, any of you, for Peter has passed through that and has balanced with it. If you'll note here and there, there are some references, even though slight. You'll get to see, we believe, a bit more of how this mechanism works in times ahead, and we should think that those will quite clearly explain to you what we are attempting to convey to you, also briefly, here.

Making comparisons, then, between entities who might depart the Earth simultaneously through accident, as you have indicated ... First of all, understand that entities do not depart the Earth unless they have accepted that departure. In the terminology of an *accident*, even in such, no matter how profound or how devastating, all entities have a choice on some level. See?

Two people, such as husband and wife, would naturally be bound, though some aren't bound through joy and love. Some are bound through obligation, contract and commitment, we note. Nonetheless, those bonds do keep a connective link between the entities for a time. If this bond is of true friendship, it will likely endure, and the two entities will have chosen that moment for purposes which are beyond the obvious ... that is, they have soul works or connections which have taken them to the point of departure simultaneously. So they will probably pass through the colors and through the experiences to some point together, possibly deviating, or one sleeping while the other experiences, if they are at varying levels of spiritual acceptance. They may emerge beyond the Veil of Darkness together and, in the case of true love and true friendship, most probably will.

We'll repeat that. These would, most assuredly, experience together and travel together for a considerable period of time, and would have consciousness of one another for considerable duration, probably to the point or limit of one another's spiritual acceptance, at which point one may choose to remain while the other goes on. See?

Two strangers would likely pass separately through their own experiences after reaching the Veil of Darkness. Once they are beyond the influences of Earth, and providing that neither are attracted to or choose to move into the Sea of Faces or such, they would travel together for a time and then enter their own individual paths of color or experience ... depending upon the level of spiritual acceptance. And you must remember that if they are in that same experience together, they have likely chosen to be. Therefore, even though they are strangers in the Earth, they may be old friends here.

Interestingly, two enemies are usually bound by the same type of energy as close friends: emotion. The stronger the force of their opposition (or *enemy-ship*, if you might call it that) the longer they'll stay close together in close proximity. Such an attitude, again ... Remember, we pointed to emotion above. Emotion is a very strong bond, and that type of energy doesn't discern between love or hatred.

Be careful whom you hate and how intensely, for that's a glue of sorts (given with a note of gentle humor, but seriousness, see). Whatever you do with intensity creates like a magnetic attraction, and that attraction may cause that thing, that object, that habit, or that entity, to be bound or tied to you to some degree. Try to release those things when they are not of your choice nor joyful.

One gains spiritual acceptance through many factors, the most common of which are reincarnative cycles. There could be other pathways of choice. The example here, of course, is Peter's. Peter has chosen, at a soul level, to follow this pathway (at least for the present) rather than returning to the Earth. That is the example of his development, his spiritual acceptance. One gains spiritual acceptance from coming into experience and emerging from it without being limited.

For example, in the more recent experiences Peter has had, he wavered, he faltered, he flickered. Remember the fireworks display of his cloak ... or rather, Zachary's at the time. Those are indicators of a struggle, a conflict. If one can balance with those, they have gained in their spiritual acceptance. See?

Peter has given you a very classic example of meeting challenge, dealing with it, and emerging on the other side, unscathed but wiser. One could state that spiritual acceptance is, to a degree, wisdom. Wisdom comes through experience, through the production of knowledge which comes from experience, and the application of that knowledge in daily life or in the continuum of experiences which follow.

The easier way that you are seeking is that which we are attempting to convey to you through the earlier projects and now by sharing Peter's experiences with him, and those of the others. You may find as you look back over these that there are several ... we'll call them *golden threads*, passing through all of the experiences, which, if you go backwards and look at the other projects, you'll find them given there. Here we have attempted to point out to you through Peter's cooperation, Zachary's, Paul's, Wilbur's, David's (and all of the others whom you know of at present and some whom you don't) ... they have all contributed this to you.

It's your job now to put this together, to parallel it in your daily life; to think about these things softly, gently, in the back of your consciousness... like you have been doing.

The easiest way to gain spiritual acceptance is to take several moments to move into a deep state of meditation or prayer, to find the center of that within you, and to accept it, fully, completely. Certainly, ego will chastise you. Habit, dictums, theology, and other things will criticize you if you come forth making proclamations. However, if you come forth bearing that light and demonstrate it, and let it be exemplified in your actions, words, and deeds, any chastisement that comes to you will be as emptiness, words upon the wind. And the truth will be borne forth in your actions.

Don't cast off the ego. It's an important part of who and what you are. It's a part of the energy, the force, of this lifetime. It deserves a certain degree of honor. But it also deserves to be dealt with with balance, and that balance pointing out that this is the continuum of the growth of the ego and but one step along the way. Some egos have great trouble in dealing with that. Others find comfort and joy in realizing it. Work with that for a time. See?

Talents are, in essence, looked upon here merely as tools. Then, if you are about to take upon yourself an incarnation as a woodcarver, it would be appropriate for you to be skilled with your hands, rather than to have an intimate working knowledge of, let's say, algebraic calculations or musical notes, or some such as this.

Conversely, if you were seeking to incarnate into an area of philosophers, of thinkers, of statisticians, it would be well for you to have mental acuity. And secondly, or thirdly, were you to enter with the intent to bring music and sound as joy or healing for others, some basic intuitive awareness of the music of the spheres, the rhythm of spirit, that would be good. And those would be the talents. See?

Choices predicate talents, in the sense that talents are tools chosen by the entity selecting the incarnation. The second female entity was by choice as a gift, not as a need. As such, then, the second entity provided a temporary sense of polarity balance for Peter in the early stages. Note this has become no longer necessary, as Peter has regained his own innate balance. Follow that? If not, ask further on it.

The purpose and function of Peter's most recent incarnation were for the acquisition of balance and harmony ... sort of a polishing-off incarnation. No singular mission, save that of works with Abe and several others were noted here. His records indicate that this was a preparatory incarnation and that it was of primary importance as a balancing or a completing incarnation. This is not to presume or preclude the possibility that he may return, for he could re-enter the Earth at a much higher cycle and continue on, if he wishes.

The collage of consciousness that exists within you is unlimited. Then, each of the entities (Zachary, Peter, Paul, David, Wilbur, and many other) do, in fact, exist within you as potentials, as alternatives.

The qualities that one finds, good and/or bad, in others are, without question, also found within self. The difference here is the emphasis. One soul may have a desire for personal accomplishment, and another may consider that to be insignificant. The one who has the great desire may create a barrier towards the attainment of that because of their intense need of it, while the other who has no great need for it may find it coming to the surface easily. Need often is tempered by qualities of intensity.

If you wish to create a cloak, then create it joyfully. But if you are obsessed with having a cloakroom full of a myriad of cloaks, you'll have some difficulty, we are most certain. (Given with considerable humor here.) See?

What you strive to do, then, is to bring the best qualities of Zachary, of Peter, of Paul, of David, of Wilbur, forth in the combined sense within yourself. Look for the best in all and attempt to emulate that, the good qualities, in all that you do.

Indeed, with your hosting of the guest, this is the example where you attempt to understand and convey different perspectives, different outlooks or alternatives as relate to ways of life. These are very important. We cannot emphasize to you just how important. You must be capable of interacting with all entities beneath your level without them disrupting you or drawing you through emotional entanglements firmly into their realm. See? Part of what Peter recently learned, if you'll recall, dealing with that. See?

We do very often speak directly to the soul of the inquirer, the entity from whom the question originates. We do most often have the involvement of all of your souls in many of the works here. Certainly, some to greater or lesser degree of awareness, and dependent upon the interests, the works, the ideal, the purposes, the goals, of each of you, you'll have greater or lesser interest in varying points of experience.

Therefore, we speak to whomever is at hand in the fullness of the consciousness, or directly to the soul of the entity who has inquired. Once you ask, you have opened a portal for us to answer directly to your soul, your spirit in the more appropriate terminology. See? No, not just rhetorical commentary. See?

The relationship between our friends, our colleagues, with Peter and those of Tobar and those of the Voyagers is profound, as you have intuited. It has to do with the bringing forth of a consciousness which has to do with the awakening of the true spirit of man while he is yet incarnated in the Earth. It is probable that this will be aided by the forces of the spirit of the Christ or by the Master Himself in a time just ahead. But this we cannot foretell with specific time, as you measure it, for it would not be ours to identify here, at any rate. But the purpose has to do with this, see ... the bringing forth of consciousness of the Light.

Yes, it is possible for you to live more than one existence simultaneously, but it is not the norm, particularly for those souls, those entities, involved with the Earth. It is possible for you to be conscious on multiple levels, and this occurs with frequency, particularly among those who are seeking and particularly among your grouping. The consciousness arises through actions of prayer, of meditation, and intent. Once you intend something, then you have but only to bring it into reality, to experience it, to actualize it, to materialize it. See?

Like-minded groups can have a dramatic impact upon the overall world-thought. The way this is accomplished, first and foremost, is for the individuals and the groupings to learn how to identify themselves in terms of their unlimited nature, then to become accomplished in the, what we'll call, workings of their tools, their mechanisms, and to ultimately work together towards a common thought-form. And this must be (and here's the key)... this must be without reservation.

In other words, the grouping as it gathers would be better to be of lesser number than to be weak in the strength of its conviction. For one of doubt or weakness or uncertainty weakens the whole lot. Just as the little leavens the lot. See? So it's important that you are unified, that you are consistent in your application, your belief, your dedication, and that you apply this in accordance with your known conviction of the Law and of your potential. And it goes without saying, we should think, that that conviction needs to be as firm, as hard, and as clear as possible.

It *is* possible for you to co-create such an idea with God and not violate Universal Law, for God has offered you, and still does, the Law of Grace.

The preservation of the right of other entities' Free Will can come about in a multiple fashion. Some alternatives you would not perhaps like to think about, others perhaps you would. For example, souls who do not agree upon the internal mechanism of the primary thought-form in which they exist, have the right to separate.

Witness, then, the example as in the case of the Atlanteans. There developed the two forces, which came into opposition of one another ... both originating as Children of God but seeing certain objectives totally differently. This culminated in the separating of those souls as interacting groups. This separation came about in several ways. One, a great number of those migrated from the Earth, departed not through death, but through their own actions and through their own devices. Other groupings migrated from the Earth through the portal called death. Other entities simply ceased their existence and returned to their originating realms of consciousness from whence they entered. And there were some variations, a few, as you'd call them, odd-balls in the lot (given with a note of loving humor), that were very innovative actually (and we found them very loving and very wonderful souls who would be the first to have humor with us in being called odd-balls).

Nonetheless, you do not violate the Law when you permit the factions to continue their choice of existence, but to do so in a separateness. Now, there's much to this, and it has to do with the approaching times or the present times of the Earth. A decision will need to be made in the Earth (perhaps not fully consciously to most entities, but to some, perhaps such as yourselves) as to whether or not the thought-form will be perpetuated in a cohabitative way striving to work these things out as a collective grouping, or whether each grouping has reached their sufficient point of definition that there no longer can be cohabitation and that the realm must divide itself or that a division or separation must come about.

If the Master enters, He will attempt to bring about a healing. Those of you who are prepared to walk with Him and serve with Him will, of course, attempt that same. Some will choose to assist the Master and then to depart and form their own realm of consciousness ... in your terminology, a.k.a an alternative Earth. We're told here this is quite profound to you in the Earth. Nonetheless, it is the answer to your question. The impact upon other realms would and will be significant, and we'll probably go into that later here. It's too broad, too intense, for the present. More will come on this later.

Learning to overcome challenge, learning to meet it, to draw upon the reserves from within self, spiritually, mentally, emotionally and, as the case might be in the Earth, physically, is indeed of much import. This, then, could be thought of, in essence, as one of *the* major lessons for Peter (in answer to Ken and Nancy's questions). The importance here is recognizing one's own power. See?

You don't easily draw forth your power, your potential, until you have a need, until you are challenged. Thus, Peter is challenged to draw upon himself ... a little here, a little there. Marvelously done by Zachary and Paul and the others, skillfully, wonderfully, lovingly.

It was and is very important for it to come forth ... the perspective on Wilbur. That was very important also. But you are correct, this was the major lesson: to meet, to pass through challenge, to see challenge as only a step-stone, an illusionary creation of a sort, but real to the extent that if you have a limitation that that challenge can get a hold of, you're stuck, and you'll have to go around again and again until you can pass through that and not get stuck. See? (Given in your colloquial terms for both humor and understanding.)

Reuben should, of course, choose where he wishes to start. That would be the best. Remember, he has the highest and best guidance within him. But just to help a bit, we'd encourage him to perhaps begin with those recordings as were made in earlier projects which are for guided meditation and/or for the development of dreams. These will be, then, very helpful tools. And from here we'd move into the experiences of Judith and find that these might be very revealing in terms of understanding his own nature and his power to control his own destiny. All healing begins within self, and usually ends there, too.

In the overall of these questions, then, it's important to remember that much of what you are asking is heard by the universe. And as such, those portions of Peter's experiences as will be useful in exemplifying to you answers to your questions will no doubt be high-lighted by the grouping relaying that information to you.

And so for the present here, then, we shall conclude.

Once again, we thank those who have come forward to assist with this information, and we ask that the blessings of our Father's wisdom, His love and grace, ever guide their footsteps and, as well, yours, dear friends.

And so, for the present, then, we conclude.

Fare thee well, then, dear friends.

Q&A READING #14

Continuation of Questions After Chapter 9:
SPIRITUAL ACCEPTANCE (V-720)

Given December 6, 1990

AL MINER/CHANNEL: *This reading is code number V-741. It is questions and answers #5, and I'm titling this one "Levels and Realms" [aka "Spiritual Acceptance"]. The reason for that is perhaps obvious, that I had quite a number of questions that deal with that or those topics, and so if you've been waiting a little while to hear your question on that topic, that's why. I've combined them here, and this should make for a very, very interesting reading on the topic of different levels and realms of existence.*

QUESTIONS SUBMITTED

(The first question is from David and Leiko in Florida.)
#1 - In V-711, the Lama Sing Group speaks of levels or realms. Lama Sing Group, would you please tell us where you are? Are you in the Godhead? Is that a correct term?

(Next, from Joan in Pennsylvania:)
#2 - Please tell us about the realms beneath us that are impacted by our every thought, conscious and unconscious. I haven't given realms beneath much thought, because I guess I always thought we were the bottom rung of the ladder here on Earth. (That's probably a shared thought, Joan.) Maybe it would give us Voyagers a better perspective on where we really are if you would enlighten us on this.

#3 - Please comment on the difference of energy quality or purity between the Garden plane and the Earth plane. *(From Dave and Leiko.)*

(From Dave in Maryland:)
#4 - On page 15 of the transcript for V-720, Peter inquires about the following: "I would like to know what others do experience and what makes the difference in terms of deciding who experiences what and where." And he comments, "I wish we could know that while we are still in the Earth." Why did the entity with the Book not address and answer these questions in V-730? What are the answers to these questions? *(I wondered about that, too, Dave. I'm glad you asked the question.)*

(From Harold and Linda in Missouri:)
#5 - We assume that Peter, Paul and the others don't exist in physical body. Yet there are continual references to them helping each other up, brushing each other off, touching, et cetera. Please explain. Are Peter, Paul, Zachary and Wilbur a soul group, like the Lama Sing Group, as opposed to being parts of one being who are reuniting? *(And in parentheses, she wrote:)* Disregarding the fact that we are all a part of God and working toward that reunification. *(Well now, you know, those are really fascinating questions, and I totally overlooked that, and I'm glad you didn't.)*

(From Dorothy in California:)
#6 - Explain the thought-form system of the Earth itself, and compare it to thought-forms in other realms. What is the "overriding thought-form which enables the existence of the Earth"? *(And that's from V-651.)* How can we as Voyagers use ideas given to us in the Voyager projects to tip the scale of balance in the Earth so that the positive power in the Earth becomes the greater and that illusion, separateness, and thought-forms of habit can be seen and known for what they are?

(Another one of our deep thinkers, Dorothy, also sent this question in.)

#7 - David said to Peter in V-710 that he would be giving his finished crystal to one or two other workers, who would work in conjunction with healers or practitioners in the Earth. Please elaborate. How is this process possible? Will the recipients in Earth be Voyagers? If so, who?

(From Vic and Lita in Virginia, also having to do with crystals, Vic writes:)

#8 - When I heard the legend of the stones of Tobar, I had a dream with a crystal stone. Subsequently, thanks to Lama Sing, I got interested in healing. Now, with the experience of David and the work that he is doing, I am wanting to get my stone as to strengthen my healing work. *(I may have mis-typed that here. I believe he wrote that he had a dream prior to hearing the legend of the stones of Tobar by several days, and that had quite an impact on him when, after just having had that dream about the crystal, here comes the Stones of Tobar tape, which deals with nothing but crystals primarily.)*

(And a real eye-opening question that really wasn't a question, but more of a statement, from Joan in Pennsylvania, and I thought I'd include it here just in case Lama Sing had some comment. She wrote:)

#9 - I finally realized that Peter needs training to become a guide. I think I thought all you had to do was pass over into a realm like the Garden, and you automatically "knew."

The statement on the last tape about being able to handle the various emotional states of the person they were guiding really hit a "yes" response within me. It's similar to here in the Earth. If you've had similar experience as your friend or client, you can relate to them and help them better than if you have no idea of how they're feeling. But also, you have to allow them to explore their emotions and feelings without you falling into them along with them.

When I work with a person, I always try to create a feeling of safety for them, where they are comfortable to "let go." Even doing a massage, it's important, once you make contact with the body, not to let go. It creates safety. *(That's a fascinating point.)* Just like Paul and Zack for

Peter. I hope we get back to Wilbur and David sometime, too. For some reason I feel very connected to David. Isn't that funny? Of all the people we've met on the voyage, I feel drawn to David. Like to know more about him. *(Well, Joan, you obviously, by this time, after hearing V-740, know a little bit more about him, and I suspect we are about to know a lot more about him, and I do think that's funny that you should have been drawn to him. Sounds like he's somebody really unique, and I'll be interested in hearing more about him, too.)*

And so, Father, I present these questions prayerfully now to You, asking as I do that You would guide us to the highest and best possible information that can be given. Once again I ask for special prayers of healing for all of the Voyagers and all of the other people who have asked for our prayers (and there are so many I haven't been able to sit down and pull the names and so forth from all the different notes and letters that I have, but I will do that shortly, in order to speak them by name). Thank You, Father, and special prayers and blessings for Peter and Company and, of course, the Lama Sing Grouping and friends. Amen.

THE READING

LAMA SING: Yes, we have the Channel then and, as well, those references which apply to the grouping, the inquiries, and the intents and purposes of this collective work as it is now before us. As we commence herein, we shall first pray in this manner.

Lord God, we know that Thou art ever with us in this and all such works. And thus, it is our prayer that we might herein accomplish Thy will and Thy purpose. We pray further that Thou would grant us the presence of those souls, including the Master, The Christ, so as to illuminate this knowledge, that it might be the more passable, the more understandable, for those souls who shall become aware of same. It is in the name of the Master, The Christ, that we pray on behalf of all those souls in all realms who are presently in some need or in limitation, and for whom there are none offering prayers of enlightenment. We thank Thee, Father, for this opportunity of joyous service in Thy name. Amen.

The information that is about to be presented here in answer to your questions, dear friends, may possibly in some instances be such that you will be much akin to Peter's experiences of reactions, in that your cloaks may crackle, sparkle, and pop here and there, just a bit (given with a note of loving humor). But in recognition of the entities Kendall and Nancy, that's a good growth experience. See?

The relationship to our grouping as called here is one such in accordance with the Universal Law that spans not one realm, but many. Therefore to answer your question, that we exist in this or that realm, even so as a primary realm, would be somewhat misleading ... indeed, perhaps even a misnomer (to coin that phrase) to the extent that we have as a part of our grouping, entities who are in physical body, in the Earth and those who are, as well, a part of or in the presence of the full Consciousness of God.

Therefore, you see, there is no definitive point at which we could state to you that we exist just here and not there. One would imply the exclusion of the other, and we are of sufficient number and consciousness so as to entail the majority of those realms of existence as would be definable to you and have some meaning, and within the grasp of the others that would have no understanding or relationship to your consciousness, due to the lack of knowledge or information about same. See?

For the purposes of a more direct answer to your question, which we know that is what you are seeking: Our primary focus, as you might call it, of consciousness is to Universal Consciousness. While Universal Consciousness exists in one form or another on all levels, it is primarily concentrated near to what we would call the unlimited realms. Therefore, it is considerably beyond the Earth in terms of the informative flow of that consciousness. However, we urge you not to think of that as just one certain sphere off a great distance from the Earth. It is not measured in that sense. In actuality, it is measured in the sense of consciousness, not distance.

Use of the term *the Godhead* is a correct term in terms of understanding of some theosophical and some doctrines, and we would find it acceptable here, as we interpret it to mean the focal point of consciousness wherein one would find utterly pure existence of God. There are those in our grouping who do primarily reside therein. Though these, we might add, are not constantly among us, their spirit is projected within our grouping at all times, moreso as the overseer, the oversoul. See?

Within your realm, you consider there to be many different groupings of individuals in terms of consciousness, in terms of purpose and/or goals. As you move from continent to continent and province to province, you find this increasingly so. Delineated by an imaginary line drawn upon some chart or map or whatnot, one can find on the one side abundance, a minimal quantity of dis-ease (in the physical sense, at least), and some considerable advancement in terms of what's called the mental or intellectual. And yet, a mere handful of meters to the other side of that imaginary line, the complete opposite can exist... poverty, lack of knowledge, dis-ease, famine, pestilence, and all that sort.

Howbeit, then, that mankind cannot conceive of other realms just a hair's-breadth away from their own, when such can exist in the (quote) "reality" (end quote) of the Earth? Does that make the meaning clear? Good.

Then consider this: The Earth plane is builded upon a foundation of sorts. That foundation is derived from basic instincts. Those basic instincts derive themselves in the present not only from the historical growth or evolution of man throughout your recorded history and beyond, but, perhaps interestingly to you, parallel themselves as well from a spiritual history and spiritual geological expression. Wherein, if one were to study and to search, they would find beneath their own realm, other realms, and evidence, quite clearly, of their existence.

Some of these realms are closer to the Earth in terms of their potential of becoming (what you'd consider to be) your spiritual, mental and emotional equal. Some of them are inhabited by entities who have been upon the Earth in physical body and who have moved to these other realms beneath your own, in terms of spiritual acceptance, because of their own choice or because of desire.

Beneath the Earth, in terms of a realm of demarcation, one will find, more often than not, quite consistently, see, that desire is the bond that keeps entities in those realms. Habit, perpetuating those desires, the familiar, the comfortable—

very often the desires are expressed to extreme.

We have spoken in past, as has the Channel, of the Sea of Faces. You have perhaps considered this to be a sphere enveloping the Earth whereupon one might think, no matter they would go, moving away from the Earth, they must pass through this realm. That is quite accurate, but also understand that these in the Sea of Faces also have their own realms. If you would think of them then, in the graphic depictation, as being the underpinnings of the Earth, wherein they exist beneath you in the sense that yours is a certain level of spiritual acceptance, and theirs is just so another, and beneath them another, and beneath them another, and so forth.

We know you will, as you hear this, want examples. What are they like? What happens there? Who's there? Why? True? Not much different than Peter, eh wot?

Here's a realm which underlies the Earth in terms of spiritual acceptance. It is very dark, brownish in color, and it has very bestial energies. The energies are very much those of survival and aggression. An entity who exists here exists in this realm by choice, primarily, and one of those factors that might predicate that choice is severe aggression. It is not the norm for an entity to continue to exist in this realm for prolonged periods of time. Usually, those who are in these realms are here because of some specific need to balance a certain trait or characteristic. There are exceptions, and there are those entities who stubbornly continue to dwell here.

As above, so below ... Well then, where there are those fuels of thought-forms that precipitate down to these realms, these are substances from which these entities can perpetuate their realm. To a degree, then, they are somewhat dependent upon those of you in the Earth for their existence. We state that to you because in the forefront of the entities in this realm is very limited thinking and, therefore, the creation of a thought-form is not, as such, exemplified in the same way as in the Earth, but rather from the emotive level.

In other words, that makes a distinguishment between the

mental and the emotional. In the Earth plane, you are controlling your thinking, your emotion, based upon experience and knowledge. As you gain more information, you more or less correlate this all together, and it forms a collage of who and what you are. In this realm, much of the salient qualities of that result are filtered out by the intervening veils. And as such then, this realm receives only those things as are of aggression and primordial or bestial intent.

It should be noted here that while there are multiple entities and one might attack another brutally, in short order the victim arises completely well, and the whole fracas starts again, over and over. They steal from one another, they covet, they lay in waiting to attack one another, first one, then the other, and so it goes, until such time as one of them might call out to be free, at which point they are guided upwards. All of your thoughts, then, are like fodder, like nourishment. The greater is your hostility, your animosity, your aggression, your hatred, the greater is the power of their realm. When that is severed between your realm and theirs, they will have to draw upon the resources that are within themselves. While this will, under Universal Law, be guaranteed or assured of a continuum of existence, it will require an effort on their part to so do.

Your prayers and your efforts to purify the overriding thought-form of your realm, as you can see from this commentary, can do much to help those beneath you. You are the light above the realms beneath you, just as perhaps you might see Zachary and Paul as lights in realms above you. If they were angry and spiteful and coveted things, that would be the light emanating to you.

One of the difficulties that has been experienced in these lower or lesser realms in the recent time of the Earth has been the abandonment of conscious thought on the part of many entities, through various mechanisms or means. What you call narcotics or drugs is one of the major culprits here. It is providing great quantities of energy, raw energy, for these entities and those in the Sea of Faces collectively, to, in essence, nourish themselves, to fortify, to strengthen, to broaden their realm. It is not unlike, in a microcosmic sense, a repetition of the Atlantean times. Good parallels could be drawn here.

So while you are thinking of serving those in your realm, each time you serve one in your realm, you have perhaps served ten or twenty in realms beneath you, as called, also, the Sea of Faces. If one cannot find the satiation of their desire or needs, they must then look to another work, another focus. See? Or at least come to understand what it is, and then perpetuate it themselves, if that is their choice. See?

The difference between the Garden plane and the Earth plane has much to do with the spiritual acceptance of the entities who perpetuate or inhabit same. In the Garden Realm the entities are of like mind and consciousness and are in spiritual control of themselves to the degree that they are capable of sustaining easily the thought-form of the Garden. In other words, they are literally creating it as a part or an extension of their being (*they* being also entities who are now in other realms). Some of you Voyagers, in fact, are contributing to the Garden Realm. Now that you all know about it, you are all contributing to it to some extent. Because you know of it, you have visualized it, and some of you have actually visited it. See?

Knowledge of and awareness of and acceptance of gives strength to reality. When there is agreement in a common thought, reality is created. Because more than one agrees that it is real, it is accepted. So the difference, then, is the level of agreement, the cohesive agreement or cooperation between the entities in the Earth and in the Garden realm. There are less in number in the Garden realm than in the Earth, as might be perhaps obvious to you. But the difference in number isn't as significant as the difference in spiritual acceptance and harmony. You might create a bush in the Garden, and we might come and look upon it and see it as beautiful. Even though it may not be our choice, we see the beauty of the creative power that has brought it into reality. Thus, we are ever providing you with the right to create as is your choice, because we know beforehand that we are of the same spiritual level of acceptance. Therefore, what you do at this highest level of acceptance *must be* in agreement with our own thought and perspective. See?

You experience what you do and where you do to the degree of your acceptance. It's that simple. Now you know that in the Earth. Work to raise your spiritual acceptance, where you can see good and purpose and find understanding in all things and all entities. It doesn't mean that you must be like them, or that you must like their works or their thoughts. But you must be capable of allowing them to exist without becoming entangled in them because of a dislike for this or that. Even though it may not please you or bring you favor in the essence of its expression, you must find the capacity to love it because it is a creation.

Anything that exists, exists through God. Find the God within all existence, and you'll find the answer to your question, David. Others experience to the degree of their ability to accept. Not so much so being chosen to go here or there because they are favored or because of this or that, but because they have learned and earned the right to exist and to experience at this or that level.

Some entities will not arrive at the Garden upon departure from the Earth. And that's not a punishment. That's not depriving them of some beauty. It's because they have chosen to experience something else. From the wisdom of their own soul, they know that another experience is much more beneficial to them than moving into the Garden at that point, even if they were capable of so doing, which of course they would not be. You cannot climb to the top rung of the ladder if you have rungs beneath you missing. There's no place to step. You need all the rungs in place in order to reach the top. Does that help?

The entity did not address and answer these questions at that time for very specific reasons. They were answered to a degree in the interim times from which you had no great detail, unfortunately. But the primary purpose here was and is that Peter will actually begin to experience these things, in most graphic and revealing ways, through his interaction with Wilbur and through some experiences that will be shared as the result of his efforts to re-awaken his old friend. See?

There are several answers to your question, entities Harold and Linda (and we are joyful that you are feeling better in the Earth) ... God answers *all* prayers. See? You do not need a physical body to touch, to interact, as you would think only physical bodies can. If you cross two beams of light, there is a reaction. If you direct two electrical currents towards one another, there is a reaction, an intersect, an occurrence.

And so, then, presume for a moment that you are an illuminated electromagnetic expression. These are concentrated fields circulating around and about the core, which is the essence of that entity or that soul. For purposes of what we'll call transitional smoothness (with a note of loving humor amongst our grouping here), the expression in physical form is maintained or sustained well beyond the Earth.

The purpose for this is perhaps quite straightforward to your mind. Some entities, upon making transition, having a great deal of difficulty relating to an orb of light. Even though it may be beautiful and they may feel and experience love and warmth and compassion from it, they cannot interact with it. They become reliant upon the familiar. But when this orb of light is replaced by a radiant form in the outline or physical appearance, as it were, of the Earth, there is an immediate receptiveness, an openness, a desire for communication, an interaction.

We believe that if you remain with us long enough to observe more of Peter's experiences, you will see movement into other forms. You will understand interaction, communication, and other events or normal exchanges between entities when they are in various other expressions or forms, including sound, color, light, and other expressions which you could not understand at the moment without graphic explanation of great length. Peter is somewhat, as you might say in the Earth, destined to move into those higher realms ... and not alone. Then, the interaction between their present forms is every bit the same as interaction between physical forms or physical bodies in the Earth.

When Paul is touched by Zachary, when Zachary is touched by Peter, or the other way around for any of them, they feel, they touch. When you touch someone in the Earth, a handshake for example, do you really touch the entity? That is, do you *know* them? Do you *feel* them? Do you know what they feel? Do you get the essence of them? Or is it automatic? Do you remember if they had a ring on their finger? Which finger? Were their fingers long? Slender?

No, the real body lies beyond the Earth. The physical body is the living temple of the true body. You have the right to create, and in accordance with the primary thought-form of the realms beyond, that body or those forms are agreed upon. And so it is for the moment here in the Garden. See?

Peter, Paul, Zachary, and Wilbur are a part of a grouping. This we believe you already have knowledge of. They are not essentially as parts of one entity who are re-uniting. With your disclaimer, the last sentence, duly noted. See?

Thought-forms ... Again, we have defined these (we believe) above. The positive power of the Earth can become greater as those who make up the sum and substance or the composite of the Earth use that positive power. If the focus is upon illusion, separateness, and thought-forms of habit, then they are given strength through the supply of energy given to same. When you shift the direction of the flow of that power, the primal power from within, you are granting the objective of that focus, that power.

It's sort of like having two or three gardens, each of them requiring watering every day. If you suddenly decide you don't like the crop in one garden and you stop watering it, eventually it will go dormant and all that will remain are seeds waiting for someone else to water, while the gardens that you do water now will flourish because they are receiving even more nourishing water. Water representing spirit, and the action of watering representing, then, conformance to Universal Law, the action of expending spiritual force or power. See?

Where one puts forth power, power must return. If one puts forth power into a garden full of weeds, the harvest is weeds. The lower realms receive the harvest in accordance with their choice. If you don't supply them anything in your harvest that is of their choice, they'll have to grow their own weeds. And that's a colloquial play on words, based upon your current terminology or slang in the Earth.

So then, entity Dorothy, continue doing what you're doing, and work for the time when you can unify and diversify, incorporating all of the modalities as you are studying them at present, as you have just finished talking about them with your group. It's not one power broken into many fragments. It's many fragments waiting to be assembled into one power.

We're also told here to tell you, you have seen the fruits of your own labor and the labor of the Voyagers and others. Hold true your faith unto that, and believe that what you are doing is sowing seeds of good fruit. These will be harvested, have no doubt of that.

We are striving in the moment of pause here to comprehend the meaning of the question, also from our good friend Dorothy, with regard to the crystals …

Very well. We believe we have the reference indicated

and as you intend: It is possible for you and any of the other Voyagers to work with the crystal workers and to work with those who are the recipients of David's work. This is not a complex matter. First, you must create the thought-form, remember? You must begin with an intent. You must form it. Go within, and create the blueprint. Then come forward into consciousness and make it real. Bring it forth.

Now, we do not mean that you must defy your laws of physics or that you must become a magician (although this is entirely possible) but we are speaking first in the spiritual, the mental, and the emotional. These are your greater tools of power. They are within your right of free will. Because you are an individual, you have the right to command and control these. Anything that falls within that spectrum in your life or in your life's consciousness must then be within your control as an individual.

Where that would then intersect with the consciousness of others, if they are in agreement, it also applies there. And it is through that mechanism, then, that crystals can be used, for example by the crystal-workers and you in conjunction, because your willingness on the part of all involved to accept this ... that forms the pathway, that forms the conduit, the channel of blessings. See?

The process will also be revealed just ahead in greater depth, as we believe Peter will decide or discover to use this as a part of his mechanism to help Wilbur. We believe that Peter will think about this and come up with the conclusion that the best way to approach Wilbur is on his terms. And so that should make for some interesting discourses for you.

If it doesn't take that turn (which we believe it shall), then you are certainly free to come forward here and inquire further if you wish more specifics. But generally, it has to do with creating a channel. Any thought-form or work which involves a thought-form is supplied by an energy force. When you are of a spiritual acceptance where you can supply that thought-form from the eternal source within you, its existence is sustained with little or no effort on your part whatsoever. Actually, the only effort required is for somebody to confirm or affirm the existence, and the continued desire for that thing or essence to exist. That's all. See?

Victor, you have had experiences with these stones, these *singing crystals* and other stones such as these in the past. This has been given to you, and, of course, you have knowledge of this. The best of all, though, is to remind you, dear friend, that the true power lies within you; that these are extensions of self, creations through the grace of God and, as such, are amplifiers. They have the quality of amplifying, modifying, and toning or adjusting. This they have naturally. But the power of God within you is their true source of power. See?

Finally, let us point to the very outstanding realization by the entity Joan: It is not so much so that one becomes trained, or that one is appointed, or that one is glorified to become a guide, or a teacher, or what not; it is that one has agreed to accept that as a work, as a focal point of their effort.

In order to reach that point, then, they must be capable of passing up and down (given in a graphic term, not necessarily literally), or passing into and out of, any of the realms which are up to that point of spiritual acceptance. If they cannot do so, and they continue forth attempting to be a guide, a mentor, a teacher, or what not, and they enter into one of the lesser realms and become entangled in something there, they may have difficulty in getting out of the realm. It is for this reason that Zachary provided Peter his cloak. It is for that reason that Paul observed Peter at all times, providing his own energy, his own spiritual consciousness, when needed.

But now we wish to point out to you a subtle difference that you may not have noticed. Peter is now in Wilbur's realm without Zachary's cloak. Not even Peter has realized this, as yet. And he's functioning quite well, doing very nicely, and we believe he will continue to do so, at least to a point. And that will be another test, another opportunity of growth for him. We don't believe it will throw him back into what has been lovingly titled from our colleagues in the Earth the *Realm of Laughter*, but that's not certain here, as yet.

Of interest to all of you in terms of the questions as they were stated above are these several points: Consciousness, generally, is the deciding factor as to where one is capable of dwelling. Desire is a qualifying factor that usually is the last decisive factor in determining where that entity actually dwells. Spiritual acceptance is the upper limit, and anything from ... If you called spiritual acceptance A, and Z being the lowest level, anything between A and Z that entity should be capable of passing into and out of without being stuck or tangled therein. See?

When you reach the point wherein you can arrive at what we'll call universal or God-Consciousness, you have considerable latitude. The potential for you at that point is one of nearly unlimited nature. The factors which determine what limitations, if any, might exist, are those of your soul's individual characteristics and goals.

If you have pledged yourself at the soul level to a certain soul group work, then you will have an affinity to any realms wherein that work exists as a possibility. This is a factor which tends to create lines of demarcation (though not nearly as intensely as in the graphic illustration we gave above, relating to the Earth), but lines of demarcation, nonetheless, which denote soul groupings. Soul groupings, then, are blessings unto a work.

We have been joyful to have been with you once again, and it is our continuing prayer that this information be of light and joy to you all.

Q&A READING #15

Continuation of Questions After Chapter 9:
ONENESS (V-720)

Given December 9, 1990

AL MINER/CHANNEL: *This reading is code number V-742. It is questions and answers #6, and in this reading I have a number of questions which all relate essentially to two topics, the Great Hall and the Entity of Light, who, as you may recall, has to date continually appeared whenever our group entered the Hall.*

I am very excited about these questions. Not that they are particularly better than many of the excellent questions we've received to date, but because I share with those of you who have submitted these questions, and I'm sure with all the Voyagers, a very strong interest in both the Great Hall and the Entity of Light. And I will be very interested in hearing this reading myself.

QUESTIONS SUBMITTED

(The first question comes from Dave in Maryland, and Dave asks a question that I think is probably one that's rolling around in the minds of all of us.)

#1 - Why doesn't Zachary or Paul explain more about the Entity of Light? Why doesn't anyone give him or her a name?

(Next, from Maria in Washington state:)

#2 - Regarding the Entity in the Great Hall, I had a meditation where there was an orb of light out of which appeared Mother Mary giving a blessing. After some time she faded away in the same orb of light. Can this be compared to the experience of Zack, Peter and Paul with the Entity in the Great Hall? Is this entity a guide to Paul and Zack?

(Somewhat in that same vein, I received this from Vic and Lunita in Virginia:)
#3 - About one week before I got the tape, I had a dream with a being that had the same characteristics as the one in the Great Hall in Peter's graduation. The intensity of the eyes seemed to say everything. I was elated with the dream, and I find it's quite synchronistic that a similar event is taking place there. What is the meaning of my dream, and is there a connection to the events there? What is the name of my being? I want to stay in touch. How can I connect again?

(Interesting, isn't it, that we've had several now who have experienced this same situation? Let me go on.)

(From Harold and Linda in Missouri:)
#4 - Why did the Entity of Wisdom tell Peter that there was never any need for apology? Isn't apologizing or attempting to rectify something which we have done to hurt another a step in the healing process?

(Next, from Ken and Nancy in North Carolina:)
#5 - When Peter faces the overwhelming light from the keeper of his record, does this condition him to withstand higher vibrations? Move to higher planes? Is it like having an entity go to a sauna in which the temperature gets turned up every time they enter it until the entity can withstand a temperature that they could not initially tolerate?

(Also from Ken and Nancy:)
#6 - Who is the keeper of Peter's records? This entity seems so lofty and bright. Is this Jesus? Peter's soul? Or perhaps one of many guides who are very accepting of the light? Has the keeper been with Peter for many lifetimes or just this one? In Earthly literature in which near-death experiences are described, the entity who has died usually reviews his Earthly life in the presence of a glowing being, who is often identified as Jesus. Would this likely be Jesus? Or the keeper of the entity's records?

(From David and Leiko in Florida:)

#7 - If the entity in the Great Hall is the same entity we know as Jesus and called Master, are there any more Masters like Jesus? Please explain the verse in the Gospel of John referencing the "only begotten Son." If there are many more Masters, does each Master specialize or emphasize different virtues, such as compassion, wisdom, et cetera? In V-730, when Peter, Paul and Zack get ready to go to the Great Hall, they hear musical sound and see the golden white light, and then seem to be transported in the light to the Great Hall. This is different from their first visit to the Great Hall. Does this have to do with Peter's level of spiritual acceptance? Please tell us more about the sound and golden white light.

(Also from David and Leiko:)

#8 - In V-730, Peter endured to complete this meeting. Does this imply a control of the emotions, or the avoidance of being overwhelmed or exhausted by the experience? Would it be useful to give us an example of this in the Earth?

(And lastly, from Harold and Linda in Missouri:)

#9 - I was really touched by the questions for Peter's reflection which Lama Sing posed at the end of V-740, as they are questions which I face daily as I do therapy. I'm looking forward to the answers. *(Harold and Linda are both very active in counseling in Missouri. They have several offices. And I'm sure that the answer will be very contributive to that work, or their work. But beyond that I'm certain that we all look forward to further commentary and information on the procedure that will be chosen. I know I have questioned in my own mind how I would go about working with Wilbur, and I'll admit to being just a little bit stumped as to where I'd start.)*

At any rate, I would like to add another question here of my own. I note in all of the questions that I've just read above, there's a very intense interest in the coming forth of an entity of light. My question is simply this:

#10 - Were it to be any of us Voyagers who were in Pe-

ter's shoes, if he has any shoes, would the Entity of Light have been any different than it was and is for Peter? And if so, please explain why it would be different and what we can do to get the same entity when we do move into other realms, leave the Earth. Tell us what we can do now in this lifetime while we're still here to sort of qualify or collect enough spiritual points ... you know, to qualify (given with a note of loving humor).

And so now, Father, we turn these questions all prayerfully over to You, asking as we do that You would guide us to the highest and best possible information. I would once again ask for the highest and best prayers for all those Voyagers in need, and all souls in all realms who are in need, and for the Earth in general, that we might have peace and health and happiness, universally. Special blessings and prayers for Peter and company, and for all those loving souls who have been helping us to get this information, not the least of which, the Lama Sing Group. Thank You, Father. Amen.

THE READING

LAMA SING: Yes, we have the Channel, then, and, as well, those references which apply to the questions, those inquiring minds as presented same, the ideal, purposes and goals of this work, and those of the intents and purposes of the soul grouping involved with same. As we commence with this work, we shall first pray in this manner:

Lord God, we know that Thou art ever with us in all that we do. And thus, it is our prayer that we might herein invoke the presence of Thy spirit, completing then Thy will and Thy purpose. We pray further on behalf of all those souls in all realms who are presently in some need and for whom there are none in joyous prayer. We offer a special prayer on behalf of all those in the Voyager grouping and others who have requested same through this, our Channel. We thank Thee, Father, in humbleness and joy for this opportunity of service in Your name. Amen.

It has been to the present the choice and intent of the Entity of Light that Peter shall, rather than have a prolonged explanation, have the better choice of experiencing and evolving his own consciousness as to the Entity of Light, his nature, his involvement with this grouping. And specifically for the present with Peter, and thereafter, that a name might come forth.

For the present, you might consider him to be a part of that Consciousness which is generally associated with the Christ Consciousness, and therefore to consider the entity an expression of the Christ.

The meditation which you experienced was and is of the

same nature, the same source, which is essentially (perhaps curiously to you) through Universal Law. Universal Law provides for the flow of consciousness of all souls to be given special blessings here and there in accordance with what's called the Law of Grace. The Law of Grace, then, enables any soul to reach beyond themselves and their environ – and even, to some extent, beyond their own capacity or level of spirituality – to bring forth into their life, their work, their need, that of the highest and best. And so you could consider, entity Maria, that the entity is indeed to be compared with the Entity of Light and to be considered of that same source.

The entity is, to answer the second portion of your question, indeed a guide to Paul and Zachary, and also to Peter and Wilbur ... the latter, to know less of this for the present but will know more of it in times just ahead.

In the dream you had, entity Victor, there was no idle chance that this occurred, as you called it, *synchronistically*. But rather, just the same as with the entity Maria, that in these times there could come forth the establishment of greater consciousness for those of you who would seek it and who are willing to receive same.

For both of you, Maria and Victor (and all of you, dear friends), this is a time of particular emphasis for you to look beyond that which is the daily happenstance in your life; to look beyond that which has become the familiar, the comfortable; and to go into that which is perhaps the new perspective, the new venture to allow yourself greater latitude in order that you can perceive as broadly and as clearly as possible.

In both of your cases, this involves, to a degree, your works. For Maria's, this is well-defined and of a nature which is apparent to her. For Victor, it may perhaps seem a bit less defined at the present, but the definition is clearly, as we see it, growing with every moment.

For all of the rest of you who have not been identified here specifically by name, but could be, suffice it to state to you that the same applies in every aspect. That each of you, as you have joined together as a grouping, have formed in essence a greater thought-form which now is looked upon from these realms essentially as a soul grouping. And as such, the intent of your minds and hearts contributes to the essence of that thought-form, that ideal, that purpose. And so, in all that you do, expect a miracle. Expect there to be answers to your prayers, solutions to the problems that seem to be insoluble.

The power of God is within you. The bringing forth of this power ofttimes is in the form of challenge, of obstacle, of hardship but it needn't be this way.

But the essence of this as a challenge in the Earth (to answer some questions which haven't been spoken above) is that these are the familiar: these are the customary, the tradition, the expected in the Earth. But once you claim your own personal power, once you have gained the victory of ownership, once you have claimed your soul heritage, all of these things and more can you easily do. See? These words are only the repetition of words given to you long ago, and frequently, perhaps even just this Earth day in another form.

The choice is, then, whether or not one is willing and receptive. Those are the keys. And you will see this in very clear evidence as Peter and company continue in their efforts and experiences with Wilbur, and other events which are very near at hand and sure to transpire very soon in your time measure.

For you, Victor, and perhaps for all of you, it would be difficult to give you a name for that which is unlimited and eternal. How does one measure and create a finiteness for the infinite? You could not, perhaps, accept that this is or were God. But in every essence, God is within all souls. So therefore, such communication must bear an essence of God's spirit, is it not so?

If you would think, then, of these experiences, and others of you who have had and shall have these, to be that which is the highest and best as you are willing to accept same –

whether that be David, Jesus, Buddha, Krishna, or how so be it – you shall see the face of God. For as many as would look upon God, there shall be an equal number who shall call God by this or that name. Choose that which is of your best choice, but choose the highest and best that you are capable of accepting.

Reconnecting with the source of light or of Consciousness which is of God is not a difficult matter, and therein perhaps lies some complexity. For it is natural for each of you to have such a contact or communication continuously. You will note that when Peter reaches deeply within himself, as he only recently did, he can find the answers to his own questions, even to the point where they become seemingly self-evident, and that this potential will be invoked in Wilbur and in others in times to come, including some of you.

To connect or reconnect, one has only but to create the need, and then take the action. Experience the desire or have the purpose, and then use Universal Law and allow it to come to be. See?

The Entity of Wisdom expressed to Peter that there was never any need for apology because where Peter and the others are dwelling there is no wrongful intent. In other words, what transpires in this realm is the equivalent of the consciousness of all other souls therein… unlike the Earth in many respects, wherein there are entities of many different levels of consciousness, some who are capable of much more awareness than that which accompanies same, and others who have clouded their awareness to the point where it would outwardly seem that they have none.

When one recognizes in the healing process in the Earth that a wrong has been, in essence, committed, it is appropriate to identify this and to answer for it, as you say. It is indeed appropriate as a step in the healing process to recognize that one has been involved in a wrong.

The complexity that often ensues or follows such is that

this can invoke perspectives of guilt. And guilt then triggers an array of memories, of emotions, that can follow one upon the other, so that the act of apologizing triggers memory response of variable length, but often very broad, very deep. This can be, for some entities, so overwhelming that they would rather not perpetuate the relationship than to experience the guilt that results from same.

Conversely, here in Peter's realm, guilt does not exist in the form that you know it. For forgiveness is instantaneous. The Entity of Wisdom intended for Peter to know that before he could express any apology, he had already been forgiven. And Peter bears forth, as such, no memories of guilt. Now that's an important point, perhaps a key one, for Peter's accomplishment of existence in this, the Garden Realm, and his forthcoming, if not present, potential as a guide, and more.

Peter has balanced (if you will recall, in our just-previous meeting, in his last incarnative experience in the Earth) with all of his karma as involves the Earth. In essence, then, his guilt is non-existent. He feels no remorse or bond in the sense that you understand guilt in the Earth. He feels, rather, a sense of peace and joy, and a sense of understanding that not even he has fully comprehended to the present.

To answer your question in another way: An entity in the Earth needs to present before themselves an understanding of the complete array of influences that are involved in a situation that requires healing. In other words, in order for there to be a reaction, there must be predicating actions. Those actions may be justifiable in terms of Earth nomenclature to warrant a reaction on the part of an entity which could create a hurt.

That hurt, then, as it might later grow into hostility or antagonism or whatnot, cannot be just apologized for, for it would be out of balance. The understanding causal effects need to also be understood, for these will surely be met again, and could trigger or create the similar situation. If they do not, and the entity has simply repressed that, this can create an emotional block which will be of even greater complexity to deal with.

Therefore, as one sees pain or suffering or a need for forgiveness, it must begin within that the willingness of self is such that the events which are triggering can be searched out for their root cause, so that such events will not in future be capable of creating the potential and/or power of causing a response or a retaliation; that there is no foundation or substance from which hurt can spring forth again. For what is the difference if an entity speaks out harshly in response to something which has inwardly hurt them or aggravated them? They are responding.

Then there must be a stimuli. See? The source of that stimuli, if it is neutralized in that entity, would simply pass them by. Therefore, disarm the power of the triggering event. (Humbly given, as we perceive same from here.)

You are correct, very accurately so, with regard to the analogy to the sauna. The greater is the experiencing of the, we'll call it, *light or energy*, the greater is the capacity of self to dwell therein. And that's an important discovery, as well.

For the more one has built the capacity to, we'll call it *be pure*, the greater is one's potential for dwelling in what's called a *pure realm*. Whether that be a pure realm of music, of light, of love, of compassion, of wisdom, or whatnot, the essence of self contains an array generally of vibrational frequencies, thought-forms, memories, hopes, loves, fears, and whatnot.

But all of these circulate more or less as molecules or particles around, orbitally speaking, a central core. The central core is the source of life-force for all else. As an entity moves to a higher realm and experiences an entity whose vibrations, whose light, more closely approximates that of the core light within each soul, the greater is the power or radiative effect or field effect of that light thereafter. Only the free will of the entity involved can thereafter reduce this or diminish it. See? So yes, each time they enter into the light, they are capable of dwelling in that light to greater, longer, and more profound depths. Very good insight.

The next questions from Kendall and Nancy were answered to an extent above. But with regard to the near death experiences, we have these comments which have been prepared in answer to the questions: When an entity moves from the physical consciousness of the Earth to the nonphysical, and yet their life-force or the connective cord of light or the golden cord or the silver cord, as called by some, remains intact, they are in a position just the same as entities who are in a full transitional experience, also known as death in the Earth, of considerable potential. And, paradoxically, where there is potential there is the possibility of an opposite expression: limitation.

The reason for this is quite simple. It has to do with polarity. When one reaches a point of transition, the intensification (speaking field-wise, in terms of molecular physics) is accelerated. The preponderance of force, then, is concentrated into the more pure forms of singular polarity. You might consider this one hundred percent positive/one hundred percent negative, so that there is perfect polarized balance, whereas, in the Earth there might be 60/30 or 60/35 or 47/53, or 40-/0, with some portion disseminated in complex matters, and all that sort.

But at the point of transition, the polarized effect is amplified and created in a state of considerable balance. Thus, the presence of an Entity of Light comes forth for the preservation of the souls involved. In what you call an NDE, or a near death experience, this is particularly important because the entity is at a transitional point of choice. Were there to be disturbing influences which were less than the spiritual intent of that soul, these could, conceivably, corrupt the balance of that entity to the point where they would be disrupted in the Earth. A similar effect occurs to an entity who has taken excessive chemical or alcohol or narcotic, to the extent that they have lost their polarized balance as their singular identity, have left their body consciousness, and are vulnerable to the extent that they have not even consciousness astrally or spiritually in the nonphysical expression. They are then subjected, under Universal Law, to an array of forces.

But in the near-death experience, they are governed by Universal Law, in that that experience is assured in the law of, we'll call it *uniqueness* ... that their unique soul is assured of its uniqueness when they are in a situation that is beyond their individual consciousness in the sense of singular control over the environ. We know this is a bit complex for some, and for others there are, or will be, thoughts wishing for even greater detail. So we are attempting to walk a somewhat moderate point of balance between those two extremes (given with a note of loving humor).

In essence, then, at the near-death experience, God's grace preserves the right of each soul to continue its uniqueness, and prevents interference by those in other realms who might have less than spiritual intent for that soul. Therefore, the keeper of that entity's records illuminates the path. And illumination, as you will recall, prevents there from being any lesser vibratory energies from being expressed. This is afforded through what's called the *soul consciousness,* or to some, the *Christ Consciousness.* And therefore, the entity is perceived in the expression of the Christ, or more accurately, in the Christ Consciousness.

There may also be the appearance of those family members who have gone before, illuminated by the Christ Consciousness, with the spirit of the Christ within them awakened sufficiently that the Christ is expressed through them in that time. In some instances, the Christ may also appear or may be the appearance, may be that light. To the extent of the consciousness of the entity then, the above would be qualified accordingly. We trust that is sufficient to answer the nature of the intent here. See?

So the entity very well may be the Master, the entity known to you as Jesus, or may be in the light of the Christ Consciousness as the keeper of that entity's records—at that point, the highest and best for that entity. See?

There are other Masters. This is certain. There is one Christ Consciousness, and that is within all souls. Jesus the Christ is also a singular consciousness in the sense that you would know the man Jesus. And you would also know the man Jesus to be Jesus the Christ.

The *nature* of the Christ is, as such, your oneness with God, the spirit of God as it is formed in the individual expression of you. In this case, the question relates to the entities David and Leiko. That Consciousness, then, is the Christ Consciousness, expressed as David and Leiko in the form of the Christ Consciousness in the Earth. It may be difficult for you to accept that you are such, but the moreso you accept this, the greater is the true potential of the individual nature of your soul to reach its fullness.

The complexity of ego, the complexity of what you might face were you to attempt to express this to others, is unimportant here. Why? Quite simply this: When you reach that level which is the full potential of your soul, or you are within the Christ Consciousness as the Master Himself demonstrated for you in the Earth, these things cannot exist. For the righteousness of the full right of God will be focused upon you, and the ego will become one with God and will knoweth itself as His.

Therefore and thereafter, all that you do will be in God's light, and you will do so guided by way of God's wisdom. These things, then, are only the challenges you are meeting (speaking of the ego or doubts and fears) which are there to strengthen you, for each time you overcome one of these, the light of your own soul becomes that much brighter. See?

In the form of the Gospel of John, each can take as they

see or hear. And we would encourage each of you to do so, and not consider our words to be greater nor lesser than your own thoughts or the words of others. All perspectives of God are to be considered, here at least, with equal honor, and no one would find fault in them. Therefore, we offer you these comments in that same vein:

In that time in the Earth, the light of God was upon the man called Jesus. And as such, the soul of the entity known as Jesus had reached the point so as to be capable of claiming His heritage. This soul was singular in the Earth at that time, in that realm and, therefore, appropriately, was identified as such. In other words (quote) "the only begotten Son" (end quote).

A soul who is considered a master or an elder or one of light, from here is looked upon to be, in essence, unlimited. Such souls are given to certain works in accordance with the joy that they find in doing them. This brings forth an array, a collage, of wondrously beautiful talents and abilities which are, to a degree, unique unto that soul, just as that soul is unique unto God. And therefore, you may find, indeed, that a Master may specialize or emphasize certain virtues or qualities or essences, but is never limited to same. It is like a musician skilled in the Earth, who favors a certain composer, and because of the love for that composer's works, plays them resplendently. See? It's like that.

The greater Peter's acceptance and the more exposure that Peter has to and/or with the Entity of Light, the greater shall become his capacity of movement within and about that level of consciousness. Just as the entity Kendall and Nancy discovered in their comments or inquiries above, so it is the same for this question. And the moreso Peter works within that capacity and develops a greater and greater acceptance of it, the more easily may he find movement to and fro from the Great Hall and the Entity of Light. Indeed, even more than this will become his potential.

The sound and golden white light, as it has been called, are, in essence, the precursors or that which goes before the appearance of that vibrational level of spiritual acceptance. We offer to you our (with a note of loving humor) apologies that we have not sufficiently defined terms here before us to allow for full expression of the thought-form to answer your question, entity David.

But, in essence, the sound and golden-white light are more or less qualities that come from that level of spirituality. You will find that each level, each realm of consciousness, tends to have its own particular hallmark or qualifying precursors. Just as the group or groups in North Carolina have discovered, to some extent, the different colors, the different essences: in some cases odors, in some cases feelings, vibrations, colors, sounds, lights, so forth, all tend to typify the nature of a certain realm of expression. Color and light are the more predominant essences which are immediately available for discernment of who you are dealing with and where you are. See?

In completing an exchange with the Light, in doing or sustaining or maintaining control, much is accomplished. Just as you would exercise in a certain way to prepare for performance of a task requiring unique muscular structure or coordination, so then mentally do you prepare to accomplish certain works, and so forth. So in the spirit, then. So as you are capable of clearing your mind, your heart, your consciousness at the soul level that you can continue to exist and perform an exchange between that higher level and yourself, the greater is your capacity to work within that realm. It has to do with acceptance.

To give you an example of this in the Earth beyond what we just did: Understand that as you look for some way to prepare for a goal, an objective, or a need which lies ahead, and as you find that each time you have that particular need in the Earth, certain preparatory steps enable you to accomplish it with greater and greater ease, then do the same spiritually. If you would envision those sounds and that light, and you would reach towards it, attempting to surround or to be a part of it, the greater thereafter becomes your ease and capacity to do just that. And the more you can dwell in that realm, the greater becomes your capacity to awaken your perception and your potential to function in it. It's that simple, that straightforward. See?

We look forward, as well, to the new experiences between Peter and company, and Wilbur and David. And we believe that it is of particular value for each of you to try to sort out in your minds how you would approach Wilbur. Just as the entities Harold and Linda attempt to do so in their daily works, as do many of you.

Preparatory thought-forms are delightfully constructive and helpful. But let them be living thoughts, that they have no limitation, that their parameters are eternal, that you can conform to the need at hand and not be confined by expectation (given with, again, a note of loving humor). But in spite of this, what would you do or say to Wilbur first? See?

The Entity of Light would essentially appear to all of the Voyagers just as he has appeared to Peter. The only differentiation there would be has to do with how some of the Voyagers would perceive the Entity of Light. This has to do moreso with the individual nature of these certain Voyagers and their current expression in the Earth as it relates to, we'll call it *soul group alignment* and purposes.

Since you have come together as a soul grouping, essentially, in the Earth, seeking to expand and broaden your own spiritual perception, you would undoubtedly experience the same as Peter did. In other words, you would perceive the Entity of Light in the Great Hall ... unless you choose not to.

And that's the primary conditioning factor here. It's a matter of choice. Note one quality about Peter which has remained fairly consistent: He has kept himself comparatively open. He has not, in essence, built any confining thought-forms, but he has had many questions.

The questions, then, are a part of the inquiring mind of Peter, a part of the inquisitive nature of his soul. Peter's soul is upon a quest. A quest to know itself. Therefore, many factors that might influence other souls do not in this situation have dramatic impact upon Peter. Peter has aligned himself with his soul's intent, at least for the present.

So, if you are seeking then to perceive the Entity of Light in accordance with the Channel's question above, then you must align yourself with your soul purpose as best you can identify same.

This process, in order that you might prepare for it in the Earth, begins with stopping everything here and there throughout the Earth day, to realign yourself to certain basic principles. Who are you? What are you? Where are you? If you answer, for example, that you are Lois, or that you are Thomas, or that you are Kendall, or whoever among your grouping, then you have defined an expression of your soul.

But the true answer to that "Who are you?" is that you are a Child of God.

"What are you?" You are an expression, a form, of this Child, manifested for the purpose of accomplishing growth, and of contributing work or light or enlightenment to yourself and/or other souls. See?

Finally, "Where are you?" You are in the Earth, but not of it. You are also with God. You are less than the diminishment of an object to finiteness. And yet you are finite in the Earth because you have thrust forth a finger of light from your soul to be focused in the Earth as Lois. See? Therefore, you are. But when you reach beyond this to become the source where you are is in eternity, expressed for a moment, simply pausing upon the pathway of your soul's destiny.

❀   ❀   ❀

Upon that note, then, with some loving humor to the entity Lois in thanks for her volunteering, we now conclude.

May the grace and blessings of our Father's wisdom ever be a lamp to guide your footsteps. Fare thee well, then, for the present, dear friends.

Q&A READING #16

Continuation of Questions After Chapter 10 and 11: ONENESS (V-720)

Given January 25, 1991

AL MINER/CHANNEL: *This reading is code number V-751. It is questions and answers #7 for Voyager project number 7. The questions that I have received for this reading are quite varied and, as always, excellent so I have not really attempted to group them because I found it too difficult, frankly.*

The questions are as follows:

(First of all, interestingly, I received a phone call just perhaps an hour ago from one of the Voyagers and we discussed the following two questions and I felt they were very pertinent and also applicable to all of us at one point or another in our lives.)

QUESTIONS SUBMITTED

The first question is:

#1 - Since Peter is apparently about to become a guide and many of us are "guides" in one form or another here in the Earth (for example, we are guides to our children; we are guides to those who are dependent upon us, and in many other respects we could consider ourselves to be guides of a sort in the Earth), occasionally in the process and in the day-to-day challenges of life here in the Earth, we as guides can often become disappointed with our subjects. The more classic example of this is disappointment, frustration and even anger with trying to guide our children.

This brings up an interesting point. Do our guides, our spiritual guides in other realms, ever get disappointed with us or perhaps even angry, or is it that the relationship is different from ours here in the Earth and the pressures and challenges also different and perhaps they are beyond those expressions? What is the case here?

(The second question is based upon an observation again on the part of our North Carolina Voyagers. I could nickname him "Hawkeye," I think. He spots lots of good stuff!).

#2 - It was noted that in readings frequently (and more frequently, of late) that in the opening prayers of readings the Lama Sing group prays, as they have been for some time, on behalf of all those souls in all realms who haven't got anyone in joyous prayer on their behalf. The new added point to that has been and is, in many cases, that they offer that prayer in another person's name. For example, they might start out like this, "And so, in Charley's name, we pray on behalf of those souls in all realms, etc." Should we here in the Earth, as Voyagers, pray more often in another person's name?

Also, we think we understand what's taking place here, but just in case we don't … Outwardly it's understandable to pray for someone in God's name or Jesus' name or such as that but to pray for someone in Charley's name, that doesn't seem to equate. Our thinking is that the intent is for the prayer and to Universal Law to be returned to the person whose name was mentioned. Is that the case and, if so, should we apply that here in the Earth? What does that do? What is the mechanism here and why is it being done?

(I think that ought to cover it for us, friend Hawkeye.)

(From Dave in Maryland)

#3 - What exactly prevents Peter's family and friends still remaining in the Earth from being able to contact him? It seems as if they have only faith that he is "O.K." Why is it not possible to have more obvious "proof"?

#4 - If Zachary or Paul were to incarnate in the Earth again, after their departure from the Earth through death would they not remember the Garden and have to relearn everything again as Peter is now?

(That's also from Dave)

(From Robin in Florida)
#5 - You have touched upon some of the different levels or planes of existence and consciousness. I would like to know more about vibratory levels here on the Earth. It seems the Earth is such a hodgepodge of different levels of consciousness. Am I correct in assuming that this is usually not the case in other planes of existence, that there is generally more uniformity of consciousness?

#6 - Also, I have changed vibratory levels during this incarnation two times that I am consciously aware of. Is this a common occurrence with the Voyagers here on Earth, with the population here on Earth in general? Are we always consciously aware of this when it happens as I have been those two times? Will I experience this again during this lifetime?

(I might add to that, will the other voyagers experience that in this lifetime?)

(This is from Barry in California and, Barry, this is some questions that I think I misplaced for awhile but fortunately rediscovered them. I apologize).
#7 - When Peter left his physical body he didn't know consciously that he was an eternal being. Like the majority of us here on the Earth plane, he may have hoped he was eternal, he may have believed he was eternal, he may have had faith he was eternal but he didn't know with certainty on a conscious level that he was eternal. Is this a fair assessment of Peter's and everyone else's predicament?

#8 - In Peter's present spiritual body does he know for a certainty he is eternal? When he makes the transition from his current plane to another will he know with complete certainty that he will continue to exist? The way I understand it is this: when one is making a transition out of a physical body there is an element of doubt. But when one is making a transition from a spiritual body into a physical body—or another spiritual body if that is done, in other words, can he move from, make a transition from, one spiritual body to another?—there is no doubt and they know consciously where they are going and the existence will continue. Is this statement, this observation correct? Judith, for example, knew full well what was in store for her when she entered the Earth plane. When she got here by passing through the veil of darkness did she consciously forget where she came from and why she was here or was she somehow more advanced than the majority of us? Did Jesus know consciously His mission or did He, too, have to recall it with faith?

(Also from Barry)
#9 - Are there many other places where entities take on a physical body besides Earth? Do they pass through a veil of darkness, too?

(From Harold and Linda in Missouri. A series of really interesting questions)
#10 - We'd like to hear more about the creation of new Earths, etc. Is Lama Sing suggesting that new Earths can be created by the thought-power of a small group? Are there other Earths in existence now? If so, were they created by Earth entities who were creating an alternate Earth?

#11 - If two or more people thinking something makes it real, does that mean that the Earth was flat when most people believed that or just that people acted as though it was flat? Likewise, if two of us decide that child abuse doesn't exist, does it cease to exist? That doesn't make sense to me. What part does the concept of denial play in this?

#12 - If we choose our talents before incarnating what role does genetics play in our development? Do we choose the talents first and then choose the parents to give us the appropriate genetic material?

#13 - We found the Christmas gift tape to be the most moving of all the tapes we've heard. What happens, though, when a child is born into a home where parents have not prayed for a baby and the baby is unwanted?

#14 - While Peter acknowledges (or is acknowledged by) other entities, except for Zack, Paul, etc., there seems to be no real interaction between them. Is there opportunity for group social activities in other realms? What fun and games are there besides those of discovery, of creative materialization, which we heard about in a prior project.

(All of these last questions, again, are from Harold and Linda in Missouri)

The last question brings to mind some funny questions, which I really shouldn't express here. Ten-to-one they will backfire on me, but why not:

#15 - Are there celestial bingo parlors, for example? How about celestial bowling or celestial golf? You know ... Can you go off to another planet and play a round of golf on a weekend? All those thoughts seem like fun and maybe even a little bit serious.

And so now, Father, I present these questions prayerfully to You, asking as I do, that You would guide us to the very highest and best possible information that can be given. We ask all of this of You, Father, in the name of the Master, The Christ, and we thank You, Father. Amen.

THE READING

LAMA SING: Yes, we have the Channel then and, as well, those references which apply to the questions and the inquiring minds as indicated above. As we commence with this work, we shall first pray in this manner.

> *Lord, God, we know that Thou art ever with us in this and all such works and thus it is our prayer that we might herein accomplish Thy will and Thy purpose. We pray further that Thou would grant us the presence of the Master, The Christ, and that the power, faith and wisdom of His spirit shall transcend from here to the Earth in preservation of the integrity of this, our Channel, during the course of these works and unto each of those Voyagers and others as are seeking from these realms during these such times of intensity here and beyond as are relevant to the Earth. In the name of the Voyagers do we pray on behalf of all those souls in all realms who are presently in some need and for whom there are none in joyous prayer. We humbly thank Thee, Father, for this opportunity of joyful service in Thy name. Amen.*

As we commence with this work, dear friends, we should preface those with the following comments: During the recent Earth days in your current of the Earth progression, there have been those activities which are called, generally, war. And associated with this there are many activities which are involving realms which are adjacent to the Earth, and other activities which are extensive and too numerous to reiterate here briefly.

Suffice it to state, then, that during the course of these activities we have discouraged any excessive contact on the part of the Channel here. For the nature of those mechanisms require that the passage of the, as it were, spiritual consciousness of the Channel through those thought-forms, those essences. And such realms as are influenced by same (the actions in the Earth) could, in the sense of an extreme potentiality, minute in nature, have detrimental impact upon the mental and emotional consciousness of the Channel as a result.

Hence the opening commentary has included the invocation of a prayer for the full power of the Christ Consciousness to be awakened around the literal aspects of the Channel itself, including the Channel himself, during the course of this and works which shall proceed from here.

There should not be, as the result of this commentary, a general cause for alarm. However, there should be the renewed attention to preceding any works of meditative or prayerful nature with an affirmation firmly and strongly rooted in the foundation of your individual spiritual belief.

The purpose for this is, quite simply, as a preservation or protective mechanism, in a manner of speaking, though Universal Law guarantees that you, as an individual, have the right to the continuity of your Free Will and your free thinking. Should there be a momentary lapse in that faith or that affirmation as such which complies with Universal Law and a coinciding factor of some weakness on the part of a nature which involves a realm adjacent to that which you are traveling into or through, there is the remote possibility that an interrupt or an involvement can occur in such conditions which could be carried over into the daily life to the extent that that carry over could disrupt the thinking, the emotions and, further, as a potentiality, become a *temporary* (and that's emphasized or underlined) disruption to the physical ease. It is to this end, then, that these comments have been given and that you are as well, each one, encouraged to follow suit. See?

We turn now joyfully and humbly to the attention of your questions that those as expressed above and those which have not reached the Channel physically but which are available here for reference and in requiring of some attention. We proceed then.

To be a guide is not to, in essence, be (quote) "dead," (end quote) with a note of loving humor, though the physical body, in many instances, may be indeed quite that.

While the term *guide* applies to and connotes some level of spiritual achievement, it does not also always follow that that spiritual achievement has moved the entity fully beyond the potentiality of feeling in the emotional sense. Quite to the contrary, the quality of feeling endures, and although changes somewhat in terms of its interaction and effect, remains very much recognizable in comparison to the feeling and reactions of emotion in the Earth.

The differentiation that is being sought after here, as the intent or nature of the question, is that the disappointment is not, in the sense as such, reactive to the entity expressing or experiencing same as it is in the Earth. The disappointment may be that an opportunity has been missed or that a work has not been fully prepared and thus not observed by the entity being guided. And therefore much of the feeling (as you might call it) *disappointment* is not in the same degree emanating for the guide as a life force or a thought-form. In the Earth disappointment and anger are created in the same mechanical sense as thought-forms are. And therefore they have potentiality for the guide who may be serving in a realm which is parallel to or adjacent to the Earth or even, possibly, in the Earth. Universal Law prevents this from having a sense of permanency and therefore, as such, the guide is sheltered to an extent from any lasting effect from same.

Joy is, conversely, echoed on nearly all realms that we are cognizant of ... the exception being, perhaps, in those realms which are lesser than joyful, where, again, Universal Law assures the continuity. But, in essence, guides can feel, can sense, and do have a reactory result from what you might call disappointments, frustrations and such.

As relates to anger, we know of none who possess anger. Anger would be a portal that would connect them to a realm much less than might broadly or typically be required for service as a guide. Exceptions here: It is possible for an entity to be a guide and be in physical body. Therefore, potentially at least, all emotions are available to them but in the physical form of the Earth. See?

Generally speaking, guides do not become disappointed with you if you are being guided by them and, to our knowledge, never become angry with you, but can feel and sense joy and, occasionally, what you might call sadness but never long-lived. Sadness and disappointment might be used interchangeably here but the impact is superficial, see? It's a superficial thing. It comes from the external potentials which are, therefore, deterred, delayed or (in quotes) "lost" for a time. See?

In the aspect or mechanism of praying on behalf of those souls who are in need for whom there are none in joyous prayer in an entity's name, we are intending this to be in accordance with Universal Law, wherein the named entity shall bear the results or return, under Universal Law, of that effort of prayer. This is, indeed, an exceptional expression of prayer and opens much potential for those who would apply same. It is not to be confused with praying in the name of the Christ or praying in God's name. It is, rather, praying as though you were that entity.

For example, the Channel gave the example above, we believe, of the name Charley or Charles. "We would now pray on behalf of all those souls who are presently in some need and for whom there are none in joyous prayer in Charley's name." Or you could place that at the beginning, "In Charley's name, we now pray on behalf of ..." See? In other words, you are acting as though you are that entity uttering the prayer.

If you would envision it this way: If Charles were standing in front of you, you would stand immediately behind him and direct the prayer outward through him into the universe. Therefore, as the universe returns the bounty, the blessings of that prayer, it comes back through Charles. See? And ultimately through you as well.

It's incorporating or involving someone in need into your prayer work. It does, in fact, open them and allows for an extremely powerful and potential return which is very pure. In other words, Charles would receive this, perhaps to an extent unknowingly, and it would be pure in that he might thereafter do with it as was his wish as a spiritual power.

Generally speaking, you can use this very effectively for healing, particularly so were Charles to have asked you to pray for him. You, then, praying for others in Charles's name completes a circle, so to say, which is an ascending circle, or spiral, to be more exact. This could raise Charles and many others to a much higher level of spiritual acceptance and awareness. The by-product of which, of course, should predicate into the Earth as physical healing. See that, then?

Should you do this? We would recommend it here but under measured circumstances, not just broadly. In order for prayer to be most effective, it should have meaning and dedication, seriousness and purpose. Those prayers are the most powerful because they come from the center of your being.

Turning back for a moment to the question of guides: As one is a parent in the Earth and they observe the lack of responsiveness to well intended guidance, it might be well to adopt some of the perspectives as your spiritual guides have already accomplished, and that is to have the faith and the knowledge that no matter what the immediate condition or reaction or lack of same might be, you have sown seeds and those are seeds of joy which shall bear fruit after their own kind.

If you become frustrated, then vent that but not at the entity you are guiding but towards a work. Anger is a power just as joy is. Turn your anger, then, to something which is worthy of same. In other words, that's an energy which has power and potentiality to accomplish something. It's just energy. Fashion it, then, towards your list of things to do or other works. You will perhaps be amazed at how productive you can become drawing upon that resource. Once you have become talented at this and familiar with it, you might look for opportunities to become angry just to get your *to do* list completed. (This is met with much humor here by our colleagues.)

It is possible for you in the Earth to have what the entity, David, has called *proof* in the Earth. However, you are looking at what we would call proof through the eyes of a physical entity living within the greater thought-form called Earth. It is well to understand that this thought-form can filter, can create patterns which obscure, which block, which, through critical analysis, can break down even the most simple and evidential occurrences of what's called proof.

Each of you has had many such occurrences in your lives to date, current and past. Some of these remain with you for varying lengths of time but few, if any, remain vividly in the forefront of your consciousness as you continue on your pathway of this life, and are impacted by the expectations and what you call the demands upon your attentiveness and your time.

The suggestion here for this is: Try to incorporate yourself into a complete being, spiritual, mental, emotional and physical, that there is a unison of perspective as you move through life. Thereby you take command of an innate, but marvelously potential, power within you to meet and overcome any challenge.

The greatest of all evidence of life's continuity throughout eternity is the ability of an entity to accept and to take command of their own inner power. The greater is the effort expended in this direction, the more pronounced are the results. The moreso this is met with continuity and diligence, the moreso are the results evidential. You are also dwelling in a realm which has, under Universal Law, been guaranteed the right of its importance as well as its preservation, and as such then, these may be factors which limit what you accept as proof or evidence.

The most specific answer to your question is that we don't know the answer. What we have given to you is what we find here before us from Universal Consciousness. In truth, we do not understand completely what you consider to be *proof* in the Earth and how you would view this. If it were to be that an entity who has left the physical body could be free to move into and out of the Earth plane, then there would be no benefit nor purpose for being, as such, individual realms of existence. The order of existence, then, would be dissipated and no true progressive accomplishments could be measured which seems to be important to the soul consciousness as well as to the individual.

Most entities in the Earth look for markers, points of demarcation, to indicate movement, progression and/or growth. These, then, as levels of existence and expression, provide such in a most unique way. Once you are beyond the Veil of Darkness separating the Earth from other realms, you will understand this.

But the true growth, we should think, of actually accomplishing and realizing or actualizing some ability, is to be capable of applying it in an instance or in a situation where that is the sole or singular form of reliance or that's the only thing you have to depend upon. That causes this to become yours. You have, then, in such, a sort of pride of ownership, an accomplishment of ownership. See? Unless you have this ownership it is difficult for you to truly have faith. You must have gained it. It can't just be handed to you or given to you. Therefore, proof cometh as one gains in their faith and possesses or truly owns same.

With regard to Zachary or Paul reincarnating in the Earth and then departing through the Veil of Darkness, for example in the process you call death, they may or may not have to relearn everything, as you have stated Peter is now. But we should qualify that just a bit, for, very definitely, Peter is not relearning everything. He is regaining, rediscovering them. And many of the things that others might have to slowly evolve consciousness of he is not required to do.

In other words, Peter is moving forward in his spiritual consciousness very rapidly. He is also moving forward on multiple levels not just where you see him as Peter. He is correlating this movement with other levels of his expression or (you might think of this) he is taking this information and fitting it in here and there in the entire sum and substance of his being, and this is very productive for him. And therefore his movement is rapid, which is why Peter has volunteered and been chosen or accepted for the work in this project. See?

It is not always necessary for an entity to relearn or to reawaken. It is good for them to move from one realm to another with some degree of moderation in their haste. This is simply to be certain that all factors in their being are well placed, firmly in position, that that which is to come can be built upon a firm foundation. That, perhaps, is the better reason for this occurring in the manner which it is.

You, entity David, will probably move to your level of highest spiritual acceptance with considerable ease because of the gains in your perspective, your consciousness, your level of awareness, and you should find this to be quite easily accomplished. Each of the Voyagers should find that having this knowledge, as has been gleaned from observing Peter, to be highly contributive in that regard to each of them, to each of you, as well.

It is true that it is not usually the case that there is a

hodgepodge of levels of consciousness in realms beyond the Earth. Conversely, you will find that at points of intersect where two levels of consciousness are very close and where there is, what we would call, a metamorphosis of one realm to another or one realm to multiple realms, this is very often the case. But as we have given here very often, the Earth plane is at a point of transition or metamorphosis and is very unique in that sense. Recall that? And as such then, you are correct. A hodgepodge comes about because the Earth is at a state of evolution. Certainly, then, many forces will be at mixed points of willingness or lack of same.

The hopefulness here is to contribute as much as possible to those who are seeking and to those who are willing to hear and to see as is possible for us to do. This work as we are about it in the present and have been for some time, through this and other channels before him, is a work which we believe will be, in a manner of speaking, culminated by the emergence of the Christ Consciousness in the Earth once again.

Once this is accomplished and the Master or the Master's Consciousness is intensified in the Earth again, then we will take on a different work, in a manner of speaking, of more direct support to those who shall make the way passable for Him, which we believe will include a number of, if not all, of you. The only reason for question here is that some of you may be about other works at that point, which is your right of choice.

And from that point, then, we collectively, as you are thinking of us or know us here as speaking through this Channel, will function in that capacity of service directly to the Master and to those who are preparing the way for and with Him. Some of our grouping will enter with the Master and some will remain here and some will enter into other realms for purposes of combined effort of assisting the Earth and those who are willing to make a transition to a higher level of consciousness.

If there is insufficient, in a manner of speaking, number to sustain what you know to be the Earth, then, in fact, there will be a movement of souls, large groupings, to what will, for all intents and purposes, seem to be the Earth, period. And yet this will be a multiple division (or a division into multiples) of the Earth in the precise manner as you have defined the realms here. The Earth will continue and we believe that the Master will then, in a form of speaking, reign over same for a considerable period of Earth time. This has been prophesied and is merely being repeated here. See?

But you are correct. There is generally more uniformity of consciousness, cooperation, and harmony. It's sort of like a code of conduct or like you see upon the entry to some eating establishments in the Earth, shirt and shoes required (with a note of loving humor, see?)

The transition through vibratory levels is not always noted consciously by entities in the Earth. Those who are seeking and who have strived to attune themselves may more probably note such transitions. And they are just that, transitional times in the Earth where, for all intents and purposes, you are passing through a sort of microcosmic experience likened unto that called death. You are leaving behind, collectively, an array of old habits, attitudes, and intents and purposes, and are adopting simultaneously new ones.

These are times of jubilance for the guides and for those who are in service with you, which again returns us to the first question above and supports our comments as given. See? The population in general might not note this but they would note some difference, and most of them would do so in retrospect. See?

You will, we are almost certain, experience this again during this lifetime and you will experience it when you depart. Very similar but much more wondrously, you know ... with all the accompanying sounds, lights and experiences, much more vividly than you can imagine. Something to be looked upon with joyous anticipation even though the prospect of what you call death in the Earth is not generally thought of in that sense or term.

The other Voyagers may also anticipate feeling, as many of you are even as we speak, some transitional impact, changes in what you have called, entity Robin, vibratory level changes.

More straightforwardly, to state what this is: It is a change in the spiritual level of acceptance while yet in physical body. It is an objective to be sought after and is highly desired. Very often those who work with manipulation, massage, chiropractic, physicians, medical practitioners, those who work in a more methodical or, as you might call it (quote) "professional" (end quote) sense, with the development of the intuitive abilities, all of these, might feel these, note these more significantly than those who do not find themselves involved in such.

Entities applying and depending very much upon the creative abilities will also be involved in this more noticeably as would be those who are aggressive thinkers, astute thinkers, might also note this.

This leaves a last grouping who do not actually respond to life but generally are simply flowing with it, taking the best here and there and actually making no effort to accomplish any one thing save survival. (That is not a statement which is judgmental, but merely an observation, see.)

Peter knows he is eternal ... we think (given with a note of loving humor). There are moments when we observe him and there is some question or doubt. These, generally speaking, do not occur frequently or to any great depth, but your first statement is a fair assessment. It is not unfair. It's fair.

It's not completely what we would call factual, in the sense that there are entities in the Earth who know they are eternal and actually don't need any more evidence of it, but that doesn't diminish their intent and dedication to accomplish as much as possible in the current span of their incarnation present. This may make for some intensity of accomplishment which might give rise to the illusion that they do not believe themselves to be eternal. See the difference?

When he makes a movement or raises his consciousness or, as the entity Robin defined it, changes vibratory levels, this could be likened unto moving from one plane to another. There would be no loss of consciousness in the sense that he would be obscured from knowing who and what he is now to the next step as to who and what he is. Movement here does not correlate precisely to movement out of and into the Earth.

The Earth is a finite realm and has deliberate and firm limitations imposed upon it, since the Earth is a collage of sorts of many different vibratory levels of entities or many levels of acceptance on the part of groups of entities. It was structured in this way and evolved this way because of the choice of the entities involved. You will hear more about that as we progress and deal with the questions about the Atlantean times in questions yet to come.

Doubt is not an enemy. Doubt is a valuable asset to all entities because it causes you to examine, to test, to look for certainties, to reach into your being for that which is your strength. But when doubt is corrosive to that basic strength, then it is to be worked upon as something undesirable to that magnitude. In other words, turn the amplitude down, the volume down, the energy level down. To question, to ask, to seek, to inquire ... All of these might be facets of the term doubt, and they are not faults or flaws unless, like any other aspect of self, they are done to excess (exercise to excess, see).

Generally speaking, there is little, if any, doubt in movement from a spiritual body into a physical body. But because of the conditions and requirements of movement out of physical body and the duration of existence in a physical body, this must be recovered or discovered and drawn out as you are challenged or inspired by the events or circumstances of that life or lives. That's the purpose, after all, of incarnating in the Earth or in other more focused or finite realms.

Movement from a spiritual realm to a spiritual realm is with some considerable certainty that existence will continue. There are, on occasions, those questions when entities may wonder or question whether their own individuality might be lost and simply thrown as a drop of water into an ocean of other droplets. This does not happen. The individuality is treated with more regard as one moves higher on the spiritual ladder of progression, colloquially stating that.

Judith, as she passed through the Veil of Darkness into the Earth (the protective membrane which preserves and lovingly protects the right of those souls functioning in the Earth) left behind her spiritual consciousness to the extent that she could gain from the experience as Judith.

And, as she did so, it wasn't that she abandoned her spiritual consciousness but that it went into a state of, what we might call, *restfulness*, and as such then, focused itself as the entity Judith. The more the entity Judith interacts with entities in the Earth, the more uniquely expressed does this soul become *Judith*. And the greater is the longevity and interaction, the more opportune becomes the possibility of her accomplishing her intended works as the expression called Judith.

Judith is not more advanced than most of you, the majority of you. She is, however, at a level of spiritual acceptance (if you would consider that being advanced) that is somewhat above the average of those souls in the Earth and about equal to or perhaps just a whit higher than the general grouping of the Voyagers. You could consider her one of your grouping quite easily. She is in that vein. See?

He recalled it not so much so with faith, but the experiences as were known to Him to be present were mechanisms which afforded Him the opportunity to continually express

Himself more and more. In other words, all those souls were in a position working harmoniously to bring forth His light.

You could state that they were preparing the way, making the way possible for the return or entry of the Christ. Just so as we have given here oft in past, that you have the opportunity to make the way possible for the Christ, the Master, once again, one and the same. Therefore you would be working with Him in that regard to enable Him to express His potential. Universal Law requires that these conditions be met.

The love of all souls on the part of our Father is not rigid and unyielding. Therefore the Law of Grace can transpire here that in such circumstances as we have before us, and you before you, this process does not require it in the outward definition of the term "and Law of Grace." See?

There are many other places where entities can take on a physical body besides the Earth, yes. Do they pass through a Veil of Darkness? Yes, they do. And as such, here again consider that where there is an expression which is more finite, that veil of darkness is more defined, the greater is the definition and the intensity of the finite focus. So then is it correlated that the Veil must be in coordinated harmony with that intensity and follow suit. See?

Many entities take on a physical body which has no real properties. In other words, the physical body is there because it is agreed upon as the accepted vehicle and the medium of exchange and interaction between the entities. The physical body does not have properties which are normally correlated to the physical body in the Earth, i.e., the ingestion of foods and the elimination of waste, the need for rest to rebuild the physical cell structure and the composite of the body in the physiological sense and such as these. It does not age, it does not, as such, weary. But you see, in Peter's experiences as times of rest, these are times of spiritual and mental assimilation, not sleep for the fatigue of his body.

When the spiritual consciousness and physical consciousness become weary, there are distinct differences. The spiritual consciousness takes time (as you would consider the measurement of time) joyfully to ingest and incorporate new discoveries or awareness into the totality of that entity's being. See the difference?

The creation of new Earths and realms, etc., is continually taking place. But be cautious in considering the term *Earth* to reflect a specific colloquial creation of an Earth as you would know it in your galaxy. Other galaxies possess such spheres as the Earth and yet other galaxies and other realms, other dimensions also.

These are not, in essence, deliberately created by souls just for a playground, although this can be done. They are more likely the result of a division of consciousness between a larger grouping. The example here being that the Earth is at a point of some division. Certain groups of souls may not wish to progress spiritually, but may wish to perpetuate and therefore continue that which is familiar and that which is their choice. Others may wish something else, and yet others yet another thing. And so you would have a separation and the creation of existence which thereafter may be, for all practical purposes, unknown consciously between groupings but exist every bit as real as in the past. In some cases, the souls may not even be conscious that this has been done.

This leads us to some complex areas which we won't delve into with depth here or finiteness except to state that all things are possible and that you are unlimited. See?

In the initial involvement with the creation of the Earth there were souls of great illumination involved in the actual creation with God. This is not to say that they and not God created, for all creation is done in and of God. There are not exceptions to this. It is God's power that is used or misused for creation or destruction, albeit nothing can be eternally destroyed. It can be transformed; it can be metamorphosized, and such as this. See?

Two or more people thinking and believing and accepting and truly having faith that a certain thing is desired and is the objective is the beginning of making it real. Before you had automobiles it was a thought-form. That thought-form was fathered, builded, and shared and it became, as such, an invention. This could be said about everything that is technologically present in your Earth, could it not?

It is also true of customs, of dictums, of attitudes, of emotions. Your society's standards in the west do vary greatly now than fifty Earth years ago and one hundred Earth years ago. Now look at it compared to two hundred Earth years ago. Isn't that almost like two different worlds? You see? The creation is not, as such, capable of producing an immediate physical result, for the greater grouping, at least.

It is possible to manifest a thought-form in an environ that supports that thought-form wherein such an action does not violate Universal Law. Where Universal Law is potentially or literally violated, then the activity is not supported and will collapse, even though the intensity of the entities involved may be tenacious. Now then, the exception here is in a combined or mixed environment such as described above about the Earth. Remember the hodgepodge comment?

At some point or another in the growth of consciousness it will become realized that continuations of such thinking must reach a point of conclusive decision. Thereafter, two courses of action are possible: construction or destruction. If the latter, then a separation of the entities involved in the hodge-podge will surely occur under Universal Law. Collective groupings may move to another realm of consciousness, and immediately, with only a moment's pause, resume the activity in accordance with their agreed upon belief whether they do so by leaving the Earth through the portal called death or in other manners. See?

Consciousness is involved in the evolution and building of a thought-form. Perception is a part of consciousness. Thus if a thought-form exists, such as: the Earth is there, it's round, it sort of spins on an axis and revolves around the axial point which you accept as the sun, though not completely accurate, but close. Nonetheless, here, then, do we find that the perception is a part of the process of building a thought-form.

To hold a thought-form and to perceive that thought-form as "real" (that's in quotes), and for all to agree upon it, even if shown visual evidence or this or that proof, it's unacceptable because the perception denies it. So even though, obviously, many evenings entities who believed the Earth was flat could perceive the moon and other spheres celestially in their round state, they could not accept the fact that their Earth could also be round. And yet there was the proof, the evidence, before them each Earth evening. And there were other examples or proofs or evidences, but the perception was that the Earth was flat. It made sense in accordance with their construction of the thought-form and therefore their perception accepted it as such. See?

But the creation of something being thought of as real, you must have the faith to perceive it as real. You must allow your perception to be open to reality. All thought-forms are real. Their power and their longevity, their impact, are dependent upon the entities, the minds, and the sources of belief that power that thought-form, noting here again that all power is from God, but that power is vested within each of you. If you direct it towards a thought and that thought is given a life force, you may thereafter perceive it and create it into reality. Again, the example of the automobile or the television or the computer or the hammer and nail. See? Follow that, then?

Need is involved here and purpose is involved and the ideal is involved. If you need to fasten two pieces of wood together then you have a need to create such as the hammer and nail. You can bind them with other forms or fiber or such as this, but need created the opportunity for a thought-form to be actualized and for it to be perceived as a reality. If you did not believe in the hammer and nail would all of these structures fastened with same fall apart? We doubt that because they are builded upon a thought-form which is already in place and in existence. In order for you to disbelieve something that has such a potential power, you would have to disbelieve it in another realm. You don't have the right to destroy that thought-form unless all involved agree upon same.

Now note that last comment, and here is an adjunct to it that should be illuminating to you: One of the mechanisms involved in the reincarnative struggle or cycle is for the purpose of allowing entities to recant or to modify previously expressed thought-forms. Follow that? In other words, they can go back to their previous thought-forms and alter them (because, after all, they are their thought-forms) by reincarnating in that same environ and choosing consciously to alter the thought-form as a part of the mass mind thought of that realm.

Think about that as you think about all of the souls who have entered the Earth in recent times who are experiencing all manner of difficulty, including dis-ease, deprivation, starvation and all that sort. Perhaps in past some of these souls, at least, created those as potentials. Perhaps they dominated and controlled or ruled with vigor and took these essentials from others. They created a thought-form and had the power to make it a reality. Now they might come back (reincarnate) and exemplify the results of their own work and thus contribute to the mass mind consciousness, changing that, ending poverty, ending hunger, ending dis-ease. See?

It's not idle. These things are not happenstance or by chance. They are purposeful and they are joyously engaged in on the part of the soul when it is cognizant of such as an opportunity while in spiritual consciousness. The greatest of all joy comes when an entity reaches that level of consciousness while in that realm and then can act as a light, a beacon, an example to others that they might, too, choose to follow same. And we have two and then twenty and then an hundred, firstly the individuals, the groups, the masses, the classes, nations, the world. See?

Abusing a child does not begin with the act, does it? In other words, an entity doesn't just meander down the pathway or a by-way in the Earth and see a child and decide to abuse it. True? There are predicating factors, emotions, triggering mechanisms, and all sorts of activities which have predicated or produced an entity who has a bent towards child abuse.

There are other instances where the inability to control oneself causes a momentary lapse which or in which an entity might create an occurrence harmful to a child, such as abuse, and other variations upon these. But in all instances, there must be a portal through which that energy, constructive or destructive, helpful or abusive, can flow.

If you wish to decide, two of you, that child abuse doesn't exist, you begin with the thought of creating such an environ, and then you are responsible to the best of your ability to take action to demonstrate your faith and belief in that goal. Why? Because you are in a realm which has the dimensional expression which requires participation and action.

Here or in Peter's Garden all of the entities have passed through that in one manner or another and they have moved to pure creation, and Peter will move to even much more potentiality than at present. But in the Garden entities are not limited in their ability to create for all are intending the purpose in a similar way.

In the Earth there are entities who have subjected themselves to personal violence, to deprivation and all sorts of things in accordance with their choice of incarnation and such. And they so compose burdens in terms of karma so as to require these events as opportunities, that these can be released. Don't misinterpret these in the broader sense, that one should avoid taking any action against child abuse; or if you do and you know that to be wrong, you have just purchased a ticket on those entities' flight of karma. You've bought into the ballgame. See?

You are responsible to live up to your belief. When you do not, you impose upon yourself some need to meet that as an opportunity once again to strengthen that quality. Where two believe that child abuse should stop, they have opened a window, a portal; when twenty believe, the window is broader; when all believe, the concept of abusing a child no longer would exist. It simply would cease to exist. Until then you are responsible for action in accordance with your potential. Does that now make sense? If not, bring it back, see?

Denial is very powerful. It, again, is subject to the conditions of Universal Law, and the right of free expression as mind-thought has a right to exist. But in your own individual instances, you can use the power of denial very succinctly and you can deny the existence of that which is not chosen consciously by you in your life. Then you take action to change it and to replace it or displace it with something of your choice.

Action must now emerge as an important point, mustn't it? Remember, Zachary and Peter encouraging ... correction ... Zachary and Paul encouraging Peter to visualize, to conceptualize, to create the need and then to bring it forth, to actualize it, to bring it into reality, to allow it to express. It's no different for you. You can't say, "Lord, stop child abuse," and then walk down the street and ignore it as you see it. You are an expression of God. You stop child abuse. God will help. The God within others as they collect and agree strengthens that. Continue in that way and you will stop it. See?

When an entity is born into a home or circumstances where the parents have not prayed for the child and the baby is unwanted, has to do more often than not with karmic interactions. It also can have to do with actions on the part of a soul which are purely benevolent in nature. Where two entities may not have wished to create an entity, a baby, the benevolence of a soul may see the value and purpose in the broader sense, or longer term as it were, and volunteer to enter into an unwanted or hostile environment.

In many cases we find these entities are also souls who have created some karmic memory which has to do with a variety of other impacts upon children in the past or upon, perhaps, those entities who are now the parents and this affords the parents in this case an opportunity to see how well they will do when the tables are turned.

Karma is an opportunity. It's not a debt. It's not a burden. It's a joyous opportunity. It's what one makes of the situation that makes the difference. See?

We regret that you do not have opportunity to observe what the Channel has mischievously called celestial bingo. There are realms where entities can proliferate such activities of entertainment or social gathering as that as they would call it in the Earth, and there are many other levels and expressions of what you call social interaction.

One of the most profound of these occurs when Peter, Zachary, Paul enter into the Realm of Laughter. The colors, the lights, the sounds, the joy … You cannot know from what we have given that these are other entities who have, as well, come to the Realm of Laughter for the purpose of sharing and interacting and, what you might call, social interaction. Obviously, the entities are in a state of consciousness where they are capable of expressing themselves in an unlimited manner.

Isn't that wonderful? It awaits each of you as a potential, as a gift, as a just reward, as an accomplishment. It is not beyond your grasp nor is it to be thought of as merely something nice to hear. It is very real and it awaits you now or in the future, in your meditation, in your prayers, or even within your daily life. If you can have a bit of the Realm of joyous laughter in and about your countenance as you go through each day, you will be most awed by the effect this will create in your world, among those with whom you interact, and your success. Laughter, joy, happiness unbridled, freely given ... these are qualities of abundance. See?

The fun and games are varied. They are not limited in the sense that one might state, "Well, we can play this game or we can have this outing." They are limited only to the creative potential of the souls involved. There are realms or levels of expression where entities could have a picnic, go fishing, go skiing, play some of your games of sports (the Channel called it golf), or other such as these. The limitations are nonexistent. The creative potential is dependent upon the souls involved. You have the potential to do the same in the Earth.

Now as one moves to the, we'll call them, *higher levels* of acceptance of spirituality, what you might think of as games or sports or social activities or as fun and games becomes, as such, incredible to your current perspective, and wonderful. You can visit other realms, you can observe, you can go to higher, to lower, to parallel realms. In each case there are certain conditions involved, of course, but are there not conditions involved in your realm for your fun and games?

And so it is here that the perspective of the entities involved know Universal Law to varying degrees. The extent to which they know and can apply and live within that Law is generally the threshold which demarcates where they can enter and where they can not. But the advantage of a friend such as Zachary, one might be able to borrow a cloak from the celestial cloak room, such as our friends Ann and Lois and others of you have done. This can be freely done and journeys can be made into realms and into joys otherwise not easily attainable. See?

Well, then dear friends, we believe this concludes the questions and answers for this meeting, and as such then, we shall return the Channel to consciousness in the Earth. As we do so, know that our joyous prayers are with you all and that each of your prayers is heard and answered and that your hopes and wishes for peace and joy in the Earth are being responded to in accordance with Universal Law.

For the present then, it is our prayer that the joy, grace and wisdom of our Father's presence is as a lamp to guide your footsteps now and throughout eternity.

Fare thee well then for the present, dear friends.

Q&A READING #17

Continuation of Questions After Chapter 10 and 11:
SHARING THE GIFT (V-720)
CEREMONY OF THE CRYSTALS

Given January 25, 1991

AL MINER/CHANNEL: *This reading is code number V-761. It is questions and answers #8 for Voyager Project Number 7.*

QUESTIONS SUBMITTED

The questions that I have received for this reading are as follows.

#1 - The golden entity in the Great Hall, the unified asexual characteristic, is this a level of spiritual acceptance obtainable by "every" entity? Is this the point or level of coming out of the illusion of separation from God?

#2 - Regarding the cloak, until you reach the realm like Paul, Peter and Zachary, you do not have a spiritual cloak? Is that correct?

#3 - Regarding the Garden Realm, until then or there we cannot meet, i.e., see the source or "golden entity" in that form? Correct or not correct?

#4 - In terms of reference in the Earth plane, is the Garden Realm the first heaven? In the Bible, the Apostle Paul refers to three heavens. The Master Jesus refers to "many mansions." Is there a correlation or does the word "realm" equate with the word "heaven"? Or is heaven just a state of mind? Is heaven a realm where you directly meet the source, i.e. like the golden entity in the Great Hall?

#5 - What does the term Father God or Father-Mother-God mean?

#6 - Does Wilbur's realm have an opportunity to meet the golden entity within the Crystal Worker's Realm in the same form? In other words, as Peter experienced in the Garden?

#7 - How many are "they" in the golden white light? Are the entities who were Buddha and the Apostle Peter now in the same realm as the golden entity?

#8 - What is the difference between the God-head, Source, God, and Father-Mother God?

(Now all of those splendid questions are from David and Leiko in Florida.)

(Next, I have several questions from Joan in Pennsylvania.)

#9 - Would you please explain more about the possibility of Jesus or the Christ forces returning to Earth to help heal our differences and to see if we can continue to cohabitate here and the people who will help them and then those people forming an alternative Earth?

#10 - Would that mean our present version of Earth would remain the same, containing the people who are presently satisfied with living here the way it is now and the others would somehow create a new version of Earth and live there?

#11 - If so, how would that be accomplished? Wouldn't that take a great deal of time? How would they move there? Would they have to die and be born there like we do here? I thought the Earth was going through a rise in consciousness and the people whose vibrations did not rise with it would leave. Do I have it backwards?

#12 - Also, what exactly is the purpose of the personality or ego, since there seems to be such differences at times between what the ego desires and the soul desires?

(And she writes:)
#13 - Last, but not least, you said a person who has a great need, let's say the need is to be successful in business, is less likely to get it as easily as a person who doesn't have the great need. What is the difference between need and desire? I always thought Spirit was expedient to need. Perhaps the need it's expedient to is the soul's need and not the personality's need. Why does such great need block getting what one desires? This is confusing to me. Please explain. Thank you so much, Lama Sing, for all your help personally and with the wonderful teachings of the Voyager Project. (*That's from Joan in Pennsylvania.*)

(The next two questions should be interesting. The first is from Joan in Pennsylvania and the second is from Harold and Linda in Missouri, which sort of indicates the two of them, or three of them, were tuned in to the same celestial radio station, doesn't it? From Joan:)
#14 - How did the Atlanteans who did not use the portal of death leave the planet? Did they use what we call space ships? What do you mean by "cease their existence and return to their originating source"? HOW?

#15 - After the break up of Atlantis, was an alternative Earth formed? If so, is this it? Or is this the lower vibrational version? Interesting thoughts, aren't they?

#16 - Is the dimension that you recently described as being a lower realm than Earth an alternative Earth also? Will I wake up one morning and look out my window and see another Mother Earth sailing about the sun with me? What fun, with a note of loving humor.
(From our friend Joan in Pennsylvania. Joan has an ex-

cellent sense of humor and has really great writing talent. I hope that she gets the breaks she needs to bring that more to the public.)

(The next question.)
#17 - How did the Atlanteans who separated by means other than death separate? What's the distinction between Atlantean entities who "ceased their existence and returned to their originating realm of consciousness" and those who chose death? Where did they go? Did they continue any interaction with Earth? *(And that's from Harold and Linda in Missouri, again. They are overlapping questions but with some variations there that I felt made it worthwhile to express both of those in their completeness.)*

That, I believe, is the extent of all the questions that I have remaining for Voyager Project #7. If any of you did not have questions asked and sent them in to me and they slipped through the floorboards, as they say somewhere here, please do alert me to that. And, if you can, send in those questions and I will see they're included in future Q & A sessions for Project #8. I hope I didn't overlook any.

Finally, I would add my own question and that is, quite simply:
#18 - Do you, Lama Sing and Company, have anything that you would like to state to us about this project or on anything in general to the Voyager group at this time? And is this now the concluding reading for Voyager Project #7?

So, Father, we turn all these questions over to You, asking as we do that You would guide us to the highest and best possible information. This we ask of You in the name of the Master, the Christ. Thank You, Father. Amen.

THE READING

LAMA SING: Yes, we have the Channel, then, and as well those references which apply to the questions, the topic, the grouping gathered, as indicated above. As we commence with this work, we shall first pray in this manner:

> *Lord God, we ask that Thou would see us in this work as we attend to these requests, doing so humbly in Thy Name. We are therefore in askance of Thee, Father, that Thou would grant us the presence of the Master, the Christ, so as to impart His love, compassion, wisdom and healing grace unto these entities, awakening same within them that they might share in His glory and Thy work. We pray in the name of the Voyagers on behalf of all souls, in all realms, who are presently in some need and for whom there are none in joyous prayer. We are both humble and grateful, Father, for this opportunity of joyous service in Thy name. Amen.*

We believe that all souls are capable of reaching that point wherein the characteristics which are defined in the Earth as sexual are no longer evident nor needed. To that point, this can be accomplished well before an entity rises to the point of spiritual acceptance wherein they would be associated with or a part of those forces, generally, as you consider to be a part of the Golden entity. And as such, then, the entities can function and interact without there being those influences, tendencies, attitudes as such are the general collage associated with sexual expression or polarities, which are, in that sense, divided.

This unification comes about upon the progression of movement upwards in consciousness and can be transcended at varying levels dependent upon the entity or entities involved. See? We know of no souls who do not have this as a potential, and were we to be cognizant of some, this would be a concerning matter.

All entities have a spiritual cloak, always, though they may not be conscious of same. When the cloak becomes known, it becomes thereafter an extension of the entity in the conscious sense and can be utilized in the sense of being a tool or a functioning mechanism with which they can accomplish works of greater breadth and depth than without such knowledge.

It is not required that an entity reach the realm such as Paul, Peter and Zachary, in order to have a spiritual cloak. You have this cloak now, even as we speak. The conscious acceptance of this greatly enhances your personal power and provides an adjunct of (with a note of loving humor) a tremendous influx of *Personal Prayer Units.*[10] Remember those? It is not essential that one be dwelling in, or capable of such, the Garden Realm, in order to perceive the source or Golden entity in that specific form. Indeed, we note that a number of you among the Voyager grouping have perceived the entity and are aware of such even as we speak.

It doesn't hurt, however, to have attained that level of acceptance, for so doing enables the perception of the entity in that form much more frequently and much more easily. In fact, Peter, Paul, and Zachary could request the entity's presence at any time they so desired and, in fact, they could be in any realm when so doing. Once that connection or contact has been made, a bridge of sorts is established which is thereafter eternal and dependent, in terms of functioning, only upon the entities at the lesser level. See?

There is a correlation in a sense to the first heaven and

---

[10] Personal Prayer Units – In the Prayer Project, Kendall, a member of that project, coined the term "PPU" to mean a measure of prayer power directed towards a need.

the Garden Realm, however, with this variation: The first heaven is dependent upon the entities involved. For some, the Garden Realm might be considered the first heaven; for others, it might not. These are those souls who have come into the Earth from a higher realm than such and therefore might perceive this only to be as one of many such realms possible or having a potential of existence for they and other entities.

The Apostle Paul, referring to the three heavens, also was making reference, we believe, (given in humbleness so as to not usurp any written word or any spiritual thought-form) to three inner kingdoms, that being: the spiritual, the mental and (some would question this and others would not) the emotional. The emotional is associated to the physical in the most direct sense by many here. Others would prefer that there be a distinguishment made between the emotional and the physical so as to be indicative of three realms defined as spiritual, mental-emotional, and, thirdly, physical. Others prefer four distinct delineations, they being spiritual, mental, emotional, and physical. Hence, you may find them interchanged here from time to time in the past and in future works as these are presented.

The three heavens do correlate, in a manner of speaking, to a certain level of existence, having to do with movement from three distinct levels, commencing with the Earth and going beyond same for, in essence, three graduated steps. These are somewhat complex to explain here in definitive terms but generally have to do with moving through expressions of self. As one moves through these expressions, they come to transitional points, or *veils* (as the Channel has termed them), which could be inferred to be the three heavens. The Master's reference to many mansions is clearly the most precise, in that there are as many mansions as there are those whom would seek such. See?

There is a correlation. The word *realm* equates to the word *heaven* only to the degree that one perceives a realm as heavenly. The Earth is perceived by us here as a realm of expression. You may not perceive it as heavenly. See?

Heaven is a state of mind, but it is a state of existence. When you are in the Earth, perception of heaven is more likely associated with a state of mind or a spiritual attitude or transference. In other words, you are an eternal being and your eternal nature is defined now in the spiritual form and, for some, in the mental form and for yet others, as well, in the emotional. But that is only because you are finitely focused or expressed. See? Were you not so, you could exist, mindfully in a heavenly state in this moment.

Heaven is not necessarily a realm where you meet the Source, i.e. the Golden entity, but it can be. The definition is dependent upon the individual perceiver. See?

Father-God, as comparatively presented to the term *Father-Mother-God* is only a hair's breadth distinction, dependent upon the philosophical and spiritual posture of the entities involved.

In the case of the latter, Father-Mother God is inferring here a completeness. In other words, the polarities are unified and the energies are totally balanced and complete, whereas in some cultures, the term Father-God implies the singular source as is distinguishable from any reference to a division, as in polarity, or as in a hierarchy, which is likened unto the pyramidal form with the Father-God at the point or terminus (the upper). And the polarity, as in the pillars of righteousness in the Cabalistic or such as this, can be seen to the right and left at the lower apexes or points of the pyramid. See?

Not intended to be cryptic but it approaches same when the finite attempts to understand the infinite as it is conceived and perceived by other finite minds. That's a bridge that needs to be builded in the Earth.

Wilbur's realm has the opportunity of meeting the Golden entity essentially in the same form. David, as you may have discerned, or as it is indicated in some respects, is from the golden realm. He is not, in that colloquial term, *native* to the Crystal Worker's Realm. David is what you would call a light worker. He is a messenger and is, as such, expressed in a lower vibratory form for purposes of that work as an emissary from the higher realm.

Therefore, the entities are in the midst of such to varying degrees of awareness. They can, when they are ready, perceive the entity in the Crystal Worker's Realm. It is, however, as you have discerned (entity David and Leiko), less likely.

We cannot define to you a numerical value of the entities in the golden white light. This is near to impossible from our perspective. Also, add to this that entities are in motion, not static. They are not there seated upon an array of golden thrones, idly convening and governing. They are much more active than even we here. Generally speaking, the higher the movement in spiritual acceptance or consciousness, the more active and the more joyful becomes the soul. That's why you perceive them with such radiance. Their vibrations are so finely tuned and so much in harmony, they are approaching an unlimited expression of nature.

The entities Buddha and the Apostle Peter are often in the realm as the Golden entity but not static. Peter is more often here in this grouping helping to provide this information through this Channel to those works as are appropriate in the Earth. The Buddha is in the form as the expression of the Christ Consciousness and serving those who perceive him as such in the form Buddha. The same applies with other titles and names for the Christ Consciousness, which have been individualized in the varying incarnations as apply to the divisions of man in consciousness and to the Atlantean peoples, as they are fragmentally depicted in those divisions ... again, the five races of man, the varying cultures, and such. See?

The differences between the terms or descriptive titles

Godhead, God, Father-Mother-God, Source, and such as these, are dependent upon one's position. At times a more specific reference to God may be more appropriate. In some instances, these do have specific meanings.

For example, we might refer to the Sources here often or we might refer to the information as is provided to us. In such instances we are referring to Universal or God Consciousness, which is the repository, in essence, for all awareness, at least potentially. This can be delineated, and to an extent focused, but it is one and the same. See?

And yet, you would not, as such, in your understanding, find (quote) "God" (unquote) here upon a throne, but His Consciousness, which serves to underpin or support Universal Consciousness ... or all experience.

Father-Mother-God is used in reference to those situations which have to do with the division or the delineation wherein a work might be performed and that work involves some polarity in need of balancing, or some need to culminate or accumulate forces, and hence might involve works which are specific to the Earth. Wherein the expression Mother-God is correlative to that energy level as opposed to positive and negative depictations which are the sustaining forces of the Earth. The expression of God which then is the force of nature is also associated with this and the Mother-God. See? This could be continued on but we believe that you can comprehend from that the answer to your question. If not, bring it back in the intent that you have need (humbly given).

We believe that the next question about the forces of the Master and the Christ returning to the Earth has been spoken to in considerable length and depth in the just previous work. However, to comment specifically to the entity Joan's question, you don't have it backwards.

It's dependent upon, however, the free will choices of man and the groups and classes and masses and countries, as well those groupings who are in a state of division because their eye perceives God from a difference perspective. That division is an illusion but is a heritage which they are striving, as individual groups, to perpetuate.

There must come a time when all would perceive God as one, and recognize that each entity, from their varying position, would perceive the infinite and the unlimited in an equal manner of expression, that being infinite. See?

The personality or the ego has to do with the accomplishment of the soul's purpose in a specific interaction, incarnation, or experience in a realm. See? Not hostile and not a division apart from the soul but an expression of the soul, more finitely, for the purpose of completing or accomplishing a work.

It is unwise to quarrel with and to fight with the ego; the ego is the preserving force within self. The better is to explore, to investigate, to understand the needs and wants within self that comprise the ego: How does the ego see life, how does the ego see self, for the ego fashions that which is seen and interacted with by others.

When one becomes ego-less they have not lost their individuality, but they have reached the point wherein their ego can accept their unlimited nature and not stumble over this. Emotion, then, needs to be under the control of such an entity. No different than Peter must have control of himself in order to interact in other realms. That is the purpose and function of Zachary's gift of the cloak. And now, as have been perceived, apparently Peter can sustain himself, at least in the Crystal Worker's Realm, from within his own cloak. See?

Need and want, desire and such, are words which can be interpreted so differently, with such variation, on the part of entities. So let's arrive at a little glossary of interpretation. Need is a factor of sustaining a life in the Earth. That's one expression of it. Desire and desirous need are expressions of the ego. So one may need in the sense of the ego and another may need in the sense of survival or growth.

To consciously have a need may or may not involve the ego. If one consciously has a need for food, this can be because they are hungry or, at the extreme, dying of starvation. If they are dying of starvation, the universe must respond. If they are hungry for a certain food, in other words, not in anywise starving, the universe may or may not participate in the obtaining of that food.

The entity's purpose and will are involved here, somewhat singularly. Will and purpose are like this: If an entity is starving and has chosen to enter that circumstance for the purpose of their own soul's unburdening of its past karma as it interprets same, then the will of the entity must be honored. Until that entity has no longer the need to endure the actual experience literally, but has assimilated the benefit of that experience and has the will to release it, the universe can act.

Spirit is expedient to need. But if you have an ego-oriented need for power, to be successful in business, to be a world renowned celebrity, to be a politician or an emperor, and that need is motivated, not out of a desire to serve mankind and God but out of a need to emphasize self, you may or may not be aided by Universal Forces.

You would be aided by those forces if this in accordance with the intent and purpose of the collective grouping—in other words, was acceptable to them and to karmic conditions and to yourself, of course, as well. The example here being an entity who has been in slavery, in bondage, persecuted, punished, perhaps ... how do you call this ... terminated, or *killed* is your term, for purposes involuntary, may be offered an opportunity of power, of re-balance or retribution if the entity has borne anger, hatred, remorse and revenge, and this has grown into a powerful thought-form within that entity. The entity, upon returning to the Earth, does so only by the acceptance of the prevailing forces. This means that collective soul groupings are willing to re-balance with that because they see it as a force which limits them from their own spiritual growth. Now all of this is taking place on a spiritual level. Once they are in the Earth, the situation changes. They no longer wish to be dominated and the aggressor strongly wishes to dominate. Once they discover why, they might be able to balance with this.

Need, as an ego or as a desire which is unjustified, becomes a blocking force to the natural ability of an entity to accomplish unlimited actions, works, deeds, accomplishments. The power of God within you is unlimited; *you* are the limiting force. The environ in which you dwell in accordance with Universal Law is the next level of that potentially limiting force.

The Master was in such harmony with the Universal Forces and Universal Law and was in accordance with the soul groupings (remember, those who prepared the way and made it passable) that he was easily able to draw upon the full Consciousness of the power of God within and do all manner of works. He has also told you that you can do the same and greater. When? Now!

You are in the Earth under similar circumstances and that's an important point. Your nature to be limited is dissipating rapidly. The potential for you to accomplish all manner of work, as the Master has told you, increases daily. Even as we speak, it is beyond your comprehension. But you must believe, and hold true to the faith which enables you to manifest it ... unwavering. See? Does that help?

Your potential is limited by your need because you might need it so badly that you forget how to create. In other words, desire becomes a veil clouding your potential. When one is in harmony, they are unlimited; when one has strong personal needs, those needs can limit. The key to unlimited potential is *being* unlimited ... that simple. You possess what you are willing to possess freely. If you must possess it, you have built a barrier to allowing it to manifest.

We should reciprocate in thanking you, entity Joan, and all of you, for your participation in these works, for just as surely as we speak in this moment, each and every one of your souls has illuminated the information just that bit more, which is now before us. The presence of your souls and inquiring minds make a light here, and Universal Consciousness is illuminated by that desire and by your quest. We thank thee, each and every one, as well.

The Atlanteans who did not use the portal of death left by several means ... yes, by the lighter-than-air craft, which they had created and which were powered by the transmission of forces (very much as you broadcast television and radio and microwave signals, but this was in a manner several stages removed from your method and involved crystals).

It also was that they were aware of what we would call anomalies or *convergencies*, lines of frequency, where varying forces converge which allow for transition ... *windows*, in your space terminology; *portals*, in spiritual terminology; and *magnetic anomalies* and such, in the more of the physics terminology. They are, quite simply, where polarized force fields converge and create alternative lines of radiance upon which, when elemental structures were aligned and properly focused, they could, in essence, ride these or move upon them out of this expression, or, as you would call it, *dimension*.

Sounds a bit like a science fiction dissertation, does it not? (With a note of loving humor.) But nonetheless, not so far removed from your current potential and that which is only shortly ahead for you in the Earth. See? Very explainable, if one has that capacity and the dictionary, as it were, with which to communicate in such terms.

The break-up of Atlantis did not immediately form an alternative Earth, though one's perspective could describe it as such, for many of the souls who did depart, whose physical bodies were destroyed through the conflict and through the convergence of opposing energy fields, did reassemble and create a realm beyond the current plane of the Earth and do still dwell there.

There are some from both sides, each of them having their own realm. The realms we are familiar with and associated with from time to time, in service to God in His Name, are those who serve the one God and, as such, were not confined to the Wheel of Karma, and are serving from their position at present to help prevent the occurrence, the repetition of the Atlantean activity.

There are those also preserving and watching over the Hall of Records and other repositories emplaced into repositories in the Earth and inter-dimensionally in the Earth, awaiting the appropriate time for the Sons and Daughters of the One God to emerge in consciousness again, whereupon these might be reclaimed for the purposes of good works.

These tools will be, as well, the knowledge invaluable, restoring the pristine and native beauty of the Earth that it might become, as such, a garden and endure for an thousand years, more or less, and possibly beyond, as such, in that state. Thereafter, it could be likened unto Peter's Garden in every sense of the term and perhaps become nearly as unlimited as well. See?

You will probably not wake up one morning and perceive another Earth orbiting around the sun. Though it's not impossible, it's not indicated here as imminent (with a note of loving humor).

You are potentially able to participate in such works, though, should you wish to do so ... turning the tables on you and now with a note of loving humor and (quote) "fun" (end quote) from here. If you should choose to do so, we are aware of quite a significant grouping who would certainly be anxious to join with you. (Just as an expansion on that note of loving humor. See?)

Some of the Atlanteans who separated by a means other than death did so by simply slowing the vibrational energy of their physical bodies and, in essence, simply disappearing. (Some did not totally disappear; their bodies remained.) Others disappeared combustively, others simply as a vapor.

But the end product or summation of all these variables was that they simply willed themselves out of the Earth and back to their previous state of spiritual consciousness as just previously was their position prior to entering into the Earth.

In other words, for example, should Peter have been back in that time, in the Garden, and had moved into the Earth to serve in the Atlantean time, then determined to depart, he would have returned to the Garden. See?

Those entities, those Atlanteans, had full consciousness of their previous experiences ... their Earth experience and their current status, in other words, no lapse, no barriers. They did not deal with the Veil for they had not closed it upon themselves. These were, as you would call them, *light workers* ... workers in the Temples of Purification, Beautification, and Edification, and such as these.

Tobar was one of these, though at the time he didn't know how he did it, actually. See?

They do continue some interaction with the Earth as they are presented. They are in harmony with God and have no intent of harm.

However, it should be noted that some of them are still dealing with some of their own, we shall call them, Earthly influences. That's not bad, but they have purposes which are somewhat limiting their spirituality, in terms of their acceptance of same. Not to be confused with the Sea of Faces, for they are not in same. But they are somewhat limited by the desire to do good and, because of this, intensified that to the extent that they have forgotten their true potential as Sons and Daughters of God. See?

Very well, then ... As you would look upon all that information as has been presented to you or related to you regarding Peter, Zachary, Paul, Wilbur, David, and all the others, both named and unnamed, each moment, each experience has moved you just a whit closer to your own point of unlimited acceptance of your nature.

Now that has to do with your potential as you are in the Earth, but it also contributes to your greater potential as an eternal creation of God ... in other words, your spiritual potential, your soul. It enables you to, in essence, tidy up any karmic fragments. It should enable you to free yourself upon departure from the Earth from limitations which you have recognized more clearly as being such ... limitations. And it should enable you to move much more freely and more rapidly and with fuller consciousness than otherwise possible.

We would encourage you to share this knowledge and to demonstrate it wherever possible that you might contribute to others as they are willing or seeking in a like manner as you have unto self.

We would also encourage the Channel in that regard to make that information as given available to those who would seek it in such a manner. The intent being here, as you have perhaps grasped already, is that the greater is your number, your grouping, who have become less limited – or, more positively, *unlimited* – the greater is your potential to create a wondrous realm of consciousness which might, by the luminosity of same, reach out as rays of hope, of light, and encouragement to lesser realms and to those who have temporarily lost their way.

We are hopeful and prayerful and certain, all at once, that this is so. We are also hopeful that you will know it to be so. But only in the experiencing in your own consciousness, as the id or the ego is expressed in this time, can you have your own evidence or proof that these things are so.

And as the entity Barry had questioned and expressed,

perhaps you will only gain it as a certainly or know it to be true when it occurs. No matter, for when it does these memories and our grouping, because of these bonds, shall be of service to you then. And we mean the latter explicitly and literally, for each of you will be met by our grouping when you are in transit from the Earth. And we shall extend to you our love and our support and our assistance, as you wish it ... as an offering, not as a mandate.

And so that has been the intent and the work accomplished in this Project 7, which we would now, in response to the Channel's question, consider to be complete, a segment unto itself.

Now as we would turn to look at the works ahead, the potentials are quite vast. There has been accomplished here in ... Project 7 has been, for the most part, preparatory, even though (with a note of loving humor) you might not have seen it as such as it was unfolding. (It may have seemed to you to have been remarkable, astonishing, highly revealing, aspiring, and, even at times, just outright unbelievable.) That work, as we defined it *preparatory*, will be greatly overshadowed, we should think, by what is to come.

And in the more specific sense, we would affirm the Channel's earlier interpretation that we do believe that you will be able to have some responses directly from Paul and, of course, much to your delight we should think, from friend Zachary, and possibly others ... maybe even including Peter, if you can handle it.

You will know whether this is possible, we believe, after the next meeting where we are able to join with and to recapitulate some of the activities incurred by Peter and company, from the past to the present point. There are many.

For the most part, we will attempt to relate some of the higher points, as we perceive them as being important to you, in some considerable detail. Other points we will pass over more swiftly, allowing you, of course, the opportunity to call us to return to them in detail, if you feel the need or purpose.

Initially, we believe that you will involve yourselves, to some extent, by attempting to query Paul and Zachary, and gaining much from the responses which should evolve from that as an interaction.

Our grouping, in the greater or collective sense, will be present, of course, as always, to serve as the channel and perhaps, in a manner of speaking, as the moderator for you, in your name, for these are colleagues in their current perspective of consciousness.

It should make for great joy, great fun, and some profound exchanges of wisdom from your realm to theirs. And, curiously perhaps to you, they have some questions which we are certain they are going to ask of you as well, which will call for answers from the Voyager grouping. Quite a turnabout, eh wot?

After that, a number of events can transpire. We are unsure at this time of the choices that will be made specifically. We know the general choices but can't reveal them all here because they would potentially disrupt the proceedings much in the manner as we have defined to you in the past.

We believe you will perceive and become involved in some healing works directly with the grouping. You will be afforded some opportunities, severalfold, which will associate with that. And some of you may even become interactive between that grouping and yourself on a more personal and/or individual way. That will be your choices, which of course we won't predict here at this time as well. As so it has, as we view it, the potential of being a significant step forward for you, each of you, as you press to rediscover your infinite nature. There should be opportunity aplenty for each of you to evidence to yourselves your own potential and the potential of your unlimited nature as it is found within you and as you attempt to bring it forth. These, then, all in the most positive, hopeful and joyous sense, shall be our continuing prayer.

❀　❀　❀

We have indeed been most joyful and humble to have participated with you and Paul, Zachary, Wilbur, David, Peter, and the Golden entity, and all the others who you know little of at present. We thank you, all of you, in all of these realms, for this wondrous opportunity of joy.

May the grace, blessings, wisdom and love of our Father's spirit ever be thy continual companion on your pathway through this lifetime. Fare thee well, then, for the present, dear friends.

Books by Al Miner & Lama Sing

The Chosen: *Back Story to the Essene Legacy*
The Promise: *Book I of The Essene Legacy*
The Awakening: *Book II of The Essene Legacy*
The Path: *Book III of The Essene Legacy*

In Realms Beyond: *Book I of The Peter Chronicles*
In Realms Beyond: *Study Guide*
Awakening Hope: *Book II of The Peter Chronicles*

How to Prepare for The Journey:
      Vol I Death, Dying, and Beyond
      Vol II *The Sea of Faces*

Jesus: *Book I*
Jesus: *Book II*

The Course in Mastery

When Comes the Call

Seed Thoughts
Seed Thoughts to Consciousness

For a comprehensive list of readings transcripts available, visit the
Lama Sing library at www.lamasing.net

About Al Miner

A chance hypnosis session in 1973 began Al's tenure as the channel for Lama Sing. Since then, nearly 10,000 readings have been given in a trance state answering technical and personal questions on such topics as science, health and disease, history, geophysics, spirituality, philosophy, metaphysics, past and future times, and much more. The validity of the information has been substantiated and documented by research institutions and individuals. Those receiving personal readings continue to refer others to Al's work based on the accuracy and integrity of the information in their readings. In 1984, St. Johns University awarded Al an honorary doctoral degree in parapsychology.

Al conducts a variety of field research projects, as well as occasional workshops and lectures. He occasionally accepts requests for personal readings, but is mostly devoting his remaining time to works intended to be good for all. Much of his current research is dedicated to the concept that the best of all guidance is that which comes from within.

Al lives with his family in the mountains of Western North Carolina.